Gayle
GREGORY

Martha
KAUFELDT

Mike
MATTOS

BEST
Practices
at Tier 1

**Daily
Differentiation
for Effective
Instruction**

Elementary

Solution Tree | Press
a division of
Solution Tree

Copyright © 2016 by Solution Tree Press

Materials appearing here are copyrighted. With one exception, all rights are reserved. Readers may reproduce only those pages marked "Reproducible." Otherwise, no part of this book may be reproduced or transmitted in any form or by any means (electronic, photocopying, recording, or otherwise) without prior written permission of the publisher.

555 North Morton Street
Bloomington, IN 47404
800.733.6786 (toll free) / 812.336.7700
FAX: 812.336.7790

email: info@solution-tree.com
solution-tree.com

Visit **go.solution-tree.com/RTIatWork** to download the reproducibles in this book.

Printed in the United States of America

Library of Congress Cataloging-in-Publication Data

Gregory, Gayle.

  Best practices at tier 1 : daily differentiation for effective instruction, elementary / Gayle Gregory, Martha Kaufeldt, and Mike Mattos.

      pages cm

  Includes bibliographical references and index.

  ISBN 978-1-936763-93-1 (perfect bound) 1. Education, Elementary--United States. 2. Effective teaching--United States. 3. Response to intervention (Learning disabled children) 4. Mixed ability grouping in education--United States. 5. Teachers--Professional relationships--United States. 6. Professional learning communities--United States. I. Kaufeldt, Martha, 1954- II. Mattos, Mike (Mike William) III. Title.

  LA219.G78 2016

  371.39'4--dc23

                                        2015029727

Solution Tree
Jeffrey C. Jones, CEO
Edmund M. Ackerman, President

Solution Tree Press
President: Douglas M. Rife
Senior Acquisitions Editor: Amy Rubenstein
Editorial Director: Lesley Bolton
Managing Production Editor: Caroline Weiss
Copy Chief: Sarah Payne-Mills
Proofreader: Miranda Addonizio
Text Designer: Laura Kagemann
Cover Designer: Rian Anderson

For my granddaughters, Megan and Jessica, with the hope that all children have the opportunity to reach their potential. May their enthusiastic pursuit and joy of learning in everything they do, in school and out, be respected and encouraged through appropriate, meaningful opportunities to make sense of and improve their world for themselves and others.

—Gayle Gregory

To every college student considering entering the teaching profession, and for every educator willing to keep on dedicating the time, energy, and creativity it takes to be good at our craft. Thank you. These 21st century learners will challenge us to do our very best, and together we can exceed expectations.

—Martha Kaufeldt

To my dear friend, trusted colleague, and RTI at Work™ cocreator Dr. Austin Buffum. A chance meeting on an airport shuttle; a thoughtful gift of Barth; a lunch discussion about RTI and PLCs—events that have changed my life!

—Mike Mattos

Acknowledgments

Bringing this book from concept to completion was truly a collaborative effort, beginning with the outstanding professionals at Solution Tree. Guided by the leadership of CEO Jeffrey Jones and Solution Tree Press President Douglas M. Rife, Solution Tree has become the premier educational publishing and staff development company in the world. Specifically, we would like to thank Douglas for suggesting a collaborative book that connects response to intervention and powerful core instruction. We also appreciate Sarah Payne-Mills for her superb editing of our manuscript. We hope that this book moves Solution Tree one step closer to achieving its vision of transforming education worldwide.

We appreciate that Solution Tree leaders know that understanding how the brain learns can help teachers do their jobs more effectively. Books such as the *Mind, Brain, and Education* anthology in the *Leading Edge* series translated the work of leading neuroscientists and cognitive psychologists into valuable information for educators.

We would like to thank Austin Buffum for his influence on the RTI at Work™ elements of this book. The recommendations provided regarding how to successfully interpret and implement a multitiered system of support are based on ideas introduced in our books *Pyramid Response to Intervention: RTI, Professional Learning Communities, and How to Respond When Kids Don't Learn* and *Simplifying Response to Intervention: Four Essential Guiding Principles.*

Finally, one of the most important themes in this book is that effective teaching is not an individual pursuit; it can only be achieved when educators work collaboratively. To this end, the recommendations we offer to improve core instruction are squarely built on the Professional Learning Communities at Work® process. We thank our dear friends Richard DuFour, Robert Eaker, and Rebecca DuFour for all their efforts to develop, articulate, and promote this process for the benefit of educators and students around the world.

Visit **go.solution-tree.com/RTIatWork**
to download the reproducibles in this book.

Table of Contents

About the Authors . . . . **ix**

Introduction **1**
    Understanding Response to Intervention 2
    Recognizing Unrealized Potential 3
    Identifying the Elements of Good Teaching 5
    Using This Book 7

1   Shifting to Collaborative Core Instruction **11**
    Reviewing Past Efforts to Improve Core Instruction 12
    Synthesizing What We Know About Good Teaching 15
    Harnessing the Power of Collaborative Teams 16
    Leveraging the Power of Student Collaboration 20
    Taking the Discussion Further 21

2   Creating Brain-Friendly Learning Environments **23**
    Maintaining a Safe and Secure Climate for Learning 24
    Providing Relevant, Meaningful, and Engaging Instruction 31
    Supporting the Social Brain 35
    Utilizing Cooperative Group Learning 41
    Getting Started and Getting Better 50
    Taking the Discussion Further 52

3   Finding Each Student's Learning Sweet Spot **55**
    Teaching to Each Student's Learning Sweet Spot 56
    Recognizing Learning Preferences 58
    Leveraging Multiple Intelligences 59
    Building a Student Profile 63
    Targeting Specific Learning Needs 66
    Helping Students Identify Their Own Learning Preferences and Needs 70
    Keeping Students in Their Learning Zone 72
    Taking the Discussion Further 75

4 Developing a Powerful Core Curriculum **77**
   Incorporating Essential Standards 79
   Determining Success Criteria for Mastery 84
   Integrating 21st Century Skills 92
   Making Content Meaningful and Relevant 94
   Employing Evidence-Based Best Practices 97
   Concentrating the Core Curriculum 103
   Taking the Discussion Further 108

5 Differentiating Instruction Through Pluralized
   Teaching Strategies **111**
   Moving From Traditional to Progressive Instructional Methods 112
   Maximizing the Power of Technology 115
   Using Multiple Approaches to Develop Student Vocabulary 119
   Differentiating Instruction Through Learning Centers 123
   Implementing a Mixed-Modality, Pluralized Pedagogy 128
   Taking the Discussion Further 143

6 Using Data to Inform Instruction **145**
   Student Profiles 147
   Prerequisite Screenings 148
   Diagnostic Preassessments 149
   Formative Assessments 151
   Summative Assessments 161
   Adjustments to Student Tasks, Groups, and Processes in Response to
      Assessment Data 161
   A Commonsense Approach to Assessment 173
   Taking the Discussion Further 175

7 Building Cognitive Rigor, Depth, and Complexity **177**
   Creating Rigorous Learning Environments and Tasks 179
   Developing Students' Higher-Level Thinking Skills 182
   Going Beyond Proficiency 191
   Using Complex Texts and Text-Dependent Questions to
      Increase Instructional Rigor 193
   Increasing Rigor Using 21st Century Skills 197
   Taking the Discussion Further 202

Epilogue: Embracing the Journey **203**
   The Art of Teaching 203
   The Journey Ahead 207

References and Resources **209**

Index **225**

About the Authors

Gayle Gregory has extensive experience as a staff developer and administrator. She consults internationally on brain-friendly differentiation, research-based instruction, block scheduling, assessment practices, early literacy, gifted instruction, and facilitating school change. Gayle has worked with many districts developing school teams to build internal capacity. She has taught at the elementary, middle, and high school levels as well as in university settings.

Gayle is coauthor of *Differentiated Instructional Strategies: One Size Doesn't Fit All*, *Teacher Teams That Get Results: 61 Strategies for Sustaining and Renewing Professional Learning Communities*, and *Think Big, Start Small*. In addition, she was featured in an edition of the *Video Journal of Education* focused on differentiated instruction. She is committed to lifelong learning and professional growth for herself and others.

To learn more about Gayle's work, visit her website www.gaylehgregory.com, or follow @gaylegregory6 on Twitter.

Martha Kaufeldt is a professional development specialist and author. Since 1984, her specialty has been applying educational neuroscience into classroom practice. She travels internationally conducting workshops and trainings on curriculum development, differentiated instruction, school restructuring, assessment, and brain-friendly strategies for teachers. She serves on the Transformative Education Forum Board and has been a trainer and coach for the Mid-California Science Improvement Project.

Martha was a classroom teacher for over twenty-three years in California. As an elementary teacher, she created brain-compatible learning environments for a diverse student population. In the middle grades, Martha was a core teacher on an interdisciplinary instructional team. Her curriculum included integrated project-based and service learning, and she emphasized social and emotional well-being. Martha has also been a district staff development specialist and gifted education program director. For her work in the San Francisco Bay area, Martha was awarded the Mason-McDuffie Outstanding Teacher of the Year Award.

She has written several books, including *Begin With the Brain: Orchestrating the Learner-Centered Classroom, Teachers, Change Your Bait! Brain-Compatible Differentiated Instruction*, and *Think Big, Start Small.*

She earned a bachelor's degree from San Francisco State University and a master's degree in human behavior from City University.

To learn more about Martha's work, visit her website Begin With the Brain (www .beginwiththebrain.com).

 **Mike Mattos** is an internationally recognized author, presenter, and practitioner who specializes in uniting teachers, administrators, and support staff to transform schools by implementing response to intervention and professional learning communities. Mike cocreated the RTI at Work™ model, which builds on the foundation of the PLC at Work® process by using team structures and a focus on learning, collaboration, and results to drive successful outcomes. Additionally, he is an architect of the PLC at Work model. He is former principal of Marjorie Veeh Elementary School and Pioneer Middle School in California. At both schools, Mike helped create powerful PLCs, improving learning for all students. In 2004, Marjorie Veeh, an elementary school with a large population of youth at risk, won the California Distinguished School and National Title I Achieving School awards.

A National Blue Ribbon School, Pioneer is among only thirteen schools in the United States that the GE Foundation selected as a Best-Practice Partner and is one of eight schools that Richard DuFour chose to be featured in the video series *The Power of Professional Learning Communities at Work: Bringing the Big Ideas to Life*. Based on standardized test scores, Pioneer ranks among the top 1 percent of California secondary schools and, in 2009 and 2011, was named Orange County's top middle school. For his leadership, Mike was named the Orange County Middle School Administrator of the Year by the Association of California School Administrators.

To learn more about Mike's work, follow @mikemattos65 on Twitter.

To book Gayle Gregory, Martha Kaufeldt, or Mike Mattos for professional development, contact pd@solution-tree.com.

Introduction

As educational practitioners, authors, and consultants who have dedicated their careers to the professional advancement of educators, we know this to be true: response to intervention (RTI) is our best hope in providing every student with the additional time and support needed to succeed in school. The research and evidence supporting our claim is both comprehensive and compelling. In perhaps the most extensive study of the factors that impact student learning, John Hattie's (2012) meta-analysis, based on over eighty thousand studies and one hundred million students worldwide, finds that RTI ranks second in the most effective influences, inside or outside of school, that can increase student performance. When implemented well, RTI has the power to help students improve multiple grade levels in a year (Hattie, 2012). Imagine for a moment the practical ramifications of these findings.

▽ A student entering third grade at a first-grade reading level could, with effective RTI support, be approaching grade level by the end of the year.

▽ A fourth-grade student with significant deficiencies in foundational number sense could, with targeted supports, be prepared to enter the advanced mathematics track in secondary school.

▽ A student qualified for special education due to a significant learning discrepancy—over two standard deviations' difference between his or her perceived IQ and current level of achievement—could close this gap and be redesignated as a general education student by his or her first triannual individualized education program (IEP) review.

While these ideas may sound unrealistically optimistic, they aren't. The research we describe in this book is not reporting theory or results achieved under the ideal teaching conditions of a generously funded experimental program. We have had the honor of working with schools implementing RTI across all fifty states in the United States, every province in Canada, and many countries throughout the world. From

Alabama to Australia and South Dakota to Singapore, we have seen these results firsthand in real-life schools facing diverse student needs, limited resources, restrictive contractual agreements, and challenging governmental regulations. At a time when success in school is no longer optional for economic and social stability, RTI provides the ongoing processes necessary to ensure every student learns at high levels.

Understanding Response to Intervention

RTI's underlying premise is that schools provide timely, targeted, systematic support early, rather than delaying help until students fall far enough behind to qualify for special education (Buffum, Mattos, & Weber, 2012). Commonly referred to as a multitiered system of support (MTSS), the three tiers of RTI traditionally take the shape of a pyramid, with each tier representing a different level of support based on student needs. See figure I.1.

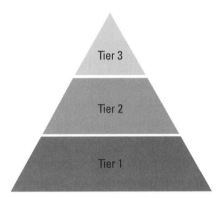

Figure I.1: Traditional RTI pyramid.

Tier 1 represents a school's core instructional program, in which all students receive effective instruction on grade-level essential curriculum. While Tier 1 should meet most students' needs a majority of the time, invariably some students will need a little extra help to succeed in core instruction. This is the primary purpose of Tier 2—to provide timely, targeted supplemental academic and behavioral interventions to ensure that those students succeed in mastering their essential grade-level curriculum. For students who enter the school year with significant deficits in reading, writing, number sense, English, and academic or social behaviors, Tier 3 supports provide intensive academic and behavioral remediation in these foundational skills.

The goal of the RTI approach isn't to move students from one tier to another; instead, RTI provides supplemental and intensive support in addition to core instruction. This approach recognizes that students who miss core instruction on essential grade-level standards in order to receive interventions are unlikely to catch up. This is because while these students receive interventions on previous learning outcomes, they miss the teaching of new content critical to future success—the proverbial "one step forward, two steps back." With the RTI approach, however, the most at-risk students receive effective Tier 1 core instruction on grade-level essential standards, Tier 2 supplemental support in meeting these critical outcomes, *and* Tier 3 intensive instruction on foundational skills that the students should have mastered years ago. Collectively, these three tiers ensure that *all* students end the school year with the essential skills and knowledge they need to succeed the following year and beyond.

When RTI is viewed this way, one point becomes very clear: the entire RTI process is built on effective, grade-level core instruction. The foundation of a successful system of interventions is effective initial teaching (Shapiro, n.d.).

Recognizing Unrealized Potential

While federal law has promoted response to intervention since the reauthorization of the Individuals With Disabilities Education Improvement Act (IDEIA) in 2004, most schools and districts are struggling to secure the student achievement results that RTI is proven to provide. Many states, districts, and schools mistakenly view RTI as a new process to qualify students for special education, with the tiers serving merely as new hoops a school must jump through in order to place students into traditional special education services. As a result, screening assessments, cut scores, and program decision protocols predetermine student identification, placement, and duration in each tier. Instead of providing students with multiple tiers of support, this misapplication of RTI moves students from tier to tier on their path toward special education.

But without question, the most common reason that schools struggle to successfully implement RTI goes back to the foundation of the process—effective core instruction. Tier 1 instruction should successfully meet the needs of a significant majority of students most of the time. When it does not, the consequences manifest in multiple ways. Some schools, for example, find that too many of their students are failing after core instruction and need interventions, and the size of that need overwhelms their system of supports and its available resources. Similarly, some schools find that significant subgroups—such as English learners (ELs) or students with special needs—struggle disproportionately in core instruction. Instead of revising their initial teaching practices to better meet these students' learning needs, many schools remove the students from grade-level core instruction and replace that instruction with remedial coursework. This decision virtually ensures that these students will never catch up. Removing students from the Tier 1 grade-level essential curriculum is nothing more than student tracking, a system that separates students into learning groups based on perceived ability. As Jeannie Oakes (1985) finds in her landmark study *Keeping Track*, this sorting continues to disadvantage those in lower-track classes. Such students have less access to high-status knowledge, fewer opportunities to engage in stimulating learning activities, and less engaging classroom experiences with teachers, peers, and learning. If the goal is for all students to learn at high levels, then all students must be taught at high levels.

When individual students struggle in core instruction, few schools begin the intervention process by assessing the effectiveness of the student's core instruction. Instead, as special education expert David Prasse (n.d.) finds, schools traditionally operate as though "failure to succeed in a general education program meant the student must, therefore, have a disability." In other words, the common assumption is that the student's innate abilities are the cause of his or her struggles. Even if these students begin receiving interventions, they mostly likely will continue to receive ineffective core instruction for a majority of their school day. Supplemental and intensive intervention cannot compensate for ineffective initial teaching that does not differentiate instruction to meet each student's unique learning needs.

Even when dedicated school staff members acknowledge that too many students are struggling in core instruction, the consensus and commitment to improve core instruction can be elusive. As a general concept, RTI is appealing to virtually all educators. Who, after all, wouldn't want to provide extra support for students in need? But, too often, the enthusiasm for intervention wanes quickly when the focus turns to Tier 1, because improving this level of instruction requires a deep level of change that affects every aspect of the school day. It requires school staff to take collective responsibility for student success, collaborate regularly, agree on essential learning outcomes and pacing, differentiate instruction, abandon traditional teaching and assessment practices that were designed to create a bell-shaped curve of student success, and make significant revisions to the school's master schedule and resource allocations—all actions required to meet each student's individual learning needs. This level of change is exceptionally difficult. In the end, many schools struggle to improve core instruction because too many adults in the building are unwilling to accept the level of temporary disequilibrium and discomfort required to significantly change what they do all day.

Because schools have resisted efforts to revise their core instructional practices, many districts have responded by purchasing a research-based textbook series and then dictating that their teachers exclusively implement it as their core program. In the name of "program fidelity," these districts often require teachers to utilize these programs' lockstep lesson plans, assessments, and supplemental materials. Such an approach assumes that the curricular design and pedagogies in the textbook represent scientifically researched-based best practice, so classroom teachers should relinquish their authority to plan and differentiate instruction and instead serve as program facilitators. Yet, Hattie's (2009) study finds that textbook series have a marginal effect on student learning. This is not to suggest that textbooks cannot serve as effective tools to assist teachers in core instruction or that educators shouldn't implement research-based programs. The concern is that when the program dictates all elements of core instruction, it limits the results teachers can achieve. In the end, no silver bullet program can ensure effective teaching for all students.

If rigid adherence to textbooks and instructional programs is not a long-term solution to improve Tier 1 core instruction, then what is? The key is to ensure more good teaching, in more classrooms, more of the time (DuFour & Mattos, 2013). When students have access to classrooms that consistently provide a learning environment and instructional practices proven to dramatically improve student learning, more students will succeed. To achieve this outcome, one must answer a critical question, What is good teaching?

Identifying the Elements of Good Teaching

Good teaching is a dichotomy. It is hard to capture in a single definition but easy to recognize when you see it. To understand the point, consider a similar example when trying to define something that is both deeply complex but apparent to the eye. When attempting to define *obscenity*, Supreme Court Justice Potter Stewart famously stated: "I shall not today attempt further to define the kinds of material I understand to be embraced. . . . But I know it when I see it" (*Jacobellis v. Ohio*, n.d.). Stewart acknowledged the difficulty in trying to write a universal, all-encompassing definition of what constitutes obscenity because any particular example or case must be weighed by the relevance and circumstances of the moment. Yet, when one sees an example of true obscenity, it's usually obvious and straightforward. Similarly, while it's difficult to create an all-encompassing definition or model of good teaching, such teaching makes itself evident to even the untrained eye. Within any school community, there is often general consensus on which instructors teach well. However, if we dig deeper and ask what makes each teacher effective, we're likely to receive a wide variety of answers. This dichotomy of what constitutes good teaching exists, in part, because effective instruction is a convergence of three critical factors.

1. **The science of teaching:** The very definition of a profession is that it encompasses research-based best practices that members are expected to know and implement on behalf of their clients. In the teaching profession, we have never had greater clarity and consensus on what is considered *best practice*, which we define as the pedagogies and methodologies that have the best chance of helping students learn at higher levels. We also know more than ever about the brain and the physiology of learning. As Mike Schmoker (2004) states, "There are simple, proven, affordable structures that exist right now and could have a dramatic, widespread impact on schools and achievement—in

virtually any school. An astonishing level of agreement has emerged on this point" (p. 424). Likewise, we also have great clarity on educational malpractice—the practices that are unlikely to significantly improve student learning. As professionals, we have ethical obligations to utilize classroom instructional strategies based on sound science and research.

2. **The art of teaching:** Teaching is a human endeavor. While we can study elements of learning through the neuroscience of the brain, what constitutes good teaching is more than a cognitive experience—it also is rooted in an instructor's heart and soul. People aren't always logical or reliably predictable in their behavior and responses. Good teaching, therefore, must take into account relationships, motivation, nurturing, constructive conflict, and mutual respect. It requires reading both people and assessment data. A hunch or an intuitive feeling for what their students need often guides master teachers. How do you quantify a teacher's passion for the subject, intellectual curiosity, or genuine concern for students? These attributes are powerful levers to inspire and connect students to learning. As Robert Marzano (2007) states in his book *The Art and Science of Teaching*, classroom instructional strategies should be based on sound science and research, but knowing when to use them and with whom is more of an art.

3. **Differentiation for individual student needs:** We know that all students don't learn in exactly the same way or develop and mature at the same speed. Every student has unique learning needs based on his or her prior knowledge and experiences, cultural values, learning styles, and aptitudes. Because of these differences, no matter how well a teacher teaches a concept, some students will grasp that concept immediately, while others in the same class will fail miserably to understand it. Effective teaching requires time to differentiate instruction to meet each student's individual learning and developmental needs.

In essence, good teaching is a convergence of all three of these factors, as each is required to achieve higher levels of learning for all students. So if a highly effective system of interventions begins with an effective core instructional program, then all students require good teaching practices on a daily basis. Therefore, good teaching requires every teacher to have knowledge and skill in the most effective teaching practices, the empowerment to practice the art of teaching, and a deep understanding of daily differentiation to meet each student's individual learning needs. That's what this book is all about!

Using This Book

In this book, we investigate the essential elements of good teaching in regard to Tier 1 core instruction. In the process of that investigation, we'll explore the science, art, and essential strategies, as well as the intuitive and affective elements, of teaching that result in powerful student learning. Specifically, here is how we have organized this book.

▽ Chapter 1, "Shifting to Collaborative Core Instruction," provides a big-picture exploration of what constitutes good teaching. The chapter begins with a discussion of some previous initiatives to improve core instruction and why those efforts have failed. The chapter also challenges the prevailing view on core instruction, which emphasizes what individual teachers do *for* their students, by offering an alternative view that emphasizes what teachers do collaboratively *with* their students.

▽ Chapter 2, "Creating Brain-Friendly Learning Environments," investigates how educators can orchestrate an optimal climate and environment for learning. The chapter outlines the fundamentals of a brain-friendly classroom based on powerful research in educational neuroscience. The chapter also illustrates that instructors can ensure that instructional best practices are most successful by implementing them in an environment that supports trial and error, risk taking, and collaboration, while also including meaningful and relevant instructional tasks.

▽ Chapter 3, "Finding Each Student's Learning Sweet Spot," describes a wide array of strategies teachers can use to identify and understand the unique abilities of every student. The chapter explains how creating a student profile and determining the student's learning preferences are helpful when selecting which best practices to use. The chapter also briefly reviews multiple intelligences—the many types of intelligence humans demonstrate—to help broaden the types of best practices and strategies educators can choose to implement first.

▽ Chapter 4, "Developing a Powerful Core Curriculum," looks at the basic question, What do we want students to know and be able to do? The chapter suggests strategies collaborative teams and professional learning communities (PLCs) can use to identify the essential power standards the Tier 1 core curriculum must include. The chapter also explores methods for clearly communicating learning targets to students. Finally, this chapter introduces the 4Cs of 21st century skills (communication, collaboration, creativity, and critical thinking) as key aspects of good problem- and project-based curriculum design.

▽ Chapter 5, "Differentiating Instruction Through Pluralized Teaching Strategies," stresses the transition from teacher-centered to student-centered instruction. This chapter is filled with practical suggestions and examples, as it explores daily differentiation—an instructional model that emphasizes effective, research-based, high-impact, and pluralized teaching strategies. The chapter also outlines dozens of classroom-tested teaching strategies that can increase instructional variety, including creating flexible groups, integrating technology, and enhancing academic vocabulary instruction.

▽ Chapter 6, "Using Data to Inform Instruction," emphasizes the power of assessments in instructional planning and their role in helping both educators and students more clearly identify and understand learning challenges and opportunities. From creating student profiles to screening for prerequisites and conducting preassessment diagnostics, ongoing formative assessments, and summative assessments, this chapter reviews the kinds of student data educators gather. Because data are only valuable when teachers use them, the chapter also discusses a number of best practices and strategies for adjusting instructional approaches, such as scaffolding and extending learning tasks, to adapt to information revealed through assessment. The chapter also explores key elements of creating adjustable assignments, also known as tiered lessons.

▽ Chapter 7, "Building Cognitive Rigor, Depth, and Complexity," offers ideas educators can use to increase dynamic instructional effectiveness by increasing their instructional rigor. The chapter also explores a variety of best practices for helping students build their own cognitive rigor by developing higher-level thinking skills, cognitive depth, and complexity. Developing learners' cognitive rigor demands that educators adjust what they teach and increase their expectations in order to ensure that each student has the opportunity to grow in ways he or she may not be able to imagine. This chapter, therefore, describes how models such as Bloom's Revised Taxonomy and Webb's Depth of Knowledge (DOK) offer educators solutions for making those adjustments in the most effective way possible. The chapter also offers a number of techniques educators can use to integrate 21st century skills into the core curriculum in ways that raise the bar for all learners.

▽ The epilogue, "Embracing the Journey," challenges teachers to work collaboratively within their collaborative teams and PLCs. The chapter explains why ongoing efforts to grow their knowledge base and skill sets are responsibilities that educators cannot ignore. It also offers suggestions for sharing information about differentiated instruction with parents in order to gain their support and assistance in efforts to provide students with the most effective educational experience possible.

Beyond a thorough discussion of the research and findings surrounding the role of differentiated instruction in improving student learning, each chapter offers specific tools and techniques for implementing the ideas and processes it describes. At the end of each chapter, therefore, we've included questions, reflections, and exercises. These sections—Taking the Discussion Further—enable educators and their teams to deepen their discussion and understanding of each chapter's content.

Finally, before we begin this journey into *Best Practices at Tier 1*, we would like to offer educators a few words of preliminary advice. We have conducted presentations on this subject for thousands of educators around the world, and while the overall response has been extremely positive, we often hear a few specific concerns.

▽ **"I already know that."** Few of the ideas in this book represent new, groundbreaking research. Instead, most of the ideas we discuss here are based on common sense and well-established practices. For example, in chapter 2, we discuss the traits of a brain-friendly learning environment. The idea that brains learn best in a safe classroom environment is neither new nor earth-shattering. We dig deeply into the topic, however, to explain that a safe learning environment requires more than order; it also must offer students clear goals for learning outcomes, specific techniques for demonstrating mastery, and the freedom to try, make mistakes, and try again. Students sitting quietly in orderly rows rarely demonstrate the high level of engagement that promotes effective learning. Yet, we find many teachers who view a safe and orderly classroom as just that—a place where students demonstrate passive compliance. Knowing that a safe and orderly classroom is critical to effective core instruction is not the point of chapter 2. Rather, the more important question is, Are all the elements of this characteristic of good teaching present in your classroom? Even when you find they are, there is still benefit in the material—it will validate your teaching and build self-efficacy that you are on the right track.

▽ **"That's a nice idea, but it won't work for the students at my school."** This response is common, especially among educators who teach a majority of at-risk youth. We also hear numerous justifications, such as "My students can't handle cooperative learning" or "My students lack the basic academic skills and self-control to do that." However, that pessimism is unfounded. The research behind our recommendations demonstrates that the educational approach we outline in this book is proven to work for all students, regardless of ethnicity, economic status, home language, or gender. Schools of every demographic makeup are successfully implementing these methods. In the end, our experience also has demonstrated that students will become whatever teachers believe them to be. If educators believe students are immature, irresponsible, and incapable of demonstrating scholarly, responsible behavior, eventually they'll be right. They will treat students as such and, as a result, create classroom rules and procedures to support their assumptions. But if educators believe students are capable of working collaboratively, demonstrating intellectual curiosity, making good choices, and self-directing their learning—and they apply the effective teaching methods necessary to promote such behaviors—they, again, will be right in their beliefs. Instead of questioning whether students are capable of achieving successful outcomes, therefore, the ideas we present in this book ask educators to consider another question: How can we help students get to those successful outcomes?

▽ **"These are great ideas, but I don't have the time to implement them because I have too much content to cover."** This is the most common concern we hear. As we discuss in chapter 4, there is an impossible amount of yearly state curriculum. However, if a school is committed to effective teaching and student learning, there is no research to support the proposition that the more content a teacher covers, the more students learn. In reality the opposite is true—the less curriculum taught to mastery, the more students achieve. There is probably not a teacher in the United States who can honestly say that he or she is currently covering all mandated material within the time constraints of the school year. It is unacceptable to deny students effective teaching in a misguided attempt to maintain the illusion that the school is covering the entire required curriculum.

Keeping these important cautions in mind, we offer a book full of proven strategies—tools that can help teachers differentiate instruction, provide engaging ways for students to learn, increase the chances for success, and avoid the need for additional intervention. Join us on a journey of continuous teacher improvement. We hope educators will use these strategies to enhance their repertoire and provide more good teaching to more students more of the time!

Shifting to Collaborative Core Instruction

Teaching matters! At a time in which successfully navigating our K–12 system of education is a mandatory prerequisite to leading a successful adult life, the greatest contributor to student success is the quality of instruction students receive each school day. Almost four decades of research into the characteristics of effective schools, such as that from Ron Edmonds (1979) and Larry Lezotte (1991), has proven that virtually all students can learn when provided with effective teaching. In his seminal work *What Works in Schools*, Robert Marzano (2003) demonstrates that highly effective schools produce results that almost entirely overcome the effects of student background. Additionally, Hattie's (2009) comprehensive study of what most impacts student learning finds that education's powerful leverage points hinge on features *within* the school, rather than outside factors like home, environmental, and economic conditions.

Teaching is also our job—the business of our career, the goal of our professional training, the criteria of our credentialing and evaluation process, the fundamental work of any school, and the very reason why most campus professionals are hired. While an unprecedented number of societal responsibilities are being thrust on educators today, one fact is undeniable: it is their responsibility to teach students the academic knowledge, skills, and dispositions they need to succeed as adults.

Fortunately, teaching also represents the area over which educators have the greatest level of direct control. While schools must work within federal, state, and local regulations and contractual agreements, many teachers have significant autonomy every school day to determine the scope and sequence of their daily lesson plans, instructional practices, assessment decisions, and classroom procedures. The law considers teachers *in loco parentis*—in place of a parent—in the classroom. In most educational decisions, teachers have much greater authority than parents. Considering that the average student will spend seven years in elementary school, educators have both an incredible opportunity and an awesome responsibility to directly impact a student's success in school and beyond.

Without question, more students will succeed in school if educators successfully fulfill their fundamental purpose. But how can we ensure that every student receives effective teaching every day? In this chapter, we examine how many of the state and national reform efforts have proven to be counterproductive to this goal.

Reviewing Past Efforts to Improve Core Instruction

The idea that better teaching improves student achievement is not new to education. Since the adoption of No Child Left Behind in 2001, myriad school-reform mandates have launched to improve teaching. Unfortunately, most efforts were doomed to fail because they advocated low-leverage practices—practices that have a limited impact on actual student learning.

To determine if a teaching practice has a high- or low-leverage effect on student learning, we look at the *effect size*, or a standardized measure of the strength of an intervention. Effect sizes above 0.40 are good, and the higher the better (Hattie, 2009). We recommend using a baseline of 0.40 standard deviation growth in student learning within a school year (Hattie, 2009). In his research, Hattie (2009) finds that the average student's academic achievement will increase yearly by 0.10 standard deviations with no instruction at all, merely as a result of the student's life experiences throughout the year. Hattie also finds that if that average student is randomly assigned a teacher for a particular grade or course, and if the teacher possesses an average level of teaching competence, the student's academic achievement will increase by 0.30 standard deviations. Combine the two factors, and the average student will improve in learning by 0.40 deviations per year, simply by living a year and regularly attending the average school.

Hattie's (2009) point is that if a school can achieve an average rate of 0.40 standard deviations in learning growth for students by doing nothing exceptional, it must specifically seek out practices proven to have a higher impact rate in order to intentionally improve student learning. Using this typical effect rate of 0.40 as our scale to judge good teaching, let's assess the most prevalent efforts to improve teaching practices and educational outcomes.

▽ **Teacher training programs:** Since the 1980s, there has been a significant increase in the collegiate coursework requirements necessary to earn a preliminary teaching credential. Beyond a subject-area degree, methods coursework, and practicum hours, most states require potential teachers to take additional classes in English language development, technology, cultural awareness, and techniques for teaching reading. Unfortunately, while teacher-preparation requirements have increased, student achievement has not. Hattie (2009) finds, in fact, that teacher-training programs have a low-leverage impact rate of 0.11 standard deviations in the annual growth of student learning—significantly lower than the 0.40 baseline of highly effective teaching strategies.

▽ **Step-and-column pay scales:** Most school districts structure their teacher-compensation scale to encourage continuing education and advanced experience. Often referred to as *step and column*, this compensation scale offers teachers higher salaries for earning continuing-education credits and postgraduate degrees, as well as for completing more years of service under the premise that greater content knowledge and teaching experience will improve teacher effectiveness. In reality, these practices produce only minimal gains in student achievement—Hattie (2009) finds that postgraduate degrees, for example, have an impact rate of 0.09. Likewise, studies that have correlated years of experience and teacher effectiveness find that teachers show the greatest productivity gains during their first few years on the job, after which their performance tends to level off (Rice, 2010). While we are not suggesting that promoting continuing education and rewarding teacher experience are nonbeneficial, it is unlikely that these practices will significantly and sustainably improve core instruction.

▽ **Ability grouping:** In the name of differentiation—in other words, in the attempt to adapt the core instructional program to meet the varying demands of individual student needs—some schools have stratified core instruction by grouping students according to their perceived ability. This practice, known as *ability grouping*, is justified with phrases such as, "We are differentiating by teaching students at *their level.*" In reality, ability grouping doesn't represent instructional differentiation; instead, it is nothing more than student tracking, a practice that has been proven controversial among educators. Hattie (2009) finds that ability grouping or tracking has minimal effects on student learning (producing just a 0.12 standard deviation) and, at the same time, can have profoundly negative effects on equity, as the students perceived to have the lowest ability are most often minorities, English learners, and students from poverty.

▽ **Flexible grouping:** Another common differentiation strategy involves the use of in-classroom flexible groupings to meet individual student needs. In this strategy, instead of grouping students by perceived ability, teachers flexibly group students within the classroom by skill. Commonly, these groups rotate through both self-guided stations and direct instruction with the teacher. Many teachers, claiming they know their students best and are in the best position to meet each student's learning needs, advocate this strategy. Hattie's (2009) meta-analysis of this practice determines an effectiveness impact of 0.18, which is hardly better than the deviation in learning improvements achieved through ability grouping (0.12)—or simply through living. (We describe using flexible grouping effectively in chapter 2, page 43.)

▽ **Class-size reduction:** During the first decade of the 21st century, many states funded class-size reduction programs to improve classroom teaching. Proponents argued that reducing class size leads to more individualized instruction, more student-centered learning, increased teacher morale, fewer student misbehaviors, and higher student engagement—all factors that should improve classroom instruction (Hattie, 2009). However, Hattie's meta-analysis of fourteen major studies on the impact of lowering class size identifies an overall impact rate of 0.21; therefore, lowering class size did not significantly impact student learning. Thus, the size of the class size itself is not as important as the quality of the instruction that takes place in it.

▽ **Teacher evaluation and merit pay:** Many states are attempting to improve teaching through a more demanding teacher evaluation process, the use of merit pay to reward teachers who demonstrate above-average results, or both. In reality, there is no evidence that either incentive-laden or overly punitive teacher evaluation processes will significantly improve instruction. In actuality, teacher evaluations do not recognize good teaching, leave poor teaching unaddressed, and do not inform decision making in any meaningful way (Weisberg, Sexton, Mulhern, & Keeling, 2009). Additionally, three out of four teachers report that their evaluation process has virtually no impact on their classroom practice (Duffett, Farkas, Rotherham, & Silva, 2008). Likewise, research consistently concludes that merit pay does not improve student achievement or change teacher behavior in a positive way. It may actually contribute to declines in student learning, as it is typically abandoned within a few years of implementation (Pfeffer & Sutton, 2006).

As you can see, each of these efforts to improve core instruction has failed to result in high-leverage education practices. There are two primary reasons for these failures.

First, the reforms have focused on the wrong outcome—ultimately, the goal of education reform is not to improve teaching but to *increase student learning*. While this difference might sound like semantics to some, in reality, it represents a seismic shift in thinking, as the effectiveness of any given teaching strategy can only be determined by evidence of its impact on student learning (DuFour & Marzano, 2011). When the goal of education reform was to improve teaching, we could logically assume that instruction could improve if teachers were required to meet more rigorous credentials and evaluation expectations, utilize research-based textbook programs, differentiate instruction in their classroom, and expect to receive bonus pay when they achieved better-than-average results in their students' learning outcomes. However, when compared to the criteria of increased student learning, all of these efforts to improve teaching fail miserably to hit the mark—wrong target, wrong result.

Second, these previous education reform efforts view teaching as primarily an individual act. That is, they assume that teaching is what each teacher does in his or her own classroom. When teaching is framed this way, then the perceived solution is to train, observe, evaluate, entice, bribe, reward, threaten, dictate, or coach each teacher into individually providing better performance—the basis of failed reform efforts previously described. We can assume that individuals with good intentions advocated, and often mandated, this litany of unsuccessful reform efforts. But as Jim Collins (2009) says in his book *How the Mighty Fall*, "Bad decisions made with good intentions are still bad decisions" (p. 148).

If coaching individual teachers into better performance has failed to significantly increase student achievement, then how does a school strengthen its core instructional program to ensure higher levels of student learning? What we will advocate for in this book, and describe in great detail, is that good teaching is not an individual act but instead a collaborative process. Good teaching is not "what *I* do *for* my students" but instead "what *we* do *with* our students." The PLC at Work process will create the framework for teacher-to-teacher collaboration, and effective differentiated instruction will engage students to be partners in learning. A review of what we know about good teaching will prove these points.

Synthesizing What We Know About Good Teaching

Based on comprehensive meta-analyses of the research on effective teaching, as well as decades of site evidence on the effectiveness of previous reform efforts, the teaching profession has never had greater consensus on what constitutes good teaching—and what does not. We know that effective teaching cannot be reduced to a single template, rubric, or checklist aligned to program fidelity, because there is no such thing as a universally effective teaching strategy, methodology, or textbook series (DuFour & Mattos, 2013). In fact, any approach that assumes such universality fails to provide teachers with the professional autonomy inherent in the art of teaching. Furthermore, requiring teachers to implement a lockstep core instructional program often restricts their flexibility, making it extremely difficult to differentiate curriculum, instruction, and assessments to meet individual student needs in the classroom.

Yet, allowing the instructional pendulum to swing completely the opposite direction, by giving teachers complete autonomy over their instructional decisions, is an equally ineffective approach to improve core instruction. As Hattie (2009) notes, "Not all teachers are effective, not all teachers are experts, and not all teachers have powerful effects on students" (p. 34). There are instructional practices that are proven to be highly effective and many that are not. Any school dedicated to ensuring that *all* students learn at high levels cannot assume that each faculty member has the knowledge, skill, or inclination to consistently use these proven practices in his or her classroom.

Based on these facts, we know that effective instruction requires an expectation that all teachers use practices proven to have the greatest impact on student learning, while simultaneously infusing their own style and offering differentiated instruction for individual student needs. The key to achieving this outcome lies in identifying and leveraging the right practices—the best practices for the kind of instruction that all students must receive, regardless of what teachers they are assigned to for core instruction. To this end, the research is abundantly clear: good teaching requires a collaborative effort. Teachers must work in collaborative teams and take collective responsibility for their students' learning. Lastly, teachers must work collaboratively with their students to engage everyone in the learning process.

Harnessing the Power of Collaborative Teams

Organizations get better results when people work collaboratively. This universal truth certainly applies to schools and the collaborative approach to good teaching. In his study of factors that most impact student learning, Hattie's (2009) first recommendation for increasing student achievement is for teachers to work collaboratively instead of in isolation. Hattie's recommendation recognizes—and experience and common sense confirm—that there is no way an individual teacher has all the time, all the skills, and all the knowledge necessary to meet every student's individual needs. The only way a school staff can achieve the mission of enabling the highest level of learning for all students is by leveraging their combined skills (DuFour, DuFour, Eaker, & Many, 2010).

If improved student learning requires a collective effort, then collaborative teacher teams are the engines that drive effective core instruction. By *team*, we do not mean loosely connected groups that assemble for traditional grade-level, department, faculty, or parent-conference meetings. Instead, to be effective, educators in teaching teams must work collaboratively to achieve the common goal of shared essential student learning outcomes. Ronald Gallimore and his colleagues find that "to be successful, teams need to set and share goals to work on that are immediately applicable to their classrooms. Without such goals, teams will drift toward superficial discussions and truncated efforts" (Gallimore, Ermeling, Saunders, & Goldenberg, 2009, p. 548). Subsequently, collaborative teams share essential student learning outcomes. Their structure could include grade-level, subject- or course-specific, vertical, or interdisciplinary teams. These common learning goals are what unite and focus the work of each teacher team.

While forming the right teacher teams is the first step in improving student achievement, just having teachers meet together does not create the collaborative effort necessary for improved teaching and learning. Teacher teams must focus their collective efforts on the instructional practices proven to best increase student achievement. This right work can be captured in the four critical questions of the PLC at Work process (DuFour et al., 2010).

1. What do we want our students to learn?

2. How will we know if our students are learning?

3. How will we respond when students don't learn?

4. How will we respond when they do?

Let's examine these critical questions and the role their answers play in efforts to promote the practices of good teaching.

What Do We Want Our Students to Learn?

Effective teaching begins with teacher teams collectively determining just what they want their students to learn. There is, perhaps, no greater obstacle to effective teaching than the overwhelmingly and inappropriately large number of standards that dictate what curriculum content students are to master in school. The elements of these mandatory curricula are so numerous, in fact, that teachers cannot even adequately *cover* them, let alone effectively *teach* them (Buffum et al., 2012).

The research supporting the need for teacher teams to collectively prioritize, analyze, and unpack the curriculum is conclusive. In their work on RTI, Buffum et al. (2012) refer to this process of analysis and prioritization as *concentrated instruction*: "a systematic process of identifying essential knowledge and skills that all students must master to learn at high levels, and determining the specific learning needs for each child to get there" (p. 10). Marzano (2003) describes this same process of instruction as offering a guaranteed, viable curriculum—one in which every student has access to the same essential learning targets and every student will receive instruction on those targets in a way that will enable him or her to master them within the allotted time.

Buffum et al. (2012) and Marzano (2003) aren't alone in addressing the need for instructional processes that focus on an agreed-on set of essential learning standards. Douglas Reeves (2002) also describes the critical importance of teacher teams identifying essential learning outcomes in *Making Standards Work*, Larry Ainsworth (2003a, 2003b) details these efforts in *Power Standards* and *"Unwrapping" the Standards*, and Grant Wiggins and Jay McTighe (2005) powerfully and comprehensively outline this essential work in *Understanding by Design*. Proponents don't claim that these essential standards represent everything the curriculum will cover in the year. Instead, the standards merely identify the most essential learning outcomes that all students must master for a higher likelihood of success in the next unit, course, or grade level. (In chapter 4, page 79, we examine more deeply the process of setting and applying these standards.) Any school dedicated to creating an effective core instructional program and a targeted system of interventions must have absolute clarity on exactly what all students must learn in each subject, course, and grade level.

Beyond just identifying essential standards, teacher teams must also understand what it looks and sounds like when students demonstrate mastery of each standard and collaboratively sequence these standards to represent a guaranteed and viable curriculum (Marzano, 2003). Finally, teachers must explicitly, clearly, and consistently model mastery. When teacher teams determine a limited number of rigorous essential learning outcomes that all students must master, and agree to how students will demonstrate mastery of each, the impact rate is 0.56—a rate much higher than the baseline of 0.40 for highly effective teaching (Hattie, 2009).

How Will We Know If Our Students Are Learning?

While the strategies for teaching a specific learning target might vary from teacher to teacher, each teacher team must commit to collectively assessing student learning at predetermined times during core instruction. This method of gauging student mastery of essential outcomes, *convergent assessment*, is "an ongoing process of collectively analyzing targeted evidence to determine the specific learning needs of each child and the effectiveness of the instruction the child receives in meeting these needs" (Buffum et al., 2012, p. 10).

Convergent assessment leverages two extremely powerful instructional practices: common assessments and formative assessments. *Common assessments* are any assessment two or more instructors give with the intention of collaboratively examining the results to assess shared learning, to guide instructional planning for individual students, and to shape instructional modifications (Erkens & Twadell, 2012). When teachers give common assessments aligned to essential standards, they are able to compare results to determine which initial instructional practices are producing the best results. *Formative assessments* are classroom and curriculum evaluations teachers use to monitor student progress toward learning outcomes and to inform instructional decision making. Rather than considering these as assessments *of* learning, assessment expert Rick Stiggins (2007) calls them assessments *for* learning, because they inform both teachers and students. Teachers embed formative assessments in the current unit of instruction and use them to diagnose where students are in their learning.

It is important to note that not all formative assessments have to be given in common, and not all common assessments need to be formative. But when teachers combine these two powerful assessment processes, Hattie (2009) finds that common formative assessments have the astonishing impact rate of 0.90. (In chapter 6, page 145, we take a closer and more detailed look at the assessment process.) Any school committed to a highly effective core instructional program would ensure that teacher-created common formative assessments, designed to guide both teachers and students in their next steps, would be the foundation of assessment practices.

How Will We Respond When Students Don't and Do Learn?

How do educators respond when students struggle to achieve essential learning targets? Furthermore, how do they respond when students succeed in achieving those learning outcomes? The purpose of RTI is to answer these two questions. Tier 1 core instruction creates the instructional focus and ongoing assessment processes necessary to effectively respond when students need additional support.

Now, consider for a moment the prerequisite conditions necessary for a school to successfully provide supplemental and intensive interventions for students who require additional support and extended learning for those who are ready to master grade-level curriculum. Asking an individual teacher to meet all these needs in his or her classroom would be unrealistic. Educators who have formed the collaborative teams of a PLC can respond collectively when students need additional time for remediation or extended learning. Yet, teachers on the same team could not collectively provide these supports unless they first agreed on essential learning outcomes and the kind of ongoing common and formative assessment information necessary to identify both student needs and the effectiveness of initial instruction. Creating a guaranteed and viable curriculum and ongoing common formative assessment processes are the foundational building blocks of an effective Tier 1 core instructional program. They are also practices that drive and depend on frequent, job-embedded teacher collaboration. These practices do not reduce teachers to the role of instructional facilitators but instead empower teacher teams to make critical decisions regarding curriculum, instruction, and assessment. Equally important, these PLC practices don't cripple an individual teacher's ability to practice the art of teaching. They give educators the freedom to determine how they will initially teach essential standards.

Leveraging the Power of Student Collaboration

As important as teacher collaboration is to good instruction, teacher-to-student and student-to-student collaboration are equally essential to the learning process. As we discuss in chapter 2, the neuroscience of learning confirms that the brain seeks social interaction, relevance, and meaning. Students are best able to develop these attributes when they are engaged in the learning process, rather than being mere idle spectators in the classroom. Student engagement begins when teachers carefully create a classroom environment that provides safety and order but also promotes student participation in the instructional process. Equally important, teachers must provide students the opportunity to answer the four critical PLC questions from their own perspective. Then, those questions become:

1. What do I need to learn?

2. How will I know if I am learning it?

3. What must I do when I am not learning?

4. What can I do to extend my learning?

Having students answer these questions can help them develop what Hattie (2009) identifies as the most powerful leverage of learning at our disposal—self-grading. Self-grading is when students:

▽ Clearly understand what they must learn

▽ Clearly know what they must be able to do to demonstrate proficiency

▽ Know how to self-assess their progress

▽ Have strategies to successfully respond when their efforts fall short

Students cannot master these outcomes through passive observation. When students develop the ability to self-grade, the impact rate is 1.44—the highest impact rate Hattie (2009) reports in his initial study. Beyond offering self-assessments of their performance, students also benefit from playing an active role in the creation and implementation of strategies to improve their performance—practices that we will describe in detail throughout this book. Unless teachers can see students successfully demonstrate what they taught, then they have no evidence that learning has taken place. Furthermore, teachers cannot observe this when students are passive participants in the learning process. Learning requires teachers working with their students and students working with each other to transform instruction into application and action.

In this chapter, we've explored the big picture of good teaching and how the PLC process is essential to an effective core instructional program. We've also taken a brief look at some of the previous attempts to improve core instruction and why those efforts failed. While all of these powerful ideas are worthy of deep and ongoing discussion, this book isn't just a collection of ideas—or guiding principles and general concepts. Instead, it offers specific recommendations and proven tools to achieve these outcomes. In the next chapter, we do just that, as we dig deeper into the process of creating a brain-friendly classroom environment and explaining how that environment contributes to the successful implementation of best practices at Tier 1.

Taking the Discussion Further

Following are some of the important ideas from this chapter that are worthy of further reflection and discussion. Educators in a PLC may want to read through this chapter with their collaborative teams and discuss each section, recording the issues related to each piece of information and considering classroom implications for students. Collaborative teams can reflect on the prompts to deepen understanding and set subsequent goals for improvement.

▽ What are some of the past efforts to improve core instruction? Why didn't they work?

▽ Revisit Hattie's (2009) quote, "Not all teachers are effective, not all teachers are experts, and not all teachers have powerful effects on students" (p. 34). Discuss its implications for your classroom and school and the core curriculum.

▽ What are the two characteristics of good teaching? How do your teams illustrate these?

▽ Revisit the quote "Good teaching is not 'what *I* do *for* my students' but instead 'what *we* do *with* our students.'" How is collaboration part of your instruction?

▽ How can you use the four critical questions of a PLC in your collaborative teams to further student learning? How can students answer these questions?

▽ What are the benefits of common assessments? How do your teams use them to plan further instruction?

Creating Brain-Friendly Learning Environments

We've seen that educators must routinely—even daily—differentiate quality learning opportunities in order to meet diverse student needs and preferences and to enable students to succeed in core instruction. Understanding specifically how to structure differentiated instruction in a way that will increase the chances of student success, however, demands that educators have some basic grounding in learners' biological and psychological needs. While a number of factors shape the brain's ability to survive and thrive, none are more critical than the classroom climate and environment. Beyond its power to influence the development of a learner's brain, classroom environment can also play a role in students' overall physical and emotional well-being. As we see in this chapter, multiple factors influence the classroom environment and climate—everything from body language to room décor affects learning.

Few teachers entered the field in order to spend more time thinking about brain science, but the more educators know and understand about how the brain operates, the more sensitive they can be to their students' needs and the better able they'll be to optimize learners' success. Fortunately, a lot of information is available on the subject of the learning environment, and more research emerges daily with implications for classroom practice. Although neuroscience will never tell us how to teach, this ever-growing bank of data on *neuroeducation* leaves little doubt about the influence of neuroscientific principles on educational practices. John Geake (2009), a professor and cofounder of the Oxford Cognitive Neuroscience Education Forum, reports, "Relevant and useful professional and classroom applications of educational neuroscience will increasingly become available as we gradually come to understand more about brain function through neuroscience research which answers educational questions about learning, memory, motivation and so on" (p. 10). The best practices educators can employ to leverage what neuroscience teaches us about the effect of environment on learning involve creating a classroom environment that supports trial and error, encourages risk taking, promotes collaboration, and includes meaningful, relevant, and engaging instruction. By understanding the fundamental elements of a brain-friendly classroom we outline in this chapter, educators can be better prepared to incorporate those elements into their own classroom environment and, in doing so, remove some of the most persistent stumbling blocks students encounter as they work to achieve learning goals.

In this chapter, we'll explore the many ways educators can create and maintain a classroom climate and environment that contribute to the optimal intellectual, emotional, and physical development of their students. From controlling stressors to creating structure, enabling a more social classroom experience, and engaging students more actively in their own learning experience and achievement, the ideas and techniques we outline in this chapter offer educators multiple opportunities to build an environment that promotes and supports student achievement.

Maintaining a Safe and Secure Climate for Learning

Creating a supportive classroom environment can maximize student engagement and create conditions for success, and it represents one of the powerful strategies educators use in delivering daily differentiated instruction. Although most brains operate in similar ways, each brain is uniquely based on the individual's genetics and environmental experiences (Shaw et al., 2006). As a result, we all have different ways in which we process information and demonstrate competence. At the same time, we each react differently to environmental stressors such as isolation, bullying, and aggressive behaviors. In the classroom, events that go unnoticed by one student may dramatically interfere with another student's ability to listen or participate in class.

Teachers intuitively know these differences exist, yet still may offer a one-size-fits-all curriculum. As teachers grow in experience and gain insight and expertise, however, their repertoire of instructional strategies and their understanding of how and where to use them evolve. The strategy of differentiated instruction is predicated on this understanding of each student's unique nature and needs. Neuroscience has much to tell us about creating a classroom environment that feels safe and supportive for *all* student brains along with a classroom climate that promotes the kind of physical and emotional nourishment that contributes to both a healthy mind and a healthy body. Because every student in the classroom comes with his or her own set of learning needs and preferences, educators can draw on the variety of techniques we outline here to create a brain-friendly environment that will help all students achieve their learning goals.

The Role of Stress in Brain Development

Perhaps the most potent factor shaping brain development in any environment is stress. The brain is a survival organ, and stress is one of the brain's survival responses to real or perceived environmental threats. Stress is a normal element of life, and brains can grow and even thrive on appropriate stress levels. Excessive stress, however, can create dramatic physical and emotional responses that can interfere with our ability to think and interact appropriately.

When we experience a real or perceived danger or other stressful situation, our brain's default system for emergencies kicks into high gear. Our amygdala (the *emotional sentinel* embedded deep in the limbic area on each side of the brain) goes on high alert. It begins scanning to identify the threat and then to decide whether to fight or flee, a reflexive automatic response that temporarily bypasses our executive, or reflective, brain functions (Posner & Rothbart, 2007; Zull, 2002). In the classroom, a student's brain may go into survival mode—or reflexive action—as a result of being ridiculed, humiliated, or bullied or in response to a fear of failure, confusion, or a task that is too far outside his or her knowledge or skill capabilities. Beyond matching challenges to student skill levels, educators also must monitor for signs of multiple other stress inducers, such as isolation from peers, unclear expectations, and lack of both physical and emotional support structures. These kinds of stress-inducing events can deeply influence a student's opinion about school. Physical and emotional support structures may include different types of seating for comfort and variety—bean bag chairs, mats on the floor, or different height and work surfaces to appeal to certain tasks. Additionally, when classrooms have rules, routines, and expectations, students' anxiety and stress will lessen.

Our attention guides us to interpret sound, movement, color, and pain, in a state referred to as *stimulus-driven attention*. When goals drive our attention, rather than environmental stimuli, our brain engages with activities that appear meaningful and interesting. Once an immediate threat has passed, our brain is able to return to the goal-driven attention of higher-level thinking. In that state, the brain can ignore stimuli and put all its energy into the task at hand (Medina, 2008). That's not to say that students learn best in a total stress-free environment. Without any pressure to learn, students have little motivation to do the hard work necessary to achieve learning goals. That's why educators must work toward creating a classroom environment marked by appropriate stress levels, which neuroscientist Antonio Damasio (2003) calls *maximal cognitive efficiency* and describes as occurring when challenge meets skill.

As you can see, high alert is not an optimal condition for classroom learning. Students thrive when they have both a high motivation to succeed and appropriate levels of stress. In an environment of excessive stress levels, student performance and engagement suffer (Goleman, 2006c). Therefore, controlling the level of stress within the classroom matters deeply in maximizing student learning.

Environmental Stressors

By controlling the types and levels of environmental stressors, educators can create a brain-friendly environment that promotes optimal learning conditions and eliminates the anticipatory anxiety students suffer when they are in constant fear of unexpected and upsetting events. A brain-friendly classroom, therefore, is one governed by clear, logical, and well-explained routines. A lack of clear and reliable routines can be one of the greatest sources of stress in any classroom. Without clear direction, consistent practices, well-defined learning goals, and established criteria for gauging learning progress, students can feel lost, unnerved, and powerless to play a determining role in their own academic success.

Rather than condemning students to a classroom experience filled with stress and anticipatory anxiety, educators who supply clarity, structure, and ample emotional and physical support in the classroom create a climate of relaxed alertness that can aid, rather than inhibit, student learning. The following list offers three practical guidelines for building a classroom environment that encourages student learning and academic success—not rules, so much as healthy habits that help teachers and students work together effectively.

1. **Develop norms or expectations for classroom behaviors:** Students can contribute their own ideas to this list, but here are some critical expectations for every classroom.

   ▸ One person speaks at a time (whether in large or small groups).

   ▸ Everyone listens respectfully.

   ▸ We can fix and correct mistakes.

2. **Build a community:** Students must know one another and respect the differences, strengths, and needs of fellow students. Early in elementary classrooms, teachers need to stress the idea that students are to learn together and help each other. That understanding sets students on the path of collaboration. In a differentiated classroom, students will work in partnerships and in groups of all sizes. Those collaborative alliances give students an opportunity to better know their classmates and to share ideas and opinions in the relative safety of a few individuals, rather than in front of the entire class where students can feel more vulnerable to ridicule (Gregory & Kaufeldt, 2012).

Furthermore, group interactions in a learning community may actually promote brain health. Edward Hallowell (2011) suggests we have a biological need to interact with others, and if that need too often goes unfulfilled, we actually lose brain cells. Hallowell's findings also support Maslow's (1968) and Glasser's (1998) basic needs theories of belonging and being included.

3. **Establish classroom organization and management strategies:** Clear classroom routines and procedures reduce anticipatory anxiety and save time and disruption in the classroom. Any confusion in this area will result in a lot of off-task behavior among students in elementary classrooms. Educators, therefore, should establish procedures that address:

   ▸ What students are to do when they come to class

   ▸ How teachers or students will distribute materials

   ▸ Where students are to hand in assignments

   ▸ What students are to do when they finish a task (such as sponge activities to absorb time in a productive way or anchor activities to extend learning)

   ▸ What students are to do when they don't know what to do

   ▸ How students get help if they need it

   ▸ How students should form groups

   ▸ How the class maintains a tidy and orderly classroom

   ▸ How students are to work with others

Besides teaching these guidelines, posting or displaying them in the classroom so students can refer to them while working provides support for successful interactions and creates autonomy and efficacy.

Healthy Brains and Bodies

Of course, the physical environment isn't the only factor that influences student learning. Students also require adequate physical movement and nutrition in order to remain alert and on task throughout the day. Fortunately, educators also have some influence over these elements of a safe and supportive classroom environment.

When students sit all day, they deplete the flow of blood to their brain. Without adequate blood flow, the brain doesn't receive the levels of oxygen and glucose necessary to support its operation at levels of high efficiency. That's why it's so important that students have an opportunity to get up and move throughout the day. Physical activity helps wake up the learner. The importance of physical activity in brain health goes beyond its role in improving blood flow. University of Illinois studies show that regular exercise can increase the basal ganglia and hippocampus in a child's brain (Reynolds, 2010), changes which improve attention, memory, and cortical functions. (The basal ganglia is found at the base of the forebrain, and its main role is to monitor and regulate activities in the premotor and motor cortexes to facilitate seamless voluntary movements. The hippocampus, a small seahorse-shaped organ in the temporal region of the brain, is part of the limbic system and thus helps regulate emotions. It is also responsible for creating long-term memory during rapid eye movement [REM] sleep and is instrumental in spatial navigation.) Furthermore, twenty minutes of exercise will increase blood calcium, which stimulates the brain's release of dopamine (the pleasure neurotransmitter). An associate clinical professor of psychiatry at Harvard Medical School, John Ratey (2008), suggests that even mild exercise releases norepinephrine and serotonin, two neurotransmitters that help regulate energy and emotions. Serotonin also supports self-esteem and learning. These neurotransmitters also benefit students with attention deficit disorder.

Yet, there is even more evidence suggesting that exercise promotes brain health. In *Spark: The Revolutionary New Science of Exercise and the Brain*, John Ratey (2008) describes a critical biological link among emotions, thought, and movement. This *brain-derived neurotrophic factor*, or BDNF, is a protein that works like a master molecule to promote growth in dendritic cells—cells that play an important role in the immune system. The BDNF, or *Miracle-Gro for the brain* as Ratey (2008) puts it, increases voltage in the electromagnetic charges of the brain's neurons, thus improving the signal strength. Additionally, it helps increase the brain's levels of serotonin. Educators can help students increase their levels of this so-called fertilizer by ensuring that classroom routines incorporate ample opportunities for physical activity. Here are just some of the ways teachers can get their students up and moving.

▽ Get students up out of their seats frequently to talk to a partner, pass out materials, or hand in work.

▽ Ask students to physically move to a new work area, such as a new group, workstation, or study center.

▽ Take stretch breaks, perhaps set to music to up the energy level.

▽ Take movement breaks to play games such as Simon Says or the Hokey Pokey.

Music can play an important role in nourishing student brains through movement and exercise. Because music can be so engaging, setting activity times to music can create a physical, mental, *and* emotional break for students. Music creates a sense of fun and spirit, even in learning tasks. Educators can, for example, use music as they help students learn hand jives that can serve as memory tools for remembering a process or concept such as number facts, letter shapes, and geometric shapes. These are just some of the ways that physical activity can nourish student brains and benefit their learning processes.

Of course, students also require whole-body nourishment. You can't learn if you're hungry, and many students come to school hungry. Even with free and reduced-cost breakfasts and lunches, many students still lack adequate nutrition. While educators can't ensure that students get to school on time to take advantage of a free breakfast or that they have adequate food at home, they can provide nutritional boosts to students throughout the day. In fact, frequent minimeals are preferable to fewer, heavier meals, in order to keep students' glucose levels up (Riby, Law, McLaughlin, & Murray, 2011). School districts that offer a balanced school day (usually consisting of three one-hundred-minute learning periods, two short recess breaks, and a longer forty-five-minute lunch) allow students to bring two snacks or lunches, which sustains glucose throughout the day. This schedule also allows for regular physical activity (Peebles & Kirkwood, 2011).

In schools with more traditional school schedules, teachers might keep some nutritious snacks (if schools permit) to help students who get into a slump. Complex carbohydrates and proteins, like granola bars or string cheese, are better choices for these snacks, since they take longer to digest and don't cause the spike and crash of simple sugars and starchy foods.

Finally, educators can teach students the need for good nutrition and model good nutritional choices by emphasizing the need to drink plenty of water during the day. Water is part of the body's nutritional arsenal for maintaining attention and alertness. The body is 75 percent water, so it requires frequent hydration. By the time we feel thirsty, we're already beginning to be dehydrated. Therefore, students should have access to water bottles or fountains as needed. In addition to giving students adequate amounts of water during the day, teachers must also offer frequent bathroom breaks.

Again, educators have an important role to play in nourishing students' minds *and* bodies. These are just some of the ways that educators can help accomplish that goal.

Mindfulness

In addition to challenging lessons, group work, physical activity, and adequate nourishment, students also need quiet time to process information and reflect on tasks. In *The Hurried Child*, David Elkind (2007), an American child psychologist and longtime professor at Tufts University, writes about young children who have their every waking minute filled with activity. Thus, they have little of the respite time necessary for metacognition, an activity that allows them to consolidate their thinking and develop the awareness of their own identity and thought patterns.

Even without a full schedule, a student's brain is constantly busy, processing data and responding to external stimuli—even a teacher's eye-rolling or sigh of exasperation can trigger the student's brain to send out distress signals and derail learning. Managing emotions and self-regulation, therefore, are key skills for success in school and life. Daniel Goleman (2006b), in his significant book *Emotional Intelligence*, suggests five components necessary for successful living.

1. Having emotional awareness

2. Managing one's emotions

3. Self-regulating and self-motivating

4. Showing empathy

5. Using appropriate social skills

How can educators help students develop and foster these characteristics as habits? One way is by teaching students techniques for developing *mindfulness*—a term with multiple definitions but that we use to describe the state of purposely paying attention to one's thoughts and feelings. Students of all ages, from elementary to high school, can benefit from mindfulness training. By incorporating some short, easy-to-do mindfulness exercises into daily classroom routines, teachers can help students learn to be more aware of—and, thus, able to control—their thoughts and actions. Not only does mindfulness training help students manage their emotions, but it also can help improve their attention and develop their abilities of concentration, conflict resolution, and empathy for others—all of which offer huge payoffs for school and life. Practicing mindfulness can help build a calm atmosphere in the classroom and improve the overall classroom environment.

Teaching mindfulness doesn't require complicated strategies. A very basic mindfulness strategy, for example, is simply teaching students to quiet themselves and take some deep breaths. Teachers also can encourage students to eliminate the distracting noise of external stimuli by taking a short walk or focusing on a short period of creative exploration, such as drawing or using noise-canceling headphones, or simply taking a short time-out to regroup thinking before moving to another learning exercise or activity. See also the Hawn Foundation (http://thehawnfoundation.org /mindup) for more on mindfulness and mindful awareness training.

In the 21st century, we are bombarded with stimuli that fight for our attention. Helping students learn to use the quiet, reflective time mindfulness affords can teach them to be more in the moment, rather than obsessing about past events or future worries. At the same time, mindfulness goes a long way to quiet student spirits and, in the process, increase their ability to focus their attention on the task at hand.

Providing Relevant, Meaningful, and Engaging Instruction

Learning new information can be a stressful experience for students and, therefore, needs special attention from educators as they attempt to build a brain-friendly classroom. The more relevant, meaningful, and engaging the learning experience, the more effective it will be for students in the classroom.

One way to make learning more engaging is to make it more accessible, something educators can accomplish by helping students anchor new ideas and understandings to familiar concepts. The brain connects new information to existing information by looking for similarities in patterns and schemas, a process Ratey (2008) refers to as *chaining*, and which pediatrician and author Mel Levine (1993) describes as *horizontal threading*. In other words, the brain can't connect new information unless there is something with which to hook it. For this reason, preassessing is an important tool for educators to use before teaching a new topic. If students have little or no prior knowledge or skills associated with new topics (which is to be expected in early-elementary students), teachers need to know so they can provide the important backfill of information necessary to help students make connections and understand. By giving students advance organizers and pointing out connections, teachers can help develop the schemas and patterns necessary to help students feel less intimidated or overwhelmed by new learning. First introduced by David Ausubel in 1968, advance organizers, sometimes called a hook or anticipatory set, are tools teachers use to introduce the lesson's content before starting a new topic. They also are helpful in gathering preassessment information. (See chapter 5, page 131, for examples of advance organizers.)

Educators also can help students find meaning in new material by engaging a number of their senses in the learning experience. Of the five acute senses—hearing, vision, touch, scent, and taste—educators often only engage the first two in the classroom. Vision is a great attention-getter and is far more powerful than hearing, as students often tune out the teacher's voice (Sousa & Tomlinson, 2010). Nevertheless, most classroom teachers try to gain and keep their students' attention through *teacher talk*. Richard Mayer (2010), a psychology professor at the University of California, Santa Barbara, indicates that students learn better from multisensory teaching than from learning that engages only one sensory modality.

Mayer is not alone in these findings. James Medina (2008), developmental molecular biologist and affiliate professor of bioengineering at the University of Washington School of Medicine, shows that memory is more accurate and retained longer when learning is multisensory. According to his studies, classrooms that provide sensory-enriched environments contribute to increased dendritic growth. When students engage in multiple rehearsals and practice using their brain's visual, auditory, and kinesthetic pathways, they actually strengthen the connections between the brain's dendritic cells and increase the efficiency of recall and use of information (Medina, 2008).

Learning also becomes more familiar and engaging when it has relevance. Students respond better to real-world situations, examples, and artifacts. Students don't always find reading information in a textbook interesting and stimulating. Here are some other simple techniques to make learning more relevant for students.

▽ Offering students the opportunity to use manipulatives, such as counting materials or using hands-on materials to represent fractions, to develop mathematics concepts and virtual reality technology to experience a new topic, location, or concept

▽ Allowing opportunities for concrete operations, such as students actually working through a science experiment or constructing a model

▽ Using field trips and guest speakers to get students out into the world and to bring the world into the classroom

In essence, the brain strives to make sense of the world and seeks to understand. The brain has a natural innate *seeking system*, an emotional system that causes us to be curious and explore to find what we need (Panksepp, 1998). Rita Smilkstein (2003) suggests that learning is an innate human need that drives us all to be curious and seek out information about our world. As we have seen, humans also respond to novelty, interest, and experiences, and these types of stimulation contribute to the growth of the brain's dendrites (Diamond & Hopson, 1998). *Dendrites* are branch-like extensions in a brain cell that receive messages from the axon of another neuron. As students learn, dendrites connect to create a larger network. Multiple rehearsals and practice using visual, auditory, and kinesthetic pathways strengthen these connections and cause *myelination*—a thickening of the connections that increases the efficiency of recall and ease of use (Medina, 2008). By providing a strong foundation of a new concept or skill, we are creating new dendrites—or pathways—to higher levels of learning. Helping students see relevance, usefulness, and the real-world applications of what they are learning increases engagement and offers purpose for the brain—and, thus, is fundamental to creating a brain-friendly learning environment.

Giving Students More Ownership of Their Learning

As the examples we've explored in this chapter indicate, activity and participation, rather than just passive participation in the educational experience, encourage student learning. One powerful technique for actively engaging students in the learning experience is by giving them more ownership over it. The work of theorists John Dewey (1938), Jean Piaget (1997), and Lev Vygotsky (1978), fundamentally the fathers of student-focused learning, enlightens us on how children learn best. As they identify, *student-centered responsibility* is an approach to curriculum planning that takes into account students' interests, learning preferences, and abilities. It is rooted in the constructive principles of learning whereby students take ownership and have choices about what, how, and why they are learning. This approach infuses the learning process with problem solving, creative thinking, and critical thinking as it develops students' metacognitive skills.

Much research and writing have focused on the idea of giving students more responsibility over the content and pace of their learning. J. Scott Armstrong (2012) claims, "Traditional education ignores or suppresses learner responsibility" (p. 2). *Self-determination theory* also supports why this type of learning works (Deci & Ryan, 2002). This theory suggests that learning is always self-directed or self-determined. If students are allowed to control their learning, it becomes their reward.

Student-centered learning offers numerous benefits. It allows students to study what they are curious about and to achieve curriculum goals. It also enables students to use a variety of strategies to suit their learning preferences and satisfy their social needs for communication, collaboration, and peer support. Student-centered learning also contributes to a supportive and nourishing classroom environment by:

▽ Promoting motivation and attention

▽ Fostering peer communication

▽ Reducing behavior issues

▽ Building teacher-student and student-student relationships

▽ Developing student responsibility for learning

▽ Improving thinking and problem-solving skills

If students can see themselves in the curriculum, recognize its relevance to their lives, and feel like they have some input into what and how they will learn, they generally feel less stressed and more committed, thus freeing the brain to be alert and engaged. In chapter 4 (page 77), we'll discuss supporting student-centered learning in a powerful core curriculum.

Promoting a Growth Mindset

In her popular book *Mindset: The New Psychology of Success*, Stanford University psychologist Carol Dweck (2006) shares her theory of *mindset*. People have one of two mental predispositions toward intelligence: either a fixed or a growth mindset. Those with a *fixed* mindset believe that they are either intelligent or not, and this condition predicts potential. Those with a *growth* mindset believe that intelligence can increase over time as the brain changes and grows (through the process of neuroplasticity). This brain plasticity, and its role in the continued growth of the brain's dendrites and neural connections, is responsible for learning even into old age. A growth mindset—among both teachers and students—plays a pivotal role in promoting student success, as it helps educators build an intellectually and emotionally nourishing classroom environment (Dweck, 2006).

Mindsets can influence how teachers and students approach school and learning. A shared belief among students and teachers in students' ability to succeed makes a significant difference in student achievement. That's why educators need to share information with students of all ages about the ability of the brain to change and grow over time with new experiences and practice. Elementary students feel encouraged when educators stress that, although they may not grasp a new concept or skill immediately, they can rehearse that idea or skill over time until they achieve or perfect it. That mastery offers multiple rewards. Through perseverance and determination, the brain produces its own incentive with a dopamine release as students get closer to their goal and anticipate achievement.

Dweck (2006) describes a New York experiment where teachers told one group of students that they were smart; rather than bestowing this label on another group of students, educators instead complimented those students on their effort during a task. When given future opportunities, the first group of students didn't engage in challenging tasks, as they didn't want to risk their smart status. They often gave up easily, reasoning that if you have to work too hard, you aren't clever. They were often defensive, blamed others, and cheated to do well. In contrast, the group of students who teachers praised for their efforts enjoyed challenge and continued to choose challenging tasks in the future. They appeared to be more resilient and were possibility thinkers who demonstrated perseverance and grit.

As these studies show, students benefit when educators promote a growth mindset. By encouraging students to believe that they can learn and master new learning, skills, and challenges, teachers prepare them for the task of succeeding in an ever-changing world. Emily Diehl (Mindset Works, 2002), a Mindset Works trainer, suggests these great feedback prompts to promote a growth mindset. (Visit Mindset Works, www.mindsetworks.com/free-resources, for more resources. Visit **go.solution-tree.com /RTIatWork** to access materials related to this book.)

When a student is struggling despite a strong effort:

▽ "If this was easy then you wouldn't be learning anything new!"

▽ "You can do this! Let's break this down into smaller chunks."

▽ "Look how much progress you have made!"

When a student is struggling and needs help:

▽ "What parts of this were hard for you? Show or tell me . . ."

▽ "Let's do one together. Describe your process out loud so I know you're thinking."

▽ "Let me show you another way to try. Maybe this will help you solve it."

When a student is making progress:

▽ "You are using the strategies we discussed. Keep it up!"

▽ "You have really stuck with this and persevered!"

▽ "Your hard work is really evident!"

When a student succeeds with strong effort:

▽ "All that hard work and effort paid off!"

▽ "What strategies did you use that contributed to your success?"

▽ "Congratulations! I am very proud of you for not giving up!"

When a student succeeds easily without effort:

▽ "You're ready for something more challenging!"

▽ "You really have that down. Let's find something that will challenge you a bit more."

▽ "What skill would you like to work on next?"

Infusing the educational process with this kind of positive energy enables students to embrace the idea that they don't have to *know* everything, they simply must be willing—even eager—to learn. That's why the growth mindset plays such a central role in creating a learning environment that stimulates and engages learners, rather than overwhelms them.

Supporting the Social Brain

Jaak Panksepp (1998)—psychologist, psychobiologist, neuroscientist, and the Baily Endowed Chair of Animal Well-Being Science at Washington State University's College of Veterinary Medicine—reminds us that humans need to connect, cooperate, and collaborate. Humans have a *contact urge* (Gopnik, Meltzoff, & Kuhl, 1999); we need both independent time and the company of others (Covey, 1989). We also need social interaction time to develop normal neurocognitive functions. Neuroscientists have discovered, for example, *mirror neurons* that are responsible for being able to replicate the brain state of others. As you watch someone else interact, express ideas, and otherwise engage in social exchanges, these mirror neurons enable you to pattern yourself after that person and his or her actions (Freedman, 2007). In essence, when creating a classroom environment designed to support and promote student learning, educators can accommodate students' social brain by encouraging healthy student relationships, cultural responsiveness, and social skills.

Socialization is an important aspect of any student's learning process and a key element of the best practices for creating a brain-friendly classroom. Still, opportunities for social development can be easy for educators to overlook. Although young students may enjoy social interaction, for example, some may lack the skills to play successfully and collaborate with partners or small groups. As a result, educators must be alert to how students perform both at play and in class work. While students often learn information by watching DVDs or working on a computer, educators fail to promote student social development when they forget to provide the kind of student follow-up discussion that is essential for developing both vocabulary and social skills.

As we addressed earlier in this chapter, emotional intelligence is key for success in life (Goleman, 2006b). Students need to be emotionally self-aware and self-managing, and they need to be able to self-motivate and self-regulate. The student's need for social and emotional intelligence extends well beyond the classroom; empathy and social skills are crucial in getting along in business, industry, and the world at large. So, let's take some time now to explore ideas and techniques for incorporating support for the social brain into the elementary classroom environment.

Developing Strong Teacher-Student Relationships

As we have noted, the brain is a social organ, and humans have an innate need to connect (Gopnik et al., 1999). The most meaningful demonstration of this connection comes through positive relationships, and the importance of that connection is evident in the influence of the teacher-student relationship on student learning. Studies show that improving teacher-student relationships can increase student achievement; when those relationships are good, students want to be at school and do better academically, and they foster resiliency (Battistich, Schaps, & Wilson, 2004; Birch & Ladd, 1997; Hamre & Pianta, 2001). Teachers who develop positive relationships with students report that attendance is better and that students are more self-directed, cooperative, and motivated (Birch & Ladd, 1997; Klem & Connell, 2004).

We also know that when students feel less lonely and isolated, their academic achievement improves. Teachers who use student-directed learning have more positive relationships and greater student engagement (Daniels & Perry, 2003; Perry & Weinstein, 1998). Hattie (2009) also places positive relationships high on the list of impactful strategies for student learning, with a 0.72 effect size on learning growth.

In contrast, students who have a history of poor relationships with teachers in their elementary years (from kindergarten days through eighth grade) often show poor academic achievement and more behavior problems than those with positive relationships. This lag in achievement is often greater for boys than girls (Hamre & Pianta, 2001). Finally, other research indicates that students with closer relationships and fewer conflicts with their teachers demonstrate better social skills by middle school (Berry & O'Connor, 2010).

Positive teacher-student relationships are evident in multiple ways. Here are just some indicators of these relationships.

▽ Teachers enjoy and find pleasure in teaching, and students know this.

▽ Teachers act in a respectful and responsive way.

▽ Teachers willingly give help and assistance to students.

▽ Teachers help students develop metacognitive skills.

▽ Teachers rarely show aggravation or disdain toward students.

▽ Teachers know details about students' lives and show an interest.

There are many ways educators can promote and maintain these strong relationships with their students. Some practices and techniques include the following.

▽ **Making the effort to know students beyond their academic ability:** By discovering what they can about students' interests, hobbies, and dreams, teachers can build stronger connections with their students and develop a deeper understanding of what motivates them. Teachers can use surveys and exit tickets appropriate for use with elementary-age students to help gather information about the students' interests, hobbies, and activities outside of school (Croninger & Lee, 2001). (We talk more about using exit tickets in chapter 3, page 70.) Some teachers make it a point to use all their students' names on the first day of school, astonishing their students and strengthening their relationship with them.

▽ **Arranging to have one-on-one time with students who are especially shy or challenging:** One-on-one interactions can help teachers understand more reserved students and identify what types of activities might help build connections with them. Research shows that such exchanges can help students see educators as people who care about them (Pianta, 1999; Rudasill et al., 2014).

▽ **Remembering the message that body language sends:** People communicate through expressions and actions as well as with words. As we have seen earlier in this chapter, head-shaking and eye-rolling can send negative messages that alienate students (Pianta & Hamre, 2001; Rimm-Kaufman et al., 2002).

▽ **Communicating frequently that all students can do well:** Teachers who consistently let their students know that they want *all* of them to succeed create a positive warm climate in the classroom and develop a supportive community of learners. This kind of ongoing assurance also fosters positive peer relationships among students (Charney, 2002; Donohue, Perry, & Weinstein, 2003).

Promoting Cultural Responsivity

Culture is the system of shared beliefs, values, customs, behaviors, and artifacts that society uses to understand our world and one another. *Cultural responsivity* is the ability to relate respectfully to—and learn from—people from your own and other cultures. Effective educators are committed to ensuring that all students can be successful and reach their potential, and they model their own cultural responsivity to English learners, immigrant students, and minorities by demonstrating an interest in and learning about these students' lives, families, and cultures. A classroom environment that teaches and promotes cultural responsivity can have a great impact on students leaving home for a school where they don't necessarily feel they fit. It also helps all students gain an increased understanding of other cultures, even as it helps them learn to eliminate cultural barriers as they collaborate effectively on shared tasks—important skills in today's global economic and social environment.

Furthermore, as Dweck (2006) tells us, teachers often have a fixed mindset when it comes to the potential of different culture groups. A growth mindset on the part of teachers makes them more positive toward students and encourages them to hold higher expectations for all students. There are many benefits to being culturally responsive in schools and classrooms. Such an environment increases students' comfort level, knowledge growth, and the freedom with which they explore new ideas. In addition, teachers who promote cultural responsivity find that they are better able to reach diverse learners, discover their students' passions, and select a greater variety of appropriate resources for learning. We cannot overstress the importance of this area of learning. Even elementary students who have no ethnic diversity in their current classroom can expect to learn—and work—with individuals of other cultures at various times throughout their lives. The more adept they become at demonstrating cultural responsivity in these early years, the more successfully they will collaborate in diverse groups later in life.

Educators have multiple tools and tactics available to them for developing a classroom environment of cultural responsivity. They can begin this effort by developing student awareness of their own *and* other cultures and ethnicities and by teaching students to appreciate the value of diversity in classrooms. Other methods for building cultural responsivity include:

▽ Encouraging students to become more cognizant of other cultures' values

▽ Discouraging students from imposing their own cultural values on others

▽ Examining cultural biases

Even everyday classroom interactions offer opportunities for students to learn cultural responsivity. As teachers become more familiar with their students' cultural influences through conversations and their own reading and research, they can try to incorporate some multicultural ideas, practices, and traditions into their classroom teaching content and practices. Students and teachers alike must also be prepared to have patience as they continue to build their knowledge base of—and responsiveness to—other cultures. There are many resources available to educators working to build their knowledge of students' culture (see, for example, Black, 2006; Brown, 2003; Ford, 2005; Gay, 2002; Montgomery, 2000). Teachers can also attend community cultural celebrations and occasions, inquire at local cultural organizations, and share and discuss cultural materials and information in collaborative teams and other professional groups.

As we continue on in the 21st century, we all can expect to learn, work, and live in culturally diverse groups at some period in our lives. In keeping with this reality, educators can't limit their focus to the late–19th century concerns of reading, 'riting, and 'rithmetic. The three Rs of most concern in education today are *relationships*, *responsibility*, and *respect*. Without these understandings, little other learning may take place in the brain. In fact, our soul and spirit are hungry for more than just survival skills and a keen ability to remain on high alert. To feed the curiosity, interest, and engagement that drive learners today, educators must engage in the critical work of building a positive classroom community of learners.

Building Students' Social Skills

Learning and demonstrating social skills is yet another essential element of a positive and nourishing learning environment. When young students receive early training in social skills, they reap the benefits of that training well into their adult lives. Many adults lose their jobs not because they lack appropriate job-specific knowledge or training, but because they can't collaborate effectively with other employees. That's why social skills are such an important part of any student's toolkit for future success (Goleman, 2006b).

Many families focus on teaching these skills in their home, but others neglect such teaching entirely. While some elementary school students may demonstrate a command of such social amenities as saying "please," "thank you," "pardon me," "pleased to meet you," and so on, many students lack training in these and other important social basics. Explicitly teaching social skills, therefore, is paramount to building a community of learners, as well as for preparing students for personal and professional success throughout life. Examples of essential social skills include:

▽ Listening to others

▽ Taking turns

▽ Encouraging others

▽ Using positive statements

▽ Using quiet voices

▽ Participating equally

▽ Staying on task

▽ Asking for help

▽ Using polite language

In the next section of this chapter, we discuss cooperative group learning (CGL), and these basic social skills are fundamental to this process. Students who learn to check for understanding, ask for clarification, follow directions, disagree agreeably, resolve conflicts, accept differences, and encourage one another become better able to participate effectively in collaborative groups.

Teaching social skills isn't like teaching "hard" skills such as reading or mathematics, where little is open to interpretation and students have direct and immediate opportunities to understand the practical application of what they're learning. To successfully teach social skills, therefore, teachers must be certain to cover the following aspects.

▽ **Why the skill is necessary:** As is often the case, examples of successes and problems associated with social skills offer more powerful learning opportunities than do lectures. Often, a teachable moment for a social skill occurs while students are working together. In those situations, educators can take time to examine the situation with students, talk about exactly what has happened, and ask the students to identify what social skill or action could solve the problems present in that experience.

▽ **What the skill looks, sounds, and feels like:** Educators can also model social skills or illustrate them through role-playing a story or watching a video or YouTube clip. Students can also create a T-chart with what the skill *looks like* and *sounds like* or a Y-chart to also identify what it *feels like* (Hill & Hancock, 1993). By helping students expand their understanding of how they demonstrate and respond to specific social skills, teachers build students' self-awareness as well as their empathy for others' feelings. Teachers can work with students to build charts that describe how people demonstrate specific social skills and the feelings those skills elicit (Hill & Hancock, 1993). Figure 2.1 illustrates such a chart for attentive listening. For younger elementary-age students, such charts may need to employ symbols, rather than words. By encouraging students to contribute ideas for the chart, teachers can ensure that the language of this teaching tool is appropriate.

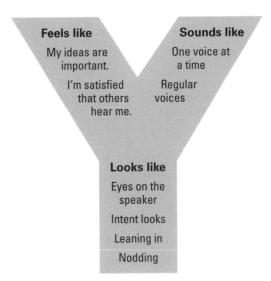

Feels like
My ideas are important.

I'm satisfied that others hear me.

Sounds like
One voice at a time

Regular voices

Looks like
Eyes on the speaker

Intent looks

Leaning in

Nodding

Figure 2.1: Attentive listening Y-chart.

▽ **How to practice demonstrating skill mastery:** Students can show that they understand a skill through multiple means—by drawing about it, role-playing a situation in which the skill is used appropriately, using puppets to demonstrate the skill in action, or writing about themselves or others using this skill in real-life situations. When guiding students through practice, teachers need to select a suitable social skill to fit the situation at hand. At first, students may feel awkward with the use of social skills and even become a little exaggerated in their use. As students practice the skills over time, however, they become more relaxed and appropriate in their use. Teachers in PLCs can assign a skill of the month to make sure students get lots of exposure and practice in using individual social skills.

As you can see, supporting the social brain offers students important tools they will leverage in every aspect of life in—and beyond—school. Of course, one of the most challenging arenas for maintaining strong social skills is in group work. Elementary school offers an early and important opportunity for learning and beginning to practice the social skills required for group collaboration, as we outline in the next section of this chapter.

Utilizing Cooperative Group Learning

Cooperative group learning is *the* key strategy for the differentiated classroom that uses heterogeneous grouping to promote success for all students. Although grouping students showed a low effect size (0.18) in Hattie's (2009) meta-analysis, especially for ability grouping, heterogeneous grouping is more beneficial for all students' ability levels (Lou et al., 1996). Cooperative group learning has also been one of the most researched strategies for educators since the 1980s. CGL not only increases student achievement but also supports the development of the 21st century skills of communication and collaboration.

When educators implement CGL carefully and thoughtfully, they can expect students to experience the following benefits (Johnson & Johnson, 2009; Johnson, Johnson, & Holubec, 1998).

▽ Greater self-esteem

▽ Higher achievement

▽ Better retention of material

▽ Increased social support

▽ Improved collaborative skills

▽ More positive attitudes toward school and teachers

▽ Higher levels of reasoning

In addition to these benefits, CGL also contributes to creating a safe and supportive classroom climate, and it provides students with opportunities to discover and develop their own learning interests and preferences. CGL contributes to vocabulary and concept development as well, since students develop higher-order thinking by using vocabulary in the context of discussion and collaboration. The dialogue of group work contributes to this development in ways the monologue of a teacher lecture cannot. Hattie's (2009) research suggests a 0.82 effect size boost in learning growth from the dialogue of group work.

For all these reasons and more, teachers are wise to consciously and consistently teach students CGL skills. Yet, in too many classrooms, true cooperative group learning is not routine. If students can't work together successfully with appropriate social skills, group work will fail most times. Teachers of such classes are prone to abandon group work, saying their students simply can't handle it.

Cooperative group learning is simple in concept, but its implementation can be complicated. Like anything else that is worthwhile, teaching CGL effectively requires careful planning, an anticipation of issues, and persistence. Marzano, Pickering, and Pollock (2001) suggest that students may need twenty-four practice trials in order to master a new skill or concept. Teachers should, perhaps, expect the same number of attempts as they learn to implement a new classroom practice or strategy. During this time, educators can leverage their own collaborative skills by discussing their practices, trials, and errors with supportive colleagues who will listen to the glitches that develop and offer their own problem-solving ideas. Now, let's examine some of the most successful best practices for implementing CGL in the classroom and for overcoming some of the most common problems educators encounter as they learn to leverage these powerful CGL strategies.

Flexible Groupings

Flexible grouping is an integral part of the brain-friendly classroom, in which teachers group students according to their needs, readiness, and interests. Such groupings can encompass any number of students, as is illustrated in the TIPS (total class, independent students, partners, and small groups) chart in table 2.1 (page 44). Educators can use the descriptions of group organization and functions in this chart to consider types and uses of grouping in the classroom for variety and purpose.

Teachers can use a variety of these flexible groupings throughout the day to offer students a change of venue and varied opportunities to interact with their classmates. Teachers can base them on student needs and readiness levels. Similarly, students can work in learning centers or stations (see chapter 5, page 123) based on need or heterogeneously to promote the cross-pollination of ideas. Heterogeneous groups are best for fostering student achievement. In readiness-level groups, students don't experience the diversity of thinking that occurs in heterogeneous groups. Homogenous groups often lack the periodic sparks of inspiration necessary to keep the group going. Lou et al. (1996) caution us that only average or grade-level students do slightly better in homogenous groups. The struggling learners in homogenous groups still struggle, and the more able students may be competitive rather than collaborative. Teachers can embed communication and collaboration skills into instruction while helping students reach targeted standards in all subject areas, thus allowing students to work in collaborative heterogeneous groups of any size. This type of group work models how the real world of business, industry, families, and organizations operates.

Student Pairs

Michael Doyle and David Straus (1976) use the analogy that the content or information is the gum that we offer learners, and dialogue is chewing the gum. Effective education demands that teachers give students less gum and more chewing. Giving students opportunities to work with partners and small groups allows them to discuss information and ideas and construct meaning from that discussion. Some teachers feel that students waste too much time in group work, through chattering and roaming off task. Yet, the benefits of dialogue far outweigh these concerns, which educators can deal with in an expedient, positive way.

Table 2.1: TIPS for Grouping

	Student Grouping	Strategy
Total Class	Instruction for the whole group at the same time	Delivery of new information New skills Guest or expert A video or DVD Jigsaw strategy Preassessment Reading a text
Independent Students	All students working independently on a variety of activities related to interest, readiness, or choice	Log or journal entry Preassessment Portfolio self-assessment and goal setting Independent study Note taking and summarizing Reflection Quick writes and exit cards
Partners	Students have a processing partner, determined by: ▽ Random selection (elbow, point and go, or other method) ▽ Teacher or student ▽ Task or interest choice	Homework review Check for understanding Information processing Peer editing and evaluation Research and investigation Interest in similar task Brainstorming
Small Groups	Groups determined by: ▽ Similar needs for skill development ▽ Cooperative groups ▽ Structured by teacher or students ▽ Random ▽ Interest or task oriented	Group projects Cooperative group learning assignments Portfolio conferences Group investigation Group brainstorming Group problem solving

Source: Gregory & Kaufeldt, 2012.

Organizing students in pairs offers them rich opportunities for such dialogue, which allows students to:

▽ Clarify their thinking

▽ Develop aural language dexterity and patterns

▽ Develop vocabulary

▽ Deepen concepts

Dialogue in student pairs also allows for a wonderful assessment tool. As teachers work the room and eavesdrop on student pairs, they can learn what students know and don't know, as well as any misconceptions students hold.

We recommend that educators have students work with partners for a while before assigning them to larger and more complicated groupings. Partners can become more engaged in the learning process, because they only have one other person to interact with and lots to do. With only two people in the group, there is also less opportunity for conflict. Furthermore, partnering with multiple classmates builds student connections and alliances, even as it prepares students to work more comfortably in larger groups of their classmates. Young students especially need experience in partnering, as it offers them ample practice in social skills. It's hard to get left out of the discussion when you're in a pair.

Because young students need such extensive practice, guidance, and coaching to improve their group skills, educators can employ special techniques when creating and guiding elementary-age student pairs. Some of the most effective techniques include the think-pair-share, write-pair-share, and draw-pair-share. Paul Black, Christine Harrison, Clare Lee, Bethan Marshall, and Dylan Wiliam's (2004) study in the United Kingdom finds that the use of think-pair-share increases students' test scores by 60 percent. That's a high payoff for such a seemingly simple strategy.

With think-pair-share, teachers give students a question and allow them to think about it silently for a set period of time before collaborating with their partner on finding a correct answer. With sufficient wait time (for the brain to recall and sort out the details) and limited pressure, more students are likely to be engaged (Rowe, 1986). Furthermore, giving students a chance to *pair* their thinking with a partner enables them to clarify their ideas and get a different perspective on the question. After discussion, clarification, and rehearsal, the student pair has an opportunity to share its solutions with the larger group. This aspect of think-pair-share has benefits for both student presenters and observers. In the process of listening to these presentations, students are also thinking about the answer and continuing to rehearse and embellish their own thoughts. The brain loves the social aspect of this approach to learning and typically responds well to the lower risk of public shame, since students are exploring their ideas with a single individual rather than the entire class. Think-pair-share also is a great strategy for ELs, as it gives them a chance to use language with a safe, small audience.

The write-pair-share strategy is similar to the process of think-pair-share, but the student pair puts its answers in writing. Students first have a chance to collect their own thoughts in writing, so they have something to refer to when they move to the pairing step. They can refine their notes through discussion with their partner. This technique is great for the tactile learner, who benefits from the act of writing as well as speaking.

The draw-pair-share strategy is another spin on the basic pair-sharing technique, but it is especially useful with the K–2 students who are more adept and comfortable with drawing symbols and pictures, rather than writing. Again, this strategy enables these students to capture their thoughts in a concrete medium, which they can refer to during shared work with their student partner. They can edit or refine their illustrations through peer discussion, which enables the visual learner to benefit fully from the pairing process.

Adding different types of partner interactions will provide variety throughout the day and alleviate boredom. Quick and easy ways to assign random partners or working pairs include *point and go*, *elbow partners*, and *turn to*. With *point and go*, teachers ask students to look at another student, point to him or her, and then move to have a conversation. With *elbow partners* and *turn to*, students work with the student closest to their elbow or nearest them. As we've seen, offering students opportunities to get up and move contributes to the brain-friendly classroom, so educators can also use other techniques for assigning partnerships between students who sit in different areas of the classroom. Such random partnerships also build the learning community by helping students become more familiar with their classmates. As students become more adept at successful cooperative learning in pairs, educators can begin organizing them into larger groups.

Common Problems in Group Work

Teachers are sometimes reluctant to use CGL because of a variety of concerns about the process. While few educators are unaware of the growing global demand for collaborative, innovative thinkers, most teachers have experienced problems with promoting group work in the classroom. Here are just some of the comments teachers make about students who demonstrate problems with group work.

▽ "They aren't on task."

▽ "They waste time."

▽ "They talk about other things."

▽ "They argue."

▽ "Some are social loafers."

▽ "Some students take over."

▽ "It takes too long to set up group work."

▽ "I can teach them this information more quickly."

▽ "I'm not sure they are all getting it."

All of these statements can be true, but none of them offers an adequate reason to abandon group work. As noted previously, teaching students appropriate social skills can prepare them for cooperative group learning. Additionally, educators can head off some of these concerns before they develop into problems, with preplanning and management solutions, such as those in table 2.2.

Table 2.2: Concerns and Solutions for Group Work

Concern	Solution
It takes too much time.	Student group activity time is well spent if students are using it to practice social skills, clarify their thinking, and expand their understanding.
Students are off task and waste time.	Students need a clear set of expectations and a realistic time frame for their group work. Use a timer. Give short and irregular amounts of time, such as eleven-and-a-half minutes. Such limits give students a sense of urgency and motivate them to get started quicker. When given too much time, students may waste it upfront. A noise monitor that alerts students when they get off task can also help to get them working.
Conflict arises.	Conflict is less likely to happen when students are working with only one other person. In a group of any size, give each member a specific role to play and hold him or her accountable. Also, teach conflict resolution.
One individual in the group does all the work, and the others become social loafers.	Ask for an independent summary from each person as an exit ticket at the end of the task. Call on random students to report an update on progress.

Of course, the concerns in table 2.2 don't represent the full range of issues and answers educators must deal with when teaching CGL to students. The following five elements of CGL increase the chances that group interactions will result in students learning and using their time together well. Additionally, by understanding and mastering these five elements of CGL, educators can anticipate and plan strategies that will enable them to construct groups and group tasks with a high probability of success.

1. **Positive interdependence:** Positive interdependence is helpful in making sure that students rely on everyone in the group to get the job done. Tasks for this element ensure collaboration is necessary and students feel engaged in and responsible for the completion of the group's task. Students understand the goal, and they are assigned roles, tasks, a task sequence, and the environment where the work is to be done. Each member knows his or her role and responsibility. Roles should be appropriate to the task, such as a research gatherer, checker, recorder, and a facilitator, to help the group stay on task; for kindergarten or first-grade students, roles might include a cutter, paster, and checker. Sequencing or chunking tasks into subtasks can help students see the complexity of the task, while breaking it into smaller pieces allows students to tackle one at a time.

2. **Individual accountability:** Every member is accountable for learning the content and concepts and skills involved in the task. Each student must help with and understand the assignment and be able to demonstrate mastery of the task at the end of the project. To ensure individual accountability, students can create their own exit ticket at the end of the group experience and explain what they've learned from and contributed to the group. Other strategies can include an individual quiz or an assessment of the part they played in the group's project or task. At the end of the activity, the teacher also can select, at random, a reporter to share the group's experience with the class.

3. **Group processing:** Students have a discussion on the process or product of the group experience in order to deepen and expand their learning. A quick discussion of the growth and development they experienced during the work helps students improve the skills they've been practicing. Problems arise when educators omit this step in the CGL process because they "just ran out of time." Group processing should be quick, and it can be as simple as "Tell someone in the group how he or she helped." A quick thumbs-up, down, or sideways or a five-finger rating system (with one finger being "We didn't understand" and five indicating "We're *really* good at this!") can give students an opportunity to reflect on and rate their group performance.

4. **Social and collaborative skills:** Beyond the basic social skills all individual students must learn, CGL offers practice in its own set of collaborative social skills, including asking for clarification, following directions, disagreeing agreeably, resolving conflicts, accepting differences, and encouraging one another. To ensure that students engage in learning these specific skills of group work, teachers must be explicit about the skills being targeted in the group interaction.

5. **Face-to-face intervention:** This element of effective CGL involves giving and receiving explanations, debating and elaborating ideas, and orally summarizing opinions and outcomes. Students who work alone on assignments are exercising only one opinion and exploring a single-minded outcome. As a group, students can combine ideas, brainstorm, debate, summarize, challenge, and build on others' perspectives. This taps into higher levels of 21st century thinking skills of collaboration, communication, critical thinking, creativity, and innovation.

To further explore how educators can use these strategies to promote and manage positive experiences in cooperative group learning, let's take a detailed look at a type of task that puts such strategies into play.

A CGL Strategy in Action

Jigsaw is an effective cooperative strategy that, as the name suggests, gives all individuals in the group responsibility for dealing with one piece of a specific "puzzle" or task (Aronson, Blaney, Stephan, Sikes, & Snapp, 1978). Jigsaw tasks help students process information, deepen comprehension, and facilitate dialogue (see also www .jigsaw.org). A jigsaw task gives students an active role in learning large amounts of material in an interactive manner that increases long-term memory and supports making connections and social learning. Here's how jigsaw works.

▽ **Simple jigsaw:** With a simple square jigsaw assignment for three students, each student becomes knowledgeable about a piece of information and then teaches the new information to the rest of the group. In this task, each group member acquires, discusses, and contemplates ideas and information, then turns those ideas into knowledge through dialogue with other group members. Individually, a student reads, finds, or watches information in an article, video, or text and then teaches what he or she has learned to his or her group members. Using a simple jigsaw can be a way of facilitating reading comprehension and dialogue about important aspects of a topic.

▽ **Expert jigsaw:** Most applicable for grades 3–5, this task is similar to that of the simple jigsaw, except students will number or letter off in their groups of three or four to become experts (for example, 1, 2, 3, 4 or A, B, C, D). Then, all ones, all twos, and so on join together with the other experts to discuss the material before teaching it back to the original group. This discussion gives the student experts an opportunity to clarify information and deepen their understanding of it, as well as gain practice in presenting the information expertly. Here's an example of the expert jigsaw process.

▶ *Step 1*—Arrange students in groups of four, and assign them a book, or ask them to gather information from a source. All together, the four students form a base or home group. Give each group member the letter A, B, C, or D. Divide the chapter or segment of information in equal or appropriate sections among the four students.

▶ *Step 2*—All the As from each group get together, read their assigned segment of the information, and summarize its key points. They then decide on the best way to share or teach their base group what they have become experts in. Similarly, Bs, Cs, and Ds do the same with their part.

▶ *Step 3*—The base group reassembles, and each student in turn teaches his or her part of the information the group has been studying with the other members of the base group. Teachers can assign an advance organizer to record the key points of each section.

▽ **Table jigsaw:** In table jigsaw, each table of students is responsible for a different piece of content. Students at each table study the material and decide how to present it to the whole class. Teachers can also use this when viewing a video; each table group might look for specific information about one aspect of the concept explained in the video. The entire group becomes an expert and presents its part to the whole class.

Strategic exercises like jigsaw are important elements in teaching and developing CGL skills in elementary students. The development of these social skills and cooperative tasks are invaluable in the differentiated classroom where students move in and out of flexible groups. These strategies encourage students to become more self-reliant, self-regulated, and on task—outcomes that promote a safe and supportive classroom climate that encourages the healthy development of each student's brain.

Getting Started and Getting Better

At this point, the number of techniques, strategies, and best practices for creating a brain-friendly classroom environment might seem overwhelming. Many educators may wonder, "So how am I supposed to plan lessons that make students feel safe and welcomed; consider each student's interests, best learning modalities, and cultural background; make the content relevant and meaningful; attend to students' physical and emotional nourishment and need for movement; and teach the social skills necessary for individual well-being *and* those necessary for succeeding in the critical arena of collaborative group efforts?"

We understand these concerns. As former classroom teachers, we know research-based best practices cannot help students if implementing them is unrealistic within the demands of today's classroom. As we mentioned in the introduction, however, we have seen the principles outlined in this chapter successfully applied in real-life classrooms across the United States. Here are some important ideas educators can bear in mind as they implement these ideas to create safe, supportive, and brain-friendly classroom environments.

▽ **Lean on your team:** When teachers work in teams, take shared responsibility for each student's success, and have weekly collaboration time to work together, their collective efforts can begin to achieve these outcomes. Instead of each teacher trying to create an interest inventory for each student, for example, a grade-level team of teachers can collectively combine this information over time. Each staff member who interacts with a student informally is likely to pick up relevant information. Combined, these observations can contribute to a very complete picture of each student. Similarly, some members might have developed a greater proficiency at using cooperative learning methods. These teachers can share this expertise across the team. Then, all teachers in the team can employ cooperative protocols across multiple classrooms and grades, which will, in turn, facilitate the implementation of the recommendations in this chapter.

▽ **Focus on essential curriculum:** As we mentioned in the introduction, teachers often feel there is insufficient time to try these practices because they are rushing to cover the required curriculum. We are not suggesting that every lesson will incorporate all the elements of brain-friendly instruction. We do believe that to maximize learning for all of their students, teachers must be vigilant in their attempts to maintain a brain-friendly classroom environment. But when a team of teachers begins by identifying the absolutely essential learning outcomes that all students must master for future success and then applies those practices to this more limited number of standards, the work becomes more doable.

▽ **Focus on students not currently succeeding in Tier 1:** In most situations, a majority of students are currently succeeding in any given classroom, which indicates that the existing classroom environment works for that group of students. For students who are struggling in that environment, however, educators should consider the following questions.

  ▸ Does this student feel safe and connected?

  ▸ Does this student clearly understand our classroom expectations, procedures, and learning outcomes?

  ▸ What are this student's interests?

  ▸ Are there cultural needs that I should consider?

  ▸ Does this student learn best through different modalities?

  ▸ How can we more actively engage this student?

These are some of the ways educators can ease into the sometimes complex, but always rewarding, process of creating a brain-friendly environment in their classrooms. Over time and with practice, teachers can expect this process to become easier—and more effective. We realize that in this chapter we have offered a multitude of ideas, but if educators think big and start small, they can find ways to benefit from all of these techniques over time. Creating a brain-friendly learning environment isn't a simple task. However, like eating an elephant, it can be pursued and accomplished one bite at a time.

Taking the Discussion Further

Following are some of the important ideas from this chapter that are worthy of further reflection and discussion. Educators in a PLC may want to read through this chapter with their collaborative teams and discuss each section, recording the issues related to each piece of information and considering classroom implications for students. Collaborative teams can reflect on the prompts to deepen understanding and set subsequent goals for improvement.

▽ Use figure 2.2 to record the issues and classroom implications for developing a brain-friendly classroom. Which of these implications are most urgent and pressing from your team's perspective?

▽ Discuss as a group the five domains of emotional intelligence and how they contribute to a student's ability to focus and learn.

▽ Discuss the upside of a growth mindset and issues in developing one in students. What are the drawbacks of a fixed mindset? What steps can teachers take in their classroom to help students understand the concept of and develop a growth mindset?

▽ Discuss ideas for developing cultural responsiveness among faculty and students. Identify initial steps for implementing those ideas.

▽ What difficulties have team members had in using flexible grouping? Brainstorm ideas for overcoming those difficulties.

▽ What sorts of issues have team members faced in using partner and group work? Explore management techniques that work.

▽ Examine the five elements of cooperative group learning. Discuss some of the ways that teachers could include these five elements to greater ensure success for students when working with others, decrease classroom management issues, and increase student responsibility and self-regulation.

Brain Facts	Issues	Classroom Implication
Stress and the brain		
Patterns and schemas		
Sensory memory		
Relevance and meaning		
Everything matters		
Social brain		

Figure 2.2: Developing a brain-friendly classroom.

Visit **go.solution-tree.com/RTIatWork** *for a reproducible version of this figure.*

Finding Each Student's Learning Sweet Spot

As most teachers look out over the sea of faces in their classrooms, they understand that no two students are identical. Children from the same family can be very different in appearance, interests, preferences, and temperaments in spite of their shared genetic and environmental influences. The fact that each student brings his or her own unique characteristics and background knowledge to the classroom forms the basis for differentiated instruction. It also emphasizes the need for preassessment tools that can enable educators to identify what students know or can do, as well as a variety of instructional methods that can maximize learning opportunities for a broad variety of student interests, abilities, and needs.

The demands for differentiated instruction can be broad as well. As we noted in chapter 2, many classes include students from multiple cultures and ethnicities, so teachers seeking ways to differentiate instruction for these groups may have to begin by demonstrating respect and tapping into that cultural milieu. In addition to ELs who are just learning to speak English, a single class may include students from a wide variety of socioeconomic backgrounds—learners who have grown up with multiple advantages and others who have struggled through great disadvantage as a result of their family's resources. Some students may enjoy an abundance of reading and writing materials, technologies, and opportunities to travel, while their classmates have few or none of these important tools for learning. Vast differences in parenting and home environment may influence the students and their mindsets about school, learning, and their potential. Still others have been taught assumptions and expectations about gender, which, even at an early age, can influence their attitudes and ideas about learning. These issues present a complex environment for teachers and students—one that doesn't support a one-size-fits-all curriculum.

Every student enters the classroom, therefore, with his or her own unique propensities for learning—abilities, mindset, aspirations, advantages, disadvantages, and expectations—all of which shape that individual's learning style and needs. By getting to know these unique elements, educators can create individual learning profiles that will help them identify each student's "sweet spot" of learning—the right combination of strategies, tactics, tools, and teaching approaches that maximizes individual learning experiences, promotes a more supportive classroom environment, and results in more successful educational outcomes for *all* students.

In chapter 2, we outlined several important methods for creating a classroom environment that is safe and supportive for all students, no matter what unique characteristics they possess. In this chapter, we explore techniques for digging further into those unique characteristics, to identify the specific learning styles and preferences that make up each student's profile. We also offer a number of tools and teaching methods educators can use to find and target the right combination of teaching and learning opportunities that will help each individual get the most from his or her learning experience. As we explain in this chapter, by understanding the unique experiences, learning preferences, and forms of intelligence students bring to the classroom, educators can create plans for presenting Tier 1 instruction in a way that boosts every student's ability to succeed.

Teaching to Each Student's Learning Sweet Spot

We often encounter references to the *sweet spot* in sports like baseball or golf. In all cases, the term refers to that place where a combination of factors results in a maximum response for a given amount of effort. For students, the sweet spot represents a point where four elements collide: (1) attention, (2) high interest, (3) positive feelings, and (4) a connection to prior successes. Figure 3.1 shows the factors that contribute to these four elements of learning and how the elements overlap to create a learner's sweet spot.

Proactive teachers look for students' learning sweet spots by assessing their prior knowledge, experiences, or skills; noting what was successful for them in the past; and predicting what interests they might have in individual topics. Here are ideas that educators can bear in mind when identifying ways to promote strong student experiences in each of the four elements of a learner's sweet spot.

1. **Attention and engagement:** Teachers promote strong attention and engagement among students by making sure that they have met students' basic needs, so they can give their attention freely to the learning tasks at hand. Creating novel and interesting ways to approach topics also helps build attention and engagement, as does focusing on content that is meaningful and relevant for students.

2. **Interest:** Teachers can consider creative ways to make learning topics or aspects of those topics match students' interests. Introducing the

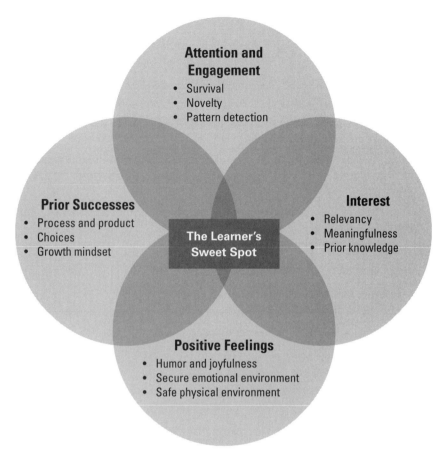

Attention and Engagement
- Survival
- Novelty
- Pattern detection

Prior Successes
- Process and product
- Choices
- Growth mindset

The Learner's Sweet Spot

Interest
- Relevancy
- Meaningfulness
- Prior knowledge

Positive Feelings
- Humor and joyfulness
- Secure emotional environment
- Safe physical environment

Source: Gregory & Kaufeldt, 2012.

Figure 3.1: The learner's sweet spot.

topic with a chance for student input and questions also will engage and motivate learners. To build interest, teachers also can develop students' background knowledge and offer them multiple choices in learning activities.

3. **Positive feelings (emotions):** Students develop positive feelings about learning in a classroom environment that is supportive of and responsive to student needs and preferences and where teachers recognize strengths. Teachers encourage positive feelings among students by considering the full range of students' affective, cognitive, physiological, and psychological needs.

4. **Prior successes:** Building on students' past successes is a certain way to move them toward their learning sweet spot. In addition to incorporating past successes in topics and learning methods, educators can offer scaffolding to incrementally advance learners' understanding and, thus, increase their chances of success.

We are not suggesting labeling or catering to students; however, connecting with learners and making the learning relevant and interesting based on student preferences are effective strategies at Tier 1. The notion of pluralized instruction (chapter 5) will satisfy more learner preferences without the need to place students in a specific category.

Recognizing Learning Preferences

As we saw in chapter 2, neuroscience has enlightened educators in the many ways they can increase success for students. Teachers recognize that all students are different, but they don't always feel able to successfully address those differences. No teacher should be expected to create a customized curriculum for each student. There are ways, however, that teachers can use daily differentiated instruction to increase success for all. A first step in this process is to recognize the different learning preferences and styles students bring with them to the classroom. Researchers often divide learning styles into four basic groups: (1) organizers, (2) analysts, (3) random learners, and (4) interpersonal learners (Dunn & Dunn, 1993, 1998, 1999; Gregorc, 1985; Kolb, 1984; McCarthy & McCarthy, 2006). The four groups have the following characteristics (Gregory & Chapman, 2007).

1. **Organizers:** To optimize learning, these learners like order, clarity, and consistency.

2. **Analysts:** While learning, these students like to examine, analyze, research, and go deeper.

3. **Random learners:** These students tend to go with the flow and appreciate variety and hands-on doing in the classroom.

4. **Interpersonal learners:** These students need to interact and feel that their classmates appreciate them. They enjoy dialogue and group work.

Neuroscientists also tell us, however, that there is no evidence that different brains use different neural networks to accomplish similar outcomes. In spite of these similarities in brain forms and functions, however, educators recognize that there are *preferences* in the way students receive information, process it, and demonstrate competencies (Sousa & Tomlinson, 2010). When given a choice of learning opportunities, students typically make those choices based on their personal preferences. These learning preferences often evolve from students' prior successes, tasks they've enjoyed, novel experiences, and natural curiosity. Geake (2009) suggests that most brains follow a normal developmental trajectory, but each is also idiosyncratic in its strengths and weaknesses when it comes to learning particular types of information. He also notes that it is more important and beneficial to provide a pluralized pedagogy than restrict instruction to target a particular student's learning preferences. Few educators have the time and resources to create a customized education experience for each student that targets that individual's specific learning preferences. But by creating an instructional plan that encompasses the broadest possible range of student learning preferences, teachers can offer the best opportunities and outcomes for all students.

A fundamental part of this solution is to provide learning opportunities that leverage all modalities, including auditory, visual, and tactile or kinesthetic. The more channels educators use, the more learners they reach. Furthermore, as we saw in chapter 2, engaging students in a wide variety of learning types and experiences helps strengthen their learning neural connections. For these reasons, we recommend that educators teach to a broad range of learning preferences by offering instruction that incorporates every modality.

Leveraging Multiple Intelligences

A student's learning style involves more than just his or her learning preferences. In fact, every student is intelligent in his or her own way. In 1984, Howard Gardner expanded our understanding of this idea when he came forward with the theory of *multiple intelligences* (Gardner, 2004). His research suggests that, rather than a fixed IQ, people have a range of different propensities of intelligence that allows them to solve problems, handle crises, and value their culture. He went on to identify the many ways humans are "smart" by defining multiple forms of intelligence. Following are Gardner's (2004) multiple intelligences.

▽ **Verbal-linguistic:** People with verbal-linguistic intelligence have a high level of verbal acuity and are often writers, actors, journalists, orators, or editors. Students with this form of intelligence enjoy the spoken and written word. Often, they are auditory learners who like to speak, listen, read, and write. Technology-enabled forms of communication, such as blogs, websites, Twitter, and email, interest these learners. Strategies that work best with this form of intelligence include the following.

  ▸ Summarize a story.

  ▸ Write a blog.

  ▸ Describe _____.

  ▸ Write an advertisement.

  ▸ Write an editorial.

  ▸ Write a news flash.

  ▸ Deliver a news update.

▽ **Musical-rhythmic:** People who enjoy using and hearing rhymes, melodies, rhythms, and beats of music and poetry have a highly evolved musical-rhythmic intelligence. Students with a high level of musical intelligence appreciate hearing and moving to music and find that music enhances their mood and enjoyment. These individuals often are drawn to careers as composers, musicians, singers, poets, and lyricists. Strategies that work best with these learners include the following.

  ▸ Compose a song, rap, jingle, or poem.

  ▸ Create a rhythmical slogan.

  ▸ Interpret a song.

  ▸ Create a video with music.

  ▸ Use a songwriting app to create a song.

  ▸ Write a rhyming poem.

▽ **Visual-spatial:** Students with a strong visual-spatial form of intelligence are able to recognize details in images, objects, and environments, and they appreciate the use of color and shape. These students gravitate to using symbols, charts, and other representations to learn, remember, and solve problems. These learners may be drawn to careers as artists, engineers, sculptors, filmmakers, videographers, and architects. Strategies that speak best to this form of intelligence include the following.

  ▸ Draw an illustration.

  ▸ Make a flipbook.

  ▸ Create graphics to represent ideas.

  ▸ Interpret a piece of art.

  ▸ Design a book cover.

  ▸ Design a diorama.

  ▸ Sketch a process.

  ▸ Create a model or sculpture.

▽ **Bodily-kinesthetic:** Students with a strong bodily-kinesthetic intelligence have a good awareness of their own body and are keen to develop fine and gross motor skills in a variety of fields. As adults, they use their dexterity in many careers from sports to surgical medicine. Strategies that speak best to this form of intelligence include the following.

▸ Create an action to represent _____.

▸ Develop a scenario, and act it out.

▸ Use your body to interpret meaning.

▸ Play a game or sport.

▸ Construct or build a model.

▸ Act out a scene from a story, play, or event.

▸ Use manipulatives to deepen understanding.

▸ Role-play.

▸ Use drama and dance.

▽ **Logical-mathematical:** Students with a strong logical-mathematical intelligence appreciate numbers, patterns, and cause and effect. They like to organize and sequence information, and they often use logic, reasoning, and data for problem solving. Careers these students may seek include accounting, programming, law, and mathematics. Strategies that work best with this intelligence include the following.

▸ Sequence items or events.

▸ Construct a timeline.

▸ Create directions for a process.

▸ Rank ideas.

▸ Classify items.

▸ Conduct a survey.

▸ Design a graph to show _____.

▸ Google _____.

▽ **Naturalist:** Students with strengths in naturalist intelligence appreciate the world of nature and the plants and animals that inhabit it. These learners are adept at recognizing the patterns and details that occur in nature and in manmade objects and environments. Students with strengths in this form of intelligence may later become botanists or environmentalists. Strategies that work best include the following.

▸ Study a variety of science topics.

▸ Invent a product.

▸ Make discoveries.

▸ Identify characteristics of groups or categories.

▽ **Interpersonal:** Students with a strong interpersonal intelligence are adept at forming positive relationships. These students tend to be empathic and sensitive to others and can easily read moods and feelings. They may seek careers as counselors, psychologists, and mediators and other professions that require a high expertise in social skills. Strategies that work best for this intelligence include the following.

▸ Work with others.

▸ Collaborate on a project.

▸ Conduct an interview.

▸ Debate an issue.

▸ Come to consensus or agreement.

▸ Discuss an idea or concept.

▸ Use a jigsaw strategy.

▸ Present a puppet show.

▸ Engage in social networking.

▽ **Intrapersonal:** Strong intrapersonal intelligence is evident in students who are introspective and in tune with their own feelings and emotions. Even young learners can begin to set goals and manage their progress through reflection and metacognition with adult facilitation and prompting. As adults, they will be drawn to philosophical issues and seek careers as counselors, therapists, or theologians. Strategies that work best with this form of intelligence include the following.

▸ Work independently.

▸ Reflect on tasks.

▸ Make a personal choice.

▸ Gather items for a portfolio.

Gardner (2004) also offers a possibility of a ninth intelligence—existential. This intelligence is the ability to ask deep questions about one's existence (a mature intrapersonal strategy). However, it does not meet all the criteria to deem it an intelligence on its own.

Gardner (2004) suggests that we all have these in various degrees and that our profile of intelligences is as unique as our thumbprint. Our thumbprint never changes, however, but our command of multiple intelligences can evolve over time with experience and practice. Again, the challenge for teachers is not to cater to each student's individual intelligence profile but to offer opportunities for learning within all forms of intelligence throughout the week, so at any given time, some students are working in their learning groove and others are stretching themselves. In groups, students working in their areas of strength will enjoy the learning process and proceed with enthusiasm; group members who are less strong in a specific form of intelligence will learn techniques from others as they solve problems or work on projects.

Educators can use surveys and inventories to determine their students' strengths and weaknesses in these multiple forms of intelligence, so they can identify areas where students need additional development. There are many inventories and surveys available online that teachers may use or modify for their students. Visit **go.solution-tree.com/RTIatWork** to access live links to the following resources.

▽ **Literacy Works, "Find Your Strengths Assessment":** www.literacy net.org/mi/assessment/findyourstrengths.html

▽ **Surfaquarium, "Multiple Intelligences Inventory":** http://surf aquarium.com/MI/inventory.htm

▽ **Edutopia, "Multiple Intelligences Self-Assessment":** www.edutopia .org/multiple-intelligences-assessment

▽ **Teachers Pay Teachers, "Multiple Intelligence Survey for Kids":** www.teacherspayteachers.com/Product/FREE-Multiple-Intelligence -Survey-for-Kids-200841

Bringing the Common Core to Life in K–8 Classrooms (Jensen & Nickelsen, 2014) also offers two helpful learning preference surveys. See also chapter 5 (page 111) for high-impact activities that support multiple intelligences.

Building a Student Profile

A student profile is a valuable tool for getting to know learners. Educators use the profile to document how students learn, what kinds of learning they enjoy, and what learning strengths and weaknesses they exhibit. The student profile is a dynamic living document (or file of documents) that changes as the learner evolves and grows.

It may not be necessary to build an entire student profile for each student, as most students' preferences are not too difficult to identify through observation. Students' choices, interests, and styles and their excitement or lack thereof as they approach tasks and pluralized, multimodal activities are usually quite telling. However, some students are not easy to engage. Student profiles can be especially helpful for helping educators reach *hard-to-serve* students who may be disconnected or disheartened with school and learning. Building a profile for more challenging learners gives the teacher opportunities for engaging the student based on preferences and ideas that have an especially strong hook for that learner. Teachers may go about building a profile in the following ways.

▽ **Informal observation:** Observation is an excellent tool for gathering data for student profiles. Through their daily work and interactions with students, teachers can observe student preferences and levels of engagement and how those levels change throughout the day or period. By jotting down such anecdotal information, teachers later can use it to tap into the student's strengths and needs. Sticky notes are a quick tool for collecting these observations, which the teacher can transfer to a log or student file.

▽ **Formal surveys:** A more formal approach to collecting data for the student profile may be to create and use inventories and surveys to collect information about students' preferences and multiple intelligences.

▽ **Trial and error:** Educators can also gather important information for student profiles by allowing students a choice of opportunities for learning and demonstrating understanding. As students exercise these choices, teachers can observe and record the student preferences and interests they illustrate.

▽ **Reflection:** As we described in chapter 2, metacognition is an awareness of one's own identity and thought patterns. Guiding students to reflect on their learning interests, preferences, and successes is a powerful way to help students develop their metacognitive skills. Reflection also is an empowering tool for building the sphere of influence that students can have over their own learning. By gathering a student's own thoughts on his or her learning experience, teachers gain important data that can greatly expand the value of the student profile. Later in this chapter, we offer specific strategies for helping students develop their metacognitive understanding.

In review, the preceding list offers just some of the ways educators can gather information to include in the student profile. Now, here are some of the kinds of information those profiles should contain about each student's unique learning preferences and intelligences.

▽ **Differences in sensory learning:** Noting which senses (auditory, visual, kinesthetic, or tactile) seem to be instrumental in engaging and helping students learn can provide teachers with valuable guidance in forming the most effective and supportive learning experiences.

▽ **Differences in multiple intelligences:** Strengths and weaknesses in multiple intelligences are important elements of the student profile. This information can help students and educators alike, as it enlightens students to their learning challenges, and it helps teachers better understand even difficult-to-engage students.

▽ **Cultural differences:** As we've noted, culture and ethnicity play a role in the student's approach to learning and needs. Such cultural specifics, therefore, are important pieces of information to include in the student profile. Identifying students as ELs is especially important. (See page 66 for more on reaching ELs.)

▽ **Interests:** Given that all students have had different experiences and opportunities in sports and the arts, they come to school with different perspectives and background knowledge.

▽ **Individualized education programs (IEPs):** If students are identified as special needs, it is very useful to consult their IEPs and special education teachers. These resources often give insight to challenges and interventions that work.

Getting to know students will allow teachers to build in relevant and meaningful activities that support their interest in certain curriculum topics. Preassessment can also help with this identification (see chapter 6, page 149). The placemat in figure 3.2 is useful for gathering and recording information to develop a dynamic student profile. Educators can adjust the content to include information to suit their particular group of students and their needs.

Learning Preferences

Visual, Auditory, Kinesthetic

Analytical, Creative, Practical

Mind Intelligence Strengths: _____

Mind Intelligence Challenges: _____

Working Preference: Group work or independent work

Performer, Producer

Outside School

Sports: _____

Music: _____

Hobbies: _____

Pop-Culture Interests: _____

Free-Time Activities: _____

Student Profile

Name: _____

Gender: M   F   Birthday: __/__/__

Grade: _____   School Year: _____

Teacher: _____

Class: _____

Family and Social Connections

Family: _____

Friends at School: _____

Other Friends: _____

Leader or Follower?

Social Network: _____

General Health: _____

Academic Strengths

Reading Level: _____

Artistic Abilities: _____

Technology Savvy: Yes   No

Favorite Subjects: _____

Figure 3.2: Student profile placemat.

*Visit **go.solution-tree.com/RTIatWork** for a reproducible version of this figure.*

Although student profiles may not be necessary for every student, they help in identifying and making a connection or hook for students who need engagement. The following information looks specifically at several groups of students with specific needs.

Targeting Specific Learning Needs

Many students have specific learning needs, such as ELs and twice-exceptional students. This section will focus on identifying, understanding, and differentiating learning for these students to find their learning sweet spot.

Working With English Learners

In most education systems, the expectation is that teachers who are knowledgeable about second- or additional-language learning will deliver Tier 1 instruction to ELs (Hill & Flynn, 2006). We also assume that these teachers are proficient in delivering culturally relevant content, literacy, and language instruction for this group. It's important for educators working with ELs to ensure that all students understand the core content (Echevarria, Vogt, & Short, 2012) and to differentiate instruction according to students' proficiency levels.

Continual assessment throughout the year is necessary in order to identify students with additional needs or greater challenges, as well as those students who need more advanced opportunities to develop their skills. For ELs, Tier 1 instruction must address both their sociocultural and academic needs. Beyond posting student-friendly content and language standards for lessons and units, educators can use a variety of tools and techniques that create more clarity for ELs, including:

▽ Sensory supports (visuals, podcasts, realia, manipulatives, video clips, and so on)

▽ Graphic organizers, charts, and tables

▽ Interactive flexible groupings (pairs, triads, and small groups)

Additionally, these tools support teachers in:

▽ Accessing students' prior knowledge and backfilling background knowledge deficiencies

▽ Fostering dialogue so students can develop oral language

▽ Engaging learners through active learning and technology

▽ Differentiating projects and assessments to match students' language proficiency levels

▽ Providing *scaffolding*—temporary support that enables a student to extend his or her current abilities—through frameworks, models, and modeling to develop literacy procedures (we talk more about scaffolding in chapter 6, page 162)

▽ Promoting academic language and domain-specific vocabulary throughout the day

By following these and other practices aimed at promoting core learning for ELs, teachers can ensure that these students have a greater chance to develop academic and domain-specific language and content understanding.

Working With Twice-Exceptional Students

Educators must also offer effective Tier 1 instruction for twice-exceptional students, who are generally high-ability students with learning challenges or advanced learners with behavioral challenges. Twice-exceptional children often enter school with frustration and low self-esteem. They may lack social skills and have a poor sense of how to fit in (King, 2005). There are generally three types of twice-exceptional students (King, 2005).

1. **Gifted students with subtle learning disabilities:** These students may have a large vocabulary, for example, but lack the mechanics of spelling. Despite their learning disabilities, these students tend to perform at grade level.

2. **Gifted students with identified learning disabilities:** These students are identified as gifted and have learning disabilities, such as attention deficit disorder. These students are bright but tend to get frustrated and often act out.

3. **Students with learning abilities and disabilities that mask one another:** Although they have superior intelligence, these twice-exceptional students may hide deficiencies in particular areas such as mathematics. These learners often perform at or under grade level.

Twice-exceptional students may be trapped between two worlds. They may feel confident in their smartness but frustrated in not being able to cope with their disabilities (King, 2005). They can have high expectations but disabilities that thwart their progress, undermine their confidence, and increase their fear of failure. It is difficult for them to keep a growth mindset when the unknown halts their learning, making them simultaneously bored and confused (Assouline, Nicpon, & Huber, 2006). Even when these students are succeeding, they often want to do better and sense that they could do better—all of which lowers their self-esteem (King, 2005).

Twice-exceptional students may also feel that they are getting mixed messages from parents and teachers, who both compliment and criticize them or who hold (according to the student) unreasonable expectations without recognizing the limitations of their disabilities (Stormont, Stebbins, & Holliday, 2001). Because they don't fully fall into either the gifted or learning-disabled categories, these students may feel socially isolated. These students may want to identify with gifted students, who tend to be more popular than those with learning disabilities. Students with learning disabilities tend to have fewer leadership skills and suffer more rejection than typical students (Stormont et al., 2001).

The first step in helping twice-exceptional students maximize their learning achievement, of course, is identifying them. This identification can be a challenge, however, especially when a disability masks an ability. If students are at grade level, sometimes educators conduct no further investigation into their abilities, and when parents and teachers allow these students to pursue their passions, they learn well. Twice-exceptional students may show some or all of the characteristics in table 3.1.

Table 3.1: Characteristics of Twice-Exceptional Students

Strengths	Challenges
▽ Strong commitment to tasks they are interested in ▽ Analytical thinking ▽ Active problem solving ▽ Creativity ▽ Excellence with abstract concepts	▽ Poor motivation ▽ Poor organization ▽ Tendencies to act out ▽ Withdrawn and shy ▽ Anxiety ▽ Depression ▽ Difficulty with memorization tasks ▽ Discrepancies between verbal and written work

Source: King, 2005.

Because standardized gifted tests do not identify twice-exceptional students, often teachers and specialists are the ones who *catch* the disabilities as they observe and work with these learners. Mary Ruth Coleman (2005) suggests keeping journal notes as to how a student performs in class, looking for talents in verbal expression, creativity, and critical thinking. William Morrison and Mary Rizza (2007) suggest looking for discrepancies between performance and standardized test scores. RTI helps teachers individually assess students and discuss them in teams so they do not miss gifts and abilities or other challenges. Addressing twice-exceptional students' needs may be more difficult if students are spending most of their time in regular or gifted classes, where teachers are not necessarily adept at recognizing and assisting students with disabilities.

Teachers can use many strategies to support the twice-exceptional student. Consider the following.

▽ **Allow students to work in their areas of interest:** Experts agree that these students need choices to offset the disabilities they are facing (Coleman, 2005; Mann, 2006; Winebrenner, 2001).

▽ **Vary sensory teaching to involve more visual and kinesthetic formats:** These students often need more doing than telling. Teachers optimize their learning experience, therefore, by using techniques that include all senses (Winebrenner, 2001).

▽ **Provide opportunities for student success:** Students whose disabilities hide their gifts need the chance to show their talents to build confidence (Coleman, 2005).

▽ **Teach concepts before teaching content:** Twice-exceptional students are often big-picture learners (Winebrenner, 2001). Educators should provide advance organizers in context and background, therefore, to set the stage for a strong learning experience.

▽ **Approach teaching skills in multiple ways:** Teachers benefit this group by tapping into students' multiple intelligences, rather than targeting a single approach (Coleman, 2005). (We offer a detailed look at pluralized instructional strategies in chapter 5, page 111.)

▽ **Use compacting:** Compacting allows students to demonstrate their knowledge and skills before a unit begins (Coleman, 2005). Prior to teaching a unit, teachers can assess students to determine what material they have already mastered. In turn, during instruction, teachers can use *compacting* to eliminate or edit such material in their lessons and cover only gaps in student understanding. (We discuss compacting in more detail in chapter 6, page 165.)

▽ **Help students with organizational skills:** In order to help twice-exceptional students self-manage, teachers can make sure they have tools necessary for their learning process, such as an agenda, timeline, rubrics, organizational note-taking materials, and a quiet place to work (Mann, 2006).

EL and twice-exceptional students often require support with targeted standards. The strategies in this section will appeal to their special needs and help them reach their potential.

Helping Students Identify Their Own Learning Preferences and Needs

As noted previously, metacognition, or thinking about thinking, is an awareness of one's own identity and thought patterns. When students analyze their thinking and how successful it has been, they may gain new insight into how they can best go about learning in the future. When solving a problem, for example, students can become more consciously aware of the processing involved in reaching a resolution if they reflect on the process. By enabling students to retain effective strategies and dismiss those that don't work, such reflection becomes a tool for lifelong learning. Hattie (2009) identifies that metacognitive strategies have a 0.69 effect size on student learning.

Teachers help students develop metacognitive strategies by providing time to reflect and by consciously helping students adopt more effective learning techniques. When teachers include metacognition as part of the lesson, students become aware of their learning preferences and can build from that knowledge (Donovan & Bransford, 2005). Exit tickets, journal entries, and surveys are just a few ways educators can foster metacognition. Now, let's take a closer look at how teachers can use these techniques to help move students into their learning sweet spot.

Exit Tickets and Journal Entries

Even K–2 students can reflect on a class or group experience through exit tickets. They are a great way to help them build metacognition. Exit tickets allow students to respond to prompts in a safe individual environment. Students answer a question based on the prompt and turn in their ticket before exiting the activity or room. In turn, teachers can respond to queries or issues student exit tickets raise and plan future instruction. Grades K–1 students can respond with symbols or emoticons (like a happy face, frowning face, or uncertain face).

Exit ticket questions might include:

▽ "What did you do well today?"

▽ "What came easy to you?"

▽ "What part of the class did you enjoy?"

▽ "Was there a different idea that you might have been more interested in?"

▽ "What was frustrating for you?"

▽ "What help do you need? From whom?"

▽ "What will you do next?"

Such questions ask students to reflect on their strengths and needs, which will help students self-regulate their thinking and facilitate their personal journey toward life-long learning.

Asking grades 3–5 students to reflect on and respond to their learning experiences, successes, and challenges in a journal is another way to encourage metacognition. To begin this process, teachers can offer students prompts to start their thinking and then ask them to make an entry in their journal that comments on their day, preferences, and interests. Such prompts may include:

▽ "If I could do anything for the day, I'd . . ."

▽ "My hobbies are . . ."

▽ "My favorite subject in school is . . ."

▽ "The things I like to do in class . . ."

▽ "I like to play these sports or games . . ."

▽ "When I have free time I like to . . ."

Surveys

By creating and gathering student responses to surveys aimed at exploring the learning experience, teachers better understand their students while, at the same time, building the students' metacognitive thinking. In the survey in figure 3.3, for example, the students circle a happy, neutral, or sad face to record their response to specific activities.

Tell me how much you like . . .			
Singing or listening to music	☺	😐	☹
Drawing and painting	☺	😐	☹
Using technology	☺	😐	☹
Working alone	☺	😐	☹
Working with others	☺	😐	☹
Using numbers	☺	😐	☹
Dancing and playing sports	☺	😐	☹
Being a leader	☺	😐	☹
Writing	☺	😐	☹
Talking	☺	😐	☹
Solving problems	☺	😐	☹

Figure 3.3: Elementary student preferences survey.

*Visit **go.solution-tree.com/RTIatWork** for a reproducible version of this figure.*

By using these and other techniques to more fully understand the types of learning experiences that resonate most strongly with students, educators accomplish multiple goals. As elementary students improve their skills of self-awareness and metacognition, they better prepare themselves for a lifetime of learning and growth. As teachers find more—and more effective—ways to appeal to learners' interests and abilities, they improve both the learning *and* teaching that occurs in their classrooms.

Keeping Students in Their Learning Zone

Hungarian cognitive psychologist and author, Mihaly Csikszentmihalyi (1990), offers the theory of *flow* and describes it as the road to success in life. Flow represents the perfect balance between challenge and skill. If the task is too difficult for the learner's perceived abilities, anxiety will emerge. If the task is not challenging enough, boredom will emerge. Through flow, there will be a gradual increase in skill development as tasks become more difficult. However, as Edward Thorndike (1932) notes, the Law of Exercise (practicing and rehearsing a skill) is required for long-term retention. Complex or challenging tasks require repetition to achieve success. Additionally, Thorndike's (1932) Law of Effect reminds us that learning is greater when there are positive feelings associated with relevant and meaningful tasks, meaning students will be better able to achieve flow. The theory of flow explains the joy students can feel and the focused motivation they can have for the pure pleasure of learning. It fosters the motivation necessary for encouraging a student's readiness to learn (Thorndike, 1932). Additionally, as we explored in chapter 2, students have an innate seeking system, and flow helps students seek by providing an appropriate level of challenge.

Six factors characterize flow (Nakamura, 1988; Nakamura & Csikszentmihalyi, 2009).

1. Sense of control over actions

2. Focus on concentration

3. Unconscious passage of time

4. Commitment to action

5. Classification of the experience as rewarding

6. Loss of self-conscious engagement

An individual achieves flow when his or her work meets three conditions.

1. The task is clear, and the teacher's feedback is constructive.

2. The task has clear goals and a structure that allows for progress.

3. The skills necessary for completing the task are in balance with its challenge.

Students can enter and thrive in a state of flow either through individual work or in groups. In any situation, finding flow can give students the most engaging, challenging, and productive learning experience possible.

Facilitating Flow

We can begin exploring the best way to help students find flow in their individual work by considering Russian psychologist Lev Vygotsky's (1978) social development theory, which has important implications for creating this critical state. Vygotsky's social development theory includes three major elements.

1. Social interaction plays a crucial role in learning and cognition. Vygotsky tells us that multiple interactions with teachers and colleagues help deepen learners' understanding. By creating positive relationships with teachers and peers and a safe, supportive environment that tolerates errors and is free of threat, educators set the stage for students to enter a state of flow in their work.

2. Learners should be clear about the goals and engage in meaningful tasks. As we've seen, clear expectations and criteria are imperative if students are to find flow.

3. The task must be doable. As in the theory of flow, tasks must incorporate a balance, or a *zone of proximal development*, between the level of challenge and learners' capabilities to perform a task on his or her own or with the help of others. Through this balance, teachers create a sense of *can do*. Preassessing students' prior knowledge helps teachers design the appropriate level of difficulty for students. (We talk more about the zone of proximal development in chapter 6, page 162.)

Students need support and resources in order to successfully experience flow in their work. This includes giving students choices that are engaging and then praising their effort and progress, not just applauding how smart they are. Constructive feedback is just one example of such support, and it's an essential condition for facilitating flow. Educators also can increase student flow by establishing personal relevancy and positive relationships and by assigning tasks that are developmentally appropriate. Students who are still being exposed to the industrial factory model of education will not receive the appropriate environment to meet their cultural and cognitive diversity.

Encouraging Cooperative Group Flow

As we've noted, flow is also a critical tool for maximizing cooperative group learning. According to Csikszentmihalyi (1990), there are several ways a group can work together so that each participant achieves flow. Characteristics for aiding the state of flow in successful group include:

▽ Norms that guide group interaction

▽ Planned work

▽ Clear goals that everyone understands

▽ An atmosphere that treats each member's differences as valuable points of view, skills, and talents and that acknowledges complementary ideas and skills as useful in solving problems and creating projects

Flow's contributions to group activities may be one of the main reasons that people play video games (Murphy, 2011). These games create challenge that balances users' current skill levels, resulting in the kind of intrinsic motivation that creates flow (Rutledge, n.d.). Furthermore, flow helps the brain release dopamine and keeps players engaged and focused (Chen, 2006). Through flow, students are more willing to meet a challenge, if within reach. Video games cater extensively to flow, as challenges increase as the player's skill level increases.

In the previous chapter, we explored how the basics of neuroscience shape overall student achievement in the classroom. In this chapter, we have tightened our focus to identify how the unique qualities of each student's brain can determine the most supportive and effective techniques for promoting learning success. By making the effort to more clearly know and gauge their students' backgrounds, interests, abilities, and challenges, teachers can ensure they are presenting Tier 1 instruction using the best practices to help *every* student find his or her optimal learning experience. Remember, finding each learner's sweet spot isn't about labeling students and catering to their preferences. It's about providing many opportunities for engaging students and helping them process new information and skills in a multiplicity of modes. When educators have identified the most effective ways to reach students—as a group and as unique individuals—they can use those techniques on a daily basis to differentiate instruction in a way that provides an effective and powerful foundation in Tier 1 essentials. In the next chapter, we take a closer look at that essential block of instruction by exploring what educators want their students to know and be able to do.

Taking the Discussion Further

Following are some of the important ideas from this chapter that are worthy of further reflection and discussion. Educators in a PLC may want to read through this chapter with their collaborative teams and discuss each section, recording the issues related to each piece of information and considering classroom implications for students. Collaborative teams can reflect on the prompts to deepen understanding and set subsequent goals for improvement.

▽ What are the multiple intelligences? Review your lesson plans for the week, and identify which multiple intelligences you have tapped. In planning the next unit of study, incorporate as many multiple intelligences as possible in the instructional plan to provide multiple entry points to learning and to satisfy students' needs.

▽ Consider students who are a challenge to engage or hook into learning. How can you focus on those students' learning needs? Use the student profile placemat (figure 3.2, page 65) to get to know their preferences and interests both in learning and in extracurricular activities.

▽ Discuss the challenges and gifts of ELs and twice-exceptional learners, and identify and discuss the specific characteristics of those students in your classroom. Which interventions or supports might best assist your students? Make observations and notations about which strategies work so you can replicate them.

▽ Discuss the concept of flow and some of the ways teachers can foster flow in the classroom. What strategies can you implement in your classroom? Discuss any at your next meeting.

▽ Discuss Vygotsky's (1978) zone of proximal development. Discuss this theory's implications for creating student engagement and success, as well as ways this theory can ease the process of planning more appropriately for student learning.

Developing a
Powerful Core Curriculum

The fundamental purpose of school is to guarantee that every student learns what he or she needs to become a successful, contributing adult in a rapidly changing world. Those needs shape the essential *core curriculum* of any effective educational system. Accordingly, the core curriculum educators teach in Tier 1 must include the skills and knowledge necessary to prepare students for college and careers. In elementary school, the core curriculum covers a wide variety of subjects, skills, and concepts. In past practices, a challenging curriculum might have been reserved for the highest-achieving students, and a less interesting or rigorous curriculum would be put in place for struggling learners. Today's educational standards specify that every student must be able to demonstrate mastery over the core curriculum. With a variety of supports, scaffolds, and differentiated best practices, most students should be able to make adequate progress at Tier 1.

In the era of standards-based instruction, teacher-designed curriculum isn't always the norm. Instead, many educators are tasked with teaching commercial, evidence-based instructional programs for reading, writing, spelling, and mathematics. Often teachers also have to follow a district pacing guide that leaves them with little flexibility regarding instructional design. With an ever-increasing emphasis on English language arts and mathematics core standards, the pressure to spend more time helping students master literacy and numeracy often overrides other content-area subjects such as social studies and science. Even formal instruction of music, art, and physical education has been reduced or even pushed aside to allow for more time to prepare students for standardized tests. In spite of these current realities, educators have a fundamental responsibility to design and present a powerful core curriculum.

A powerful core curriculum includes five key components (see figure 4.1).

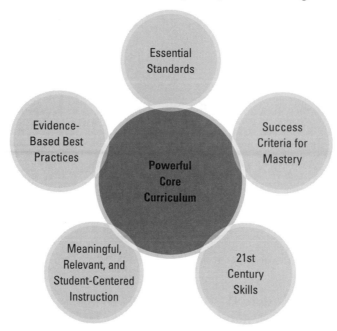

Figure 4.1: Powerful core curriculum.

So how can teachers and collaborative teams use a core curriculum design to teach the essential standards, as well as enhance student engagement, promote active learning, and help students develop skills necessary for thriving in the 21st century? The best path toward that achievement may require that educators start with the end in mind and plan backward. But even then, they must not forget under what conditions brains learn best. Collaborative grade-level or course-alike teams should examine and become familiar with the five key components that make up a powerful core curriculum. Valuable instructional improvements can happen when team members take time to review their program and analyze the effectiveness of each element to maximize the strength of the core curriculum for all students.

Additionally, teachers and teacher teams must consider the four critical questions of the PLC at Work process (DuFour et al., 2010) as the foundation for all core curriculum planning. As introduced in chapter 1, those questions include:

1. What do we want our students to learn?

2. How will we know if our students are learning?

3. How will we respond when students don't learn?

4. How will we respond when they do?

In this chapter, we're going to explore the first question and outline an effective pathway for how educators can determine the essential standards of a powerful core curriculum. In the following chapters, we'll also introduce practical tools and techniques teachers can use to make that core curriculum even more adaptable and responsive to the ever-changing needs and opportunities that shape the progress educators and students make throughout the year. With these and other supports, scaffolding, and differentiated best practices we describe in this book, *all* students can make adequate progress with a rigorous curriculum at Tier 1.

Incorporating Essential Standards

Before educators can begin implementing any instructional plan, they first must take the time to determine the essential standards for each unit—those standards that, among all others, are absolutely fundamental to the core curriculum. Identifying these standards in grade-level or course-based teams is also a primary responsibility for educators in developing an RTI plan. As Austin Buffum and his colleagues (2012) tell us, "Schools that attempt to build an intervention program before they have clearly identified what is essential for all students to learn are placing the cart before the horse" (p. 48).

Teachers and teacher teams typically use their state standards to guide them as they determine the first critical question of a PLC, What do we want our students to learn? While those standards set grade-specific goals, however, they do not define how educators should teach the standards or which materials they should use to support students. The standards, in other words, are just standards. Developing a powerful core curriculum from those standards—one that will serve as the substance of instruction—is a multistep process.

Many educators discover that state standards dictate teachers to cover an overwhelming amount of content in a given time frame. When that is the case, teachers or teacher teams must prioritize some of the standards. Categories within this prioritization might include:

▽ Essential to know and do

▽ Important to know and do

▽ Worth being familiar with

▽ Nice to know

Now, let's examine how educators identify which standards fall into the essential category.

Identifying Essential Standards

One of the key features of the Common Core State Standards for English language arts (ELA) and mathematics is that they are specifically designed to include fewer, more rigorous standards, but they can still be daunting. In Larry Ainsworth's (2003a) book *Power Standards*, he proposes a system for prioritizing standards (Ainsworth,

2003a). Ainsworth defines *power standards*, a term Doug Reeves (2002) first coined, as "prioritized standards that are derived from a systematic and balanced approach to distinguishing which standards are absolutely essential for student success from those that are 'nice to know'" (pp. 1–2). In other words, power standards are essential standards—a subset of the standards that represent the *most important elements* that must be taught, no matter what.

A key identifier for essential standards is their ability to best prepare students for subsequently hitting another important target and learning other key objectives in the future. When educators are tasked with selecting which learning targets they should prepare students to approach *first*, they can begin by building consensus about which standards best represent the key skills, concepts, and processes that students must master at a given grade level. Ainsworth (2003a) encourages teachers to keep asking this question when trying to prioritize standards: "What do your students need for success—in school (this year, next year, and so on), in life, and on your state tests?" (p. 14). An agreed-on list of essential standards doesn't relieve teachers of the responsibility for teaching all standards, but it does identify which standards are *critical* for student success. Other standards can receive less emphasis.

Educators can use the following three key criteria to help select essential standards.

1. **Endurance:** Does the standard or indicator provide students with knowledge and skills that will be of value beyond a single test date? Essential standards should focus on skills, concepts, and processes students are likely to draw on throughout their lives.

2. **Leverage:** Does the standard provide knowledge and skills that will be of value in multiple disciplines? Essential standards should offer skills, concepts, and processes that have wide applicability to other areas of study.

3. **Readiness for further study:** Does the standard provide students with essential knowledge and skills that are necessary for success in the next grade or level of instruction? Essential standards should provide students with an opportunity to master skills, concepts, and processes that will form the necessary foundation for success in future studies.

When a standard fulfills all three of these criteria, educators can consider it a nonnegotiable essential standard. When a standard fulfills two of the three criteria, it is more likely to be an *important standard*. If the standard appears to really only fulfill one of the three criteria points, it probably is a *nice-to-know standard*.

As teacher teams participate in active discussions about prioritizing standards, they should also review the vertical alignment, or learning progression, for each standard. The learning progression indicates whether the standard is or will be considered an essential standard at an adjacent grade level. (We talk more about learning progressions later in this chapter; see page 86.)

Rewriting Essential Standards

Taking some time to systematically rewrite each grade-level essential standard can help teachers clarify exactly what students need to know, do, and demonstrate. Additionally, rewriting essential standards (also known as *unwrapping*, *unpacking*, or *deconstructing*) helps teachers:

▽ Develop a deeper understanding of the standards for planning instruction

▽ Simplify the language into student-friendly terminology

▽ Determine the level of rigor demanded for proficiency

▽ Identify the prerequisite skills necessary for students to learn the standard

Elements that educators must consider when rewriting standards include the following.

▽ **Important skills and strategies:** These skills and strategies describe what students should be able to do in fulfilling the standard, as identified by the standard's verbs.

▽ **Key concepts:** These concepts describe specifically what students must know and understand in relation to the standard, as identified by the important nouns and noun phrases in the standard.

▽ **Selected learning activities and tasks:** The rewritten standard also must describe what students must be able to demonstrate in relation to the standard, through a particular context or topic, as identified by a specific task or product in the standard.

Figure 4.2 (page 82), for example, illustrates the process of rewriting standard six of the Common Core English language arts Reading Standards for Informational Text at grade 4 (RI.4.6). We've circled the important skills and strategies in the standard and underlined key concepts that support selected learning activities and tasks.

The process of rewriting the standard can help teachers better identify what exactly the standard is demanding. With this clarification, teachers can orchestrate a learning task that is more likely to hit the target standard. The rewriting process, however, can become tedious and time consuming. Rather than rewriting all of the standards, therefore, educators and teacher teams can train their focus on rewriting only those standards they have collaboratively identified as the essential standards for an upcoming designated unit.

(Compare) and (contrast) a <u>firsthand</u> and <u>secondhand account</u> of the same <u>event</u> or <u>topic</u>; (describe) the <u>differences</u> in <u>focus</u> and the <u>information</u> provided. (RI.4.6)

Skills and Strategies	Key Concepts	Activities and Tasks
Compare	Differences (regarding the focus and information provided)	Describe how the information is presented in each account. Find and compare similarities and differences of the two perspectives.
Contrast	Secondhand account (of the same event or topic)	What is the author emphasizing in the secondhand account?
Describe	Firsthand account (of the same event or topic)	What is the author emphasizing mostly in the firsthand account?

Source: NGA & CCSSO, 2010a.

Figure 4.2: Rewriting RI.4.6.

Visit **go.solution-tree.com/RTIatWork** for a reproducible version of this figure.

Even the most carefully written essential standard may not fully articulate the standard's specific expectations for learning in terms that are understandable and informative for educators, students, and parents alike. To do that, educators also must identify and clearly describe the specific *learning targets* for each standard they include in the core curriculum. A learning target is any achievement expectation we have for students on the path toward mastery of a standard. It clearly states what we want students to learn, and both teachers and students should understand it. Teachers should formatively assess learning targets to monitor progress toward a standard. *Collaborating for Success With the Common Core* (Bailey, Jakicic, & Spiller, 2014) is a rich resource designed to help teaching teams unwrap standards and identify learning targets.

To create effective learning targets, educators must write them in student-friendly language, make them specific to a daily lesson, and connect them directly to some form of assessment. To help students and parents fully understand learning standards and expectations they represent, teachers can write them as "I can" statements. These statements not only give students a clear set of expectations for the learning goals they're working toward but also help teachers and teacher teams in their planning. Curriculum Corner (www.thecurriculumcorner.com) is a terrific resource for "I can" statements for the K–5 Common Core standards.

Here are some examples of rewriting state essential standards in student-friendly language.

▽ **Language arts writing for grade 3 (3.2.2.e):** "Compare various mentor texts and/or exemplars to create a similar piece." (Nebraska Department of Education, 2014, p. 5)

▷ **Student-friendly learning target:** "I can analyze examples of writing and write a similar piece."

▽ **Language arts speaking skills for grade 1 (1.3.1):** "Students will develop and apply speaking skills to communicate key ideas in a variety of situations." (Nebraska Department of Education, 2014, p. 12)

▷ **Student-friendly learning target:** "I can communicate ideas with my words."

▽ **Reading Foundational Skills for kindergarten (RF.K.1b):** "Recognize that spoken words are represented in written language by specific sequences of letters." (NGA & CCSSO, 2010a)

▷ **Student-friendly learning target:** "I can understand that words I say can be written using letters in a certain order."

▽ **Operations and Algebraic Thinking for grade 4 (4.OA.A.2):** "Multiply or divide to solve word problems involving multiplicative comparison, e.g., by using drawings and equations with a symbol for the unknown number to represent the problem, distinguishing multiplicative comparison from additive comparison." (NGA & CCSSO, 2010b)

▷ **Student-friendly learning target:** "I can solve word problems involving multiplication and division by using drawings."

▽ **Writing for grade 1 (W.1.6):** "With guidance and support from adults, use a variety of digital tools to produce and publish writing, including in collaboration with peers." (NGA & CCSSO, 2010a)

▷ **Student-friendly learning target:** "I can log on to the computer and use the keyboard and mouse to create a picture story using a story app."

When teacher teams have determined the essential standards and learning targets, it is imperative that they let students in on the game plan. One of the strongest recommendations in *Visible Learning* (Hattie, 2009) is that educators need to clearly communicate the intentions of lessons and the criteria for success to students. We've seen that clear learning targets describe the skills, knowledge, attitudes, and values that the student needs to learn. In helping students pursue these targets, teachers need to know the goals and success criteria of the lessons, as well as how well *all* students in their class are progressing and where the teaching and learning need to go next. Communicating all of this to students along the way is a proven method for generating student success. Such communication helps students become assessment capable, so they can self-report their own grades.

A final step in rewriting standards is to determine what level of thinking each standard demands from the learner. By examining the elements of the task and targeting in on the process verbs, teachers can often determine whether the activity generates only low-level responses or demands higher-level thinking. Tools such as Bloom's Revised Taxonomy and Webb's Depth of Knowledge model are useful in determining and developing rigor. (We describe this process in more detail in chapter 7, page 184.)

Charting Essential Standards

As we've seen, choosing and rewriting essential standards is a multistep process. By working in collaborative teams when possible, examining all relevant documents (CCSS, state standards, district essential standards, and so on), and applying the three key criteria for essential standards, educators can determine which standards *all* students must master. To help them with this process, teams can answer the following questions.

▽ What essential standards do students need to learn? Describe them in student-friendly language.

▽ What does proficient student work look like? Provide an example or description.

▽ What prior knowledge, skills, or vocabulary does a student need to master this standard?

▽ When will this standard be taught?

▽ What assessments will we use to measure student mastery?

▽ What will we do when students have already learned this standard?

To make sure they have described all aspects of essential standards, teachers can use a chart similar to the one in figure 4.3. Filling out the chart by the second or third week of each instructional period or semester is most effective.

With these questions in mind while identifying and charting essential standards and describing all aspects of essential standards, teams can consider the next key component of a powerful core curriculum: determining success criteria for mastery. *Success criteria for mastery* is a vital piece of identifying and incorporating essential standards into the curriculum.

Determining Success Criteria for Mastery

Determining success criteria for mastery is another critical aspect of the core curriculum design and planning. How do teachers know when students have met their goals? In what ways can teachers gather information regarding a student's progress toward mastery? How will students demonstrate mastery? What will be acceptable evidence?

What Do We Want Our Students to Learn?					
Grade:	Subject:	Semester:	Team Members:		
Description of Standard	**Example of Rigor**	**Prerequisite Skills**	**When Taught?**	**Common Summative Assessment**	**Extension Standards**
What is the essential standard to be learned? Describe in student-friendly vocabulary.	What does proficient student work look like? Provide an example or description.	What prior knowledge, skills, or vocabulary are needed for a student to master this standard?	When will this standard be taught?	What assessments will we use to measure student mastery?	What will we do when students have already learned this standard?

Source: Adapted from Buffum, Mattos, & Weber, 2012.

Figure 4.3: Essential standards chart.

Visit go.solution-tree.com/RTIatWork for a reproducible version of this figure.

Learning progressions and student-friendly proficiency scales are two tools to incorporate into the core curriculum to assess progress toward essential standards and provide students with meaningful feedback.

Learning Progressions

Learning progressions describe the increasingly sophisticated levels of understanding and expertise that students should develop over time. They represent the pathway students will travel as they progress toward mastery. As the Glossary of Education Reform states, learning progressions articulate:

> the purposeful sequencing of teaching and learning expectations across multiple developmental stages, ages, or grade levels. The term is most commonly used in reference to learning standards—concise, clearly articulated descriptions of what students should know and be able to do at a specific stage of their education. (Great Schools Partnership, 2013)

Examining how a standard progresses in complexity from grade to grade can facilitate the planning of rigorous standard-based curriculum and instruction. By reviewing the learning progressions for each standard, teachers can get better at sequencing learning and avoiding repeating material that was taught in earlier grades. When teachers know the sequence, they are better able to help students progress through their learning at a slightly faster (or slower) pace based on their ability to learn the required material and demonstrate proficiency. Learning progressions can also provide educators with fundamental learning milestones that can help guide the development of assessment tools. Many teachers find that using a vertically aligned chart is an easy way to see the progression of complexity that develops at each grade level.

In regard to the CCSS, learning progressions are arranged as grade-level standards. Figure 4.4 illustrates an example of a K–12 learning progression for CCSS Reading anchor standard six for Craft and Structure, which asks students to "Assess how point of view or purpose shapes the content and style of a text" (CCRA.R.6; NGA & CCSSO, 2010a). Anchor standards represent what students should know and be able to do by the end of high school. The Reading Informational Text standards progress through each grade level K–12. Upper-elementary teachers should be familiar with the standards' progression throughout the grades. Some students may be working beyond their grade-level expectations. Likewise, secondary teachers should be familiar with lower grades, as students may be working below grade level.

Figure 4.5 (page 88) illustrates a sample K–5 learning progression for Writing anchor standard three for Text Types and Purposes. Note how for each grade level the new challenge is in boldface (sometimes highlighted in yellow). This helps teachers, parents, and students easily identify what has been added from the previous grade level.

A strong criticism regarding the Common Core has been the attempt to make curricula more rigorous by placing some standards in lower grades than they previously

Common Core ELA	K–12 Learning Progression
Anchor Standard	**CCRA.R.6:** Assess how point of view or purpose shapes the content and style of a text.
Grades	**Craft and Structure—Reading Informational Text**
Kindergarten	Name the author and illustrator of a text and define the role of each in presenting the ideas or information in a text. (RI.K.6)
Grade 1	Distinguish between information provided by pictures or other illustrations and information provided by the words in a text. (RI.1.6)
Grade 2	Identify the main purpose of a text, including what the author wants to answer, explain, or describe. (RI.2.6)
Grade 3	Distinguish his or her own point of view from that of the author of a text. (RI.3.6)
Grade 4	Compare and contrast a firsthand and secondhand account of the same event or topic; describe the differences in focus and the information provided. (RI.4.6)
Grade 5	Analyze multiple accounts of the same event or topic, noting important similarities and differences in the point of view they represent. (RI.5.6)
Grade 6	Determine an author's point of view or purpose in a text, and explain how it is conveyed in the text. (RI.6.6)
Grade 7	Determine an author's point of view or purpose in a text, and analyze how the author distinguishes his or her position from that of others. (RI.7.6)
Grade 8	Determine an author's point of view or purpose in a text, and analyze how the author acknowledges and responds to conflicting evidence or viewpoints. (RI.8.6)
Grades 9–10	Determine an author's point of view or purpose in a text, and analyze how an author uses rhetoric to advance that point of view or purpose. (RI.9–10.6)
Grades 11–12	Determine an author's point of view or purpose in a text in which the rhetoric is particularly effective, analyzing how style and content contribute to the power, persuasiveness, or beauty of the text. (RI.11–12.6)

Source: NGA & CCSSO, 2010a.

Figure 4.4: CCRA.R.6 sample learning progression.

appeared. Therefore, some learning expectations may be developmentally inappropriate for students. By representing the steps and building blocks toward success, learning progressions can help assuage this concern. Teachers and teacher teams should carefully examine new versions of learning progressions to understand how each standard has been realigned in the continuum. For each standard, teachers should be well versed in identifying how the standard is stated in the prior grade level and how it is developed in the following grade.

Student-Friendly Proficiency Scales

After teams have identified essential standards, educators can use *proficiency scales* to provide meaningful feedback to students, track their progress over time, determine when students have mastered a given task or standard, and what the student's next level

Common Core ELA	K–5 Learning Progression
Anchor Standard	**CCRA.W.3:** Write narratives to develop real or imagined experiences or events using effective technique, well-chosen details, and well-structured event sequences.
Grades	**Text Types and Purposes—Writing**
Kindergarten	**Use a combination of drawing, dictating, and writing to narrate a single event or several loosely linked events, tell about the events in the order in which they occurred, and provide a reaction to what happened.** (W.K.3)
Grade 1	**Write narratives in which they recount two or more appropriately sequenced events, include some details regarding what happened, use temporal words to signal event order, and provide some sense of closure.** (W.1.3)
Grade 2	Write narratives in which they recount **a well-elaborated event or short sequence** of events, include details **to describe actions, thoughts, and feelings,** use temporal words to signal event order, and provide a sense of closure. (W.2.3)
Grade 3	Write narratives to develop real or imagined experiences or events using effective technique, descriptive details, and clear event sequences.
	▽ **Establish a situation and introduce a narrator and/or characters; organize an event sequence that unfolds naturally.**
	▽ **Use dialogue and descriptions** of actions, thoughts, and feelings **to develop experiences and events or show the response of characters to situations.**
	▽ Use temporal words **and phrases** to signal event order.
	▽ Provide a sense of closure. (W.3.3)
Grade 4	Write narratives to develop real or imagined experiences or events using effective technique, descriptive details, and clear event sequences.
	▽ **Orient the reader** by establishing a situation and introducing a narrator and/or characters; organize an event sequence that unfolds naturally.
	▽ Use dialogue and description to develop experiences and events or show the responses of characters to situations.
	▽ Use **a variety of transitional words** and phrases to manage the sequence of events.
	▽ **Use concrete words and phrases and sensory details to convey experiences and events precisely.**
	▽ **Provide a conclusion that follows from the narrated experiences or events.** (W.4.3)
Grade 5	Write narratives to develop real or imagined experiences or events using effective technique, descriptive details, and clear event sequences.
	▽ Orient the reader by establishing a situation and introducing a narrator and/or characters; organize an event sequence that unfolds naturally.
	▽ Use **narrative techniques, such as** dialogue, description, **and pacing**, to develop experiences and events or show the responses of characters to situations.
	▽ Use a variety of transitional words, phrases, **and clauses** to manage the sequence of events.
	▽ Use concrete words and phrases and sensory details to convey experiences and events precisely.
	▽ Provide a conclusion that follows from the narrated experiences or events. (W.5.3)

Source: NGA & CCSSO, 2010a.

Figure 4.5: CCRA.W.3 sample learning progression.

of mastery should involve. As Marzano (2013) defines, "A proficiency scale presents knowledge or skills as a continuum of simpler, target, and complex goals that students work toward sequentially" (p. 11). By working with a team, teachers can build an understanding of how to use proficiency scales with essential standards and embed those progressions in scoring rubrics. Teacher teams can use commonly planned assessments when everyone on the team measures mastery with the same proficiency scale. Teachers can analyze the data to reflect on their effectiveness, determine next steps for reteaching or extension, and promote meaningful dialogue among their colleagues.

A useful generic model for determining proficiency comes from Marzano Resources (see table 4.1). The scale ranges from 0.0 (Even with help, no understanding or skill demonstrated) to 4.0 (Mastery of a complex learning goal). Teams can customize this model by inserting specific complex, target, and simple learning goals. (See also www.marzanoresources.com/resources/proficiency-scale-bank for more proficiency scales.)

Table 4.1: Generic Proficiency Scale

Score 4.0		Complex learning goal
	3.5	In addition to score 3.0 performance, partial success at score 4.0 content
Score 3.0		Target learning goal
	2.5	No major errors or omissions regarding score 2.0 content and partial success at score 3.0 content
Score 2.0		Simple learning goal
	1.5	Partial knowledge of score 2.0 content, but major errors or omissions regarding score 3.0 content
Score 1.0		With help, partial success at score 2.0 and score 3.0 content
	0.5	With help, a partial understanding of the score 2.0 content, but not score 3.0 content
Score 0.0		Even with help, no understanding or skill demonstrated

Source: Marzano, Yanoski, Hoegh, & Simms, 2013, p. 49.

In accordance with this scale, the 3.0 level represents that the student has mastered the target learning goal. A score of 4.0 includes not only mastery of the content knowledge or skill but also a complex learning goal, such as the 21st century skill critical thinking. For sample team-customized proficiency scales, see tables 4.2 and 4.3 (pages 90–91) for reading and mathematics, respectively.

Table 4.2: Proficiency Scale for ELA Text Structures and Features for Grade 1

Reading		
Text Structures and Features		
Grade 1		
Score 4.0	In addition to score 3.0 performance, the student demonstrates in-depth inferences and applications that go beyond what was taught.	
	3.5	In addition to score 3.0 performance, partial success at score 4.0 content
Score 3.0	The student will: ▽ Explain major differences between books that tell stories and books that give information (RL.1.5)	
	2.5	No major errors or omissions regarding score 2.0 content and partial success at score 3.0 content
Score 2.0	The student will recognize or recall specific vocabulary, such as: ▽ *Book, information, story* The student will perform basic processes, such as: ▽ Recognize the differences between books that tell stories and books that give information	
	1.5	Partial knowledge of score 2.0 content, but major errors or omissions regarding score 3.0 content
Score 1.0	With help, partial success at score 2.0 and score 3.0 content	
	0.5	With help, a partial understanding of the score 2.0 content, but not score 3.0 content
Score 0.0	Even with help, no understanding or skill demonstrated	

Source: Marzano et al., 2013.

When designing a proficiency scale, teacher teams should follow these guidelines.

▽ Identify the target learning goal, remembering that mastery will equal 3.0 on the scale.

▽ Select a strategy or task that would best demonstrate a student's proficiency score of 3.0 for the goal.

▽ Determine what simple learning goal would represent a score of 2.0, or partial success with some errors in mastering the target goal.

▽ Add additional depth, complexity, and critical thinking to the target goal to raise it to a complex learning goal with a score of 4.0.

Following are suggestions teachers can use when designing assessment tasks to use with a proficiency scale.

▽ Tasks associated with a 2.0 score should involve simpler details and processes that have been explicitly taught.

Table 4.3: Proficiency Scale for Mathematics Place Value for Grade 4

Number and Quantity	
Place Value	
Grade 4	
Score 4.0	In addition to score 3.0 performance, the student demonstrates in-depth inferences and applications that go beyond what was taught.
	3.5 In addition to score 3.0 performance, partial success at score 4.0 content
Score 3.0	The student will: ▽ Compare two multidigit numbers based on meanings of the digits in each place using <, >, and = (4.NBT.A.2) ▽ Use place value understanding to round multidigit whole numbers to any place (4.NBT.A.3)
	2.5 No major errors or omissions regarding score 2.0 content and partial success at score 3.0 content
Score 2.0	The student will recognize or recall specific vocabulary, such as: ▽ Base-ten numeral, compare, digit, expanded form, multidigit number, number name, place, place value, round, whole number The student will perform basic processes, such as: ▽ Recognize that in a multidigit whole number, a digit in one place represents ten times what it represents in the place to its right (4.NBT.A.1) ▽ Read and write multidigit whole numbers using base-ten numerals, number names, and expanded form (4.NBT.A.2)
	1.5 Partial knowledge of score 2.0 content, but major errors or omissions regarding score 3.0 content
Score 1.0	With help, partial success at score 2.0 and score 3.0 content
	0.5 With help, a partial understanding of the score 2.0 content, but not score 3.0 content
Score 0.0	Even with help, no understanding or skill demonstrated

Source: Marzano et al., 2013.

▽ Tasks associated with a 3.0 score should involve complex ideas and processes that have been explicitly taught.

▽ Tasks associated with a 4.0 score should involve inferences and applications that go beyond what was taught (including one or more 21st century skills).

Teachers can create several assessment items for scores of 2.0, 3.0, and 4.0 and determine how to score the items. For example, when assessing student work, some teachers may want to differentiate completely correct, completely incorrect, and partially correct answers.

▽ Completely correct (C)

▽ Completely incorrect (I)

▽ Partially correct (P)

Figure 4.6 illustrates an assessment item to accompany a proficiency scale.

Student Responses	Proficiency Level
Student misses all items—even when helped. (I)	0.0
Student misses all items, but with help and prompts, he or she answers some correctly. (P)	1.0
Student answers score 2.0 items correctly but not scores 3.0 or 4.0 items. (P)	2.0
Student answers scores 2.0 and 3.0 items correctly but not score 4.0 items. (C)	3.0

Figure 4.6: Sample assessment item based on student responses and proficiencies.

When developing a powerful core curriculum, determining clear, rigorous learning targets and communicating them to students are essential. By helping students understand how teachers will determine mastery, educators provide them with specific criteria for success.

As we've seen, whenever possible, curriculum planning should involve a student-centered approach and be meaningful and relevant to students. Even then, teachers can anticipate some missed opportunities when meeting all of the mandates to deliver a rigorous standards-based curriculum.

Working in teams to determine the essential standards and the necessary success criteria for each one allows teachers to strengthen the foundation of their core curriculum. While commercial textbook programs may profess to be aligned with the CCSS and have a logical sequence, identifying essential standards allows teachers to thoughtfully consider reordering chapters and lessons to better serve their students' needs. Ultimately, the essential standards need to be connected to meaningful, relevant learning experiences. The lesson's context, content, and topic become the vehicle for how to present the standard to the student.

Integrating 21st Century Skills

To prepare students for an unknown future in a rapidly changing world, many experts recommend that curriculum design should give less attention to covering content, facts, and general knowledge and focus more closely on the important skills students will need to navigate in the world—skills such as problem solving, analysis, perseverance, self-control, and curiosity. These life skills, also known as *habits of mind*, can be the keys to ongoing success in education, careers, and life (Costa &

Kallick, 2008). As educational writer and communications consultant Sam Chaltain (2014) notes, "Content is merely the means by which young people develop new skills and habits to carry them successfully through life and to equip them to solve problems we can't even conceive of."

The Partnership for 21st Century Skills (P21), formed in 2002, explores the education needs of the ever-changing digital world. P21 advocates for standards that adequately address both the core academic knowledge and the complex thinking skills necessary for success in college, life, and careers in the 21st century (see figure 4.7).

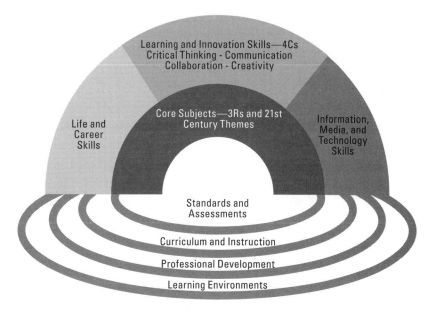

Source: P21 Framework for 21st Century Learning. www.P21.org. All Rights Reserved. 2009.

Figure 4.7: 21st century student outcomes.

In addition to these 21st century student outcomes, the Partnership for 21st Century Skills urges educators to integrate the 4Cs of 21st century skills—*communication, collaboration, critical thinking,* and *creativity*—into the Common Core State Standards, or state standards, as they build powerful core curricula. Additional life and career skills teachers should incorporate into any standards-based curriculum plan for ELA and mathematics include *self-direction, flexibility, adaptability, productivity,* and *responsibility.* These skills represent important competencies for all students as they learn the standards and become college and career ready. (We describe using the 21st century skills to create more rigorous lessons in chapter 7, page 197.) As the Common Core states:

> The Standards define what all students are expected to know and be able to do, not how teachers should teach. . . . The Standards must therefore be complemented by a well-developed, content-rich curriculum consistent with the expectations laid out in this document. (NGA & CCSSO, 2010a, p. 6)

Identifying the essential standards launches the development of the core curriculum plan. Teachers must then look for integration opportunities to include essential 21st century life skills to better equip students with the competencies they need for success.

Making Content Meaningful and Relevant

Beyond identifying and revising essential standards and incorporating 21st century skills, teachers engaged in the work of building a powerful core curriculum have the additional challenge of ensuring the content's concepts and skills are relevant to learners. That's how educators help students understand the connection between what they're learning in school and the things they find important in their world. Students rarely engage in curriculum content or activities that appear to have no meaning or relevance in their everyday life. Before they present any lessons, therefore, teachers must help students connect to the instruction. When students clearly understand the meaningfulness and usefulness of what they're learning, teachers are less likely to have to continually answer questions like "Why do we need to know this?" and "When are we ever going to use this?"

These findings serve as just some of the compelling evidence that the curriculum's context makes a distinct difference in learning.

▽ Knowledge of both the culture and the student should influence the curriculum (Dewey, 1938). A culturally responsive curriculum can build meaningfulness between home and school experiences. Teaching to the whole child not only includes the importance of academic achievement but also cultural identity and heritage (Gay, 2000).

▽ Student work should be worth doing (Darling-Hammond, 2006). Time is often a teacher's greatest nemesis. However, busywork is not effective. Every single minute is a learning opportunity. The teacher should select every task, discussion, reading, and lesson as a worthwhile pursuit. Student engagement will lack if students don't feel the task is worth it or it doesn't matter or count.

▽ Presenting content in more authentic ways is beneficial (Spillane, 2000). Authentic learning experiences and genuine real-life tasks, or simulated tasks, engage all senses and allow learners to create a meaningful connection to the real world. Instead of regurgitating information, authentic learning provides students with opportunities to create tangible, useful products worth sharing with their community.

▽ Students will both understand and remember best when teachers have them apply information in a relevant, practical setting (Daggett, 2008). Students should have opportunities to create real things that matter.

They should write newspaper articles, plays, and brochures; create campaigns; make videos; compose music; and so on for a real potential audience. Students shouldn't be asked to create a PowerPoint presentation on a topic they don't care about for an imaginary audience.

▽ Students are motivated and their learning will be advanced if we provide a socially relevant curriculum (Cammarota, 2007). Students care about the welfare of their communities, friends, and families. Learners become empowered when they discover they have a voice and may be able to initiate social changes or influence global issues.

▽ A lack of integrated and relevant curriculum continues to be one of the main barriers for minority students to transition successfully from school to work (Wentling & Waight, 2001). A key to engaging all learners is to ensure that a powerful standards-based core curriculum makes connections to a student's world—that means *every* student's world. Connecting projects, tasks, and lessons to students' communities assures them that the learning is relevant.

Thus, to ensure that Tier 1 content is relevant and meaningful to students, teachers must focus on authenticity and student-centered instruction.

Authenticity

Meaningful learning typically is authentic learning, involving students in the kinds of real-world tasks that are clearly connected to their everyday lives. Authentic intellectual work, according to M. Bruce King, Fred Newmann, and Dana Carmichael (2009), involves careful study of the topic's or problem's details and the application of knowledge and skills to a problem, project, or presentation relevant beyond school. King et al. (2009) offer the following three criteria for identifying and measuring authentic instruction and assessment.

1. **Knowledge construction:** Students create new meaning personally from the opportunity to organize, interpret, synthesize, and evaluate knowledge.

2. **Disciplined inquiry:** Students use prior information to investigate important concepts and real-world problems while expressing in-depth understanding.

3. **Relevance beyond the classroom:** Students apply the new understanding to face real-world issues. The work doesn't merely meet curriculum standards, but it also has value in the global community.

As we've seen, the brain loves a challenge and will be attracted to and will willingly embrace novel situations. Traditional stand-and-deliver curriculum—a teacher monologue with little or no student input or involvement—does not engage students in the same way because it has little personal meaning or relevance. When building core curricula, therefore, educators are wise to ensure content authenticity. King et al.'s (2009) three criteria are a good place to start in that effort.

Student-Centered Instruction

When teacher teams really keep students in mind as they build a core curriculum, the curriculum plan has a different focus. Then, the instruction becomes targeted on what learners need and want. With a student-centered focus, educators design every aspect of the curriculum around how it can support *learning* rather than how it can make sure *teaching* happens. Topics of such student-centered curricula reflect students' interests, and instructional strategies are more likely to be developmentally appropriate and culturally responsive. Beyond attending to the content's authenticity, therefore, educators and planning teams should keep these three elements in mind in creating a powerful core curriculum that supports the learning process.

1. **Clear learning targets in student-friendly language:** As we mentioned previously, students should be in on the game plan through clear learning targets in language students can understand. Students should know the agenda for each day and understand their short- and long-term goals.

2. **Student voice:** Students have unique perspectives, and their insights warrant attention. When designing a curriculum plan, leave some flexible space for students to make suggestions and contributions. By recruiting students to make decisions or solve problems, teachers can build student engagement and offer valuable learning opportunities.

3. **Less us, more them:** Gary Stager (n.d.), executive director of the Constructivist Consortium, a group dedicated to empowering learners, always ends his talks with the same four words of advice to teachers: "Less us, more them." With that statement, he reminds listeners not to confuse teaching and learning. While it is important that the teacher crafts a dynamic lesson or learning experience, the school experience really is about students learning. Well-designed curriculum plans, therefore, should focus on learning experiences rather than teaching experiences.

When we offer students real-world authentic tasks that go beyond the classroom, creativity is sparked, and engagement and motivation are inevitable through communicating, researching, analyzing, decision making, producing, and contributing. As we learn in the next section of this chapter, students can expand their knowledge by solving problems and applying new learning to complex projects.

Employing Evidence-Based Best Practices

The fifth element of a powerful core curriculum is the actual content and processes of the lessons, activities, tasks, textbooks, and programs teachers use as the vehicles to teach the essential standards. Selecting and implementing instructional strategies based on scientifically validated research will ensure that all students at Tier 1 are more likely to master the core curriculum. We've dedicated chapter 5 (page 111) to an overview of a variety of instructional approaches, strategies, and evidence-based best practices. Here, however, we review just a couple practices—problem-based learning and project-based learning—and demonstrate their critical role in a powerful core curriculum.

Problem-Based Learning

Problem-based learning (PBL) is a student-centered, constructivist curriculum strategy that challenges students to learn about the subject matter by *seeking* out information they need in order to solve problems: "Challenges, especially real-world challenges, invite students to use their imagination to extend thinking about what is known in order to solve real problems" (Drapeau, 2014, p. 62). Authentic, complex, real-world problems with many possible solutions are attention grabbers especially for all learners. Problem-based learning taps into student autonomy through self-directed learning and fosters skills of developing flexible knowledge, problem solving, resource gathering, reasoning, critical thinking, and collaborating. As the Northwestern University Feinberg School of Medicine (n.d.) notes:

> PBL is a learner-centered educational method. In PBL, learners are progressively given more and more responsibility for their own education and become increasingly independent of the teacher for their education. PBL produces independent learners who can continue to learn on their own in life and in their chosen careers.

In its most basic form, problem-based learning includes:

▽ **A problem for students to solve or a question to answer**—"How might we rearrange the tables and chairs in our classroom to make sure there are enough seats for three new students who arrive tomorrow?"

▽ **Students working in small collaborative groups brainstorming what they already know about the topic and deciding on a hypothesis**—"We saw how quickly the seeds sprouted last week on the damp paper towels and without any soil. This week we will be planting seeds in small cups of soil. How long do you predict it will take before we see any sprouts appear? Decide with your group what your hypothesis is. Can you propose what a growth chart might look like at the end of two weeks?"

▽ **Students identifying what they need to know to be successful and making a plan to validate or discard their hypothesis**—"We have brainstormed many ideas and gathered lots of information about our school's new lunch schedule that will begin next week. What has your group decided to propose as an alternative suggestion? If it is accepted, how will you know if it is successful? Create a review plan for how you will evaluate it in two weeks."

This type of strategizing requires active learning. As we mentioned in chapter 2 (page 32), the seeking system energizes our behaviors and attitudes and plays a key role in learning, connections, and motivation. Problem-based learning engages students' seeking system, and they receive a dopamine release as they move forward to solve the problem. This active learning also satisfies social needs as students work together.

Not only does problem solving engage learners, but it also fosters intelligence behavior. Gardner (2004) defines *intelligence* as one's ability to handle crises, solve problems, and create innovations that would benefit society. Robert Sternberg's (1996) theory of successful intelligence defines it as the ability to be analytical, practical, and creative. In other words, successful intelligence is not just what you know but also what you can do with what you know. Art Costa and Bena Kallick (2008) offer that, "The critical attribute of intelligent human beings is not only having information but also knowing how to act on it" (p. 16). Costa and Kallick (2008) remind us that developing a skill set of habits of mind will help you know how to behave intelligently even when you don't know the answer. All of these demonstrations of intelligence are fostered and supported in the problem-based learning experience.

Students involved in problem-based learning develop skills to generate hypotheses, apply knowledge, provide coherent explanations, support their claims with evidence, and evaluate their results (Barron & Darling-Hammond, 2008). In elementary classrooms, encourage students to do the following.

▽ **Ask lots of questions:** "What do you need to know?" "What are you curious about?"

▽ **Compare new information to what they already know:** "What does this remind you of?" "Where could you go to find out more information?"

▽ **Make predictions:** "What do you think will happen next?" "What changes could be made that could make a real difference in the outcome?"

▽ **Test ideas:** "How could you prove that?" "What could you do to find out if that would work?"

All of these skills are emphasized in most state standards and the Common Core State Standards. By including meaningfulness, relevancy, and choices, problem-based learning can engage and challenge all learners. Here are just some of the other benefits problem-based learning offers.

▽ It develops students' social skills through collaborative problem solving.

▽ It helps students achieve multiple learning outcomes by integrating several disciplines (cross-disciplinary).

▽ It encourages students to find their level of challenge within the zone of proximal development.

▽ It fosters creative and critical thinking.

Working Through the Problem-Based Learning Process

Although problem-based learning can take several forms, in general, there are six steps involved in incorporating the process into curriculum planning.

1. Use minilectures to set the context and introduce the problem (Duch, Groh, & Allen, 2001; Gallagher, 1997), or students may identify the problem. For example, showing a photo of a current event, presenting a concern in the neighborhood, or offering a possible unsafe situation might introduce a problem that needs attention.

2. To activate prior knowledge, have students discuss and identify the problem.

3. Students collaboratively generate a hypothesis or initial course of action (listening to suggestions from the teacher and having discussions to clarify the task).

4. Provide students with templates and suggestions for how to gather data and resources.

5. As a class, students and the teacher orchestrate time and plan steps for investigation.

6. Students generate solutions and evaluate the outcomes.

As you can see, students need to clarify and identify the problem to launch the problem-based learning process. Teachers or students may generate the problem or issue based on learning standards. The greater the student involvement in the process, the greater their engagement will be. The teacher's role is to activate, facilitate, and resource the plan with support and guidance while monitoring the process.

Teachers play only a guiding role as students work to select a good question for investigation in the process. Closed questions—those with simple, short, black-and-white answers—typically aren't good for this process. Instead, good questions for problem-based learning are open ended and may have multiple answers. Here are three ways to frame open-ended questions that foster thinking and encourage seeking.

1. **How?** How could things be made better or different? This question is the basis for problem solving, synthesis, and evaluation. Example questions include: How might things be different if school started at 10:00 a.m.? How can our community help reduce garbage? How might the school's cafeteria be redesigned to make it more friendly and so students get to know each other better?

2. **Why?** Why do or did things happen? This type of question requires analysis of cause and effect and the relationship between variables. It encourages students to compare and contrast. Example questions include: Why would some people want fast food restaurants to close? Why have more students been absent from school this year? Why is it important to recycle paper and plastic?

3. **Which is best?** Which would we choose? Such questions require deep learning through research, the weighing of evidence, and thoughtful decision making. Example questions include: Can you think of a daily food menu to give your body energy during the day and good nutrition? Which types of transportation to school should you choose if you wanted to create the least amount of pollution?

Other types of good problems might include:

▽ Should children your age have a limit to how much screen time they have each day?

▽ Our class has raised money to help students in need. How should we decide to whom we should give it?

▽ The school board is considering altering the calendar for the next school year. What recommendations for changes should our class make?

▽ What would be a safe, but more efficient, plan for an evacuation at our school?

Open-ended problems may prove to be quite a challenge for younger students. The following criteria will help guide the development of good questions and problems.

▽ The questions or problems include the standards and content teachers will target in the unit.

▽ Students have resources available to them to find additional information about the questions or problems.

▽ The questions or problems have multiple solutions that students can support.

▽ Students can adjust or modify their hypothesis.

▽ The questions or problems foster controversy and interest and extend students' thinking.

▽ Solving the problems or questions demands more than mere recall, as they are open ended and complex.

▽ The questions or problems foster critical and creative thinking through collaboration.

▽ The questions or problems examine subject content in an authentic way.

Figure 4.8 can help students organize and clarify their thinking related to an open-ended problem.

Problem:			
What do we know?	What is our hypothesis?	What do we need to know?	What is our plan?

Figure 4.8: Problem-solving question chart.

*Visit **go.solution-tree.com/RTIatWork** for a reproducible version of this figure.*

Facilitating Problem-Based Learning

Teachers must modify their typical role to become a facilitator in the problem-based learning process. Students become more active in their learning by seeking solutions to a challenging task, as the teacher's role shifts to:

▽ Guiding the group process

▽ Encouraging participation

▽ Asking students more questions

▽ Insisting that they support their ideas with evidence

▽ Modeling good reasoning

▽ Offering instruction when needed in the form of minilessons

▽ Providing and facilitating access to resources

As active participants in the learning process, rather than passive receivers of information, students develop strong connections between learned concepts through problem-based learning (Gallagher, 1997; Ronis, 2007; Torp & Sage, 2002). Students engaged in problem-based learning are not just regurgitating facts but are going deeper to develop understanding of issues and events, as well as analyzing, applying, assimilating, and adapting new information. Teachers, too, benefit from the problem-based learning approach, which is a powerful addition to the evidence-based practices that contribute to the most effective core curricula. As University of Delaware professor Hal White (1995) notes in "'Creating Problems' for PBL," "One must reconsider what students really need to learn and the environment in which they learn. Much of the enthusiasm for the problem-based approach to learning comes from instructors who feel revitalized by the creative energy it releases."

Project-Based Learning

Including complete, complex projects is another evidence-based practice that plays an important role in creating a powerful and dynamic core curriculum, even as it builds content relevance and student engagement. An effective project-based curriculum helps students *transfer* their learning to real-world situations. Students move beyond surface content and facts when they complete complex tasks that result in a realistic product, event, or presentation to an audience. Students typically find project-based learning more enjoyable, engaging, and motivating than the traditional *sit and get* approach to education.

Powerful projects incorporate local resources and issues, as they build students' 21st century skills. Great projects also help the community and spark ongoing community awareness. Table 4.4 offers a detailed comparison between project-based learning and traditional instructional design.

Table 4.4: Project-Based Learning Versus Traditional Instructional Design

Project-Based Learning	Traditional Instructional Design
▽ Student centered	▽ Teacher directed
▽ Real informative sources	▽ Textbooks
▽ Student-planned tasks as needed	▽ Workbooks—packets of worksheets
▽ Authentic summative assessment	▽ Quizzes and tests
▽ Students working in groups and partners	▽ Students working alone
▽ Project's success provides authentic assessment	▽ Grades to inform abilities

When elementary students work in teams on real projects, they develop many skills. For example, social skills improve as students develop compassion and cooperation and learn to manage conflict. In the process, students develop feelings of efficacy, self-worth, inclusion, and contribution. Leadership skills increase as well, through project-based learning, and students also develop perseverance and tenacity as they pursue the project's goal.

Some project-based learning ideas to incorporate in the curriculum include:

▽ Designs and a 3-D model for a new playground structure that could fit in the existing area and be more accessible to students with physical handicaps

▽ School garden projects

▽ Solutions for making a neighborhood safe with an action plan that includes grade-appropriate informational brochures, public service announcements, and community meetings

▽ Intergenerational projects utilizing local retired teachers

▽ Projects supporting the phrase: "Think Globally, Act Locally!"

Brigid Barron and Linda Darling-Hammond (2008), in *Teaching for Meaningful Learning*, present that:

▽ Active learning has a more significant impact on student performance than student background and prior achievement

▽ Students learn more deeply when they are allowed to apply learned knowledge to real-world problems and when they apply it to projects that sustain engagement and collaboration

▽ Students are more successful when they are taught how to learn as well as what to learn

Project-based and problem-based learning include many of the essential strategies Hattie and Yates (2014) cite as having a significantly high impact on student learning: higher-order thinking, collaborative learning, formative assessment, effective feedback, goal setting, learning from errors, and self-monitoring. Including a problem to solve and a project to work on will provide multiple opportunities for students to engage and maximize their learning (Boss, 2014).

Even the most carefully constructed core curriculum can be improved over time. Let's examine that process now.

Concentrating the Core Curriculum

As we continue to investigate the elements of a core curriculum, it's important to remember that through modest modifications, or a *concentrated* effort, teams can offer additional opportunities to engage students and enhance the core curriculum. At the same time, if educators discover that elements they've included in the core curriculum no longer seem as effective or valuable as they once did, they can consider eliminating those elements and investing the time in more meaningful, productive pursuits. In this section of the chapter, we're going to examine the process of concentrating the core curriculum. We offer these suggestions not to impose a greater burden on an already overloaded curriculum ("One more thing to do!") but as considerations that might, if implemented, make the job of teaching the curriculum more manageable.

▽ **Interdisciplinary (cross-discipline) connections:** Whenever possible, connect the content across disciplines to create opportunities for students to even more so develop meaning and relevance. Even though core essential standards are written around individual subject areas, in reality, most real-world projects and tasks are a blend of a variety of disciplines. Curriculum plans that encourage interdisciplinary connections will provide more opportunities for students to see how learning subjects and tasks are related. Reading and writing about social studies, history, or science content allow two or more disciplines to be "taught" at the same time. For example, a commercial reading program may have a passage about an endangered species. Teachers could use this text as the perfect opportunity to introduce local endangered species and address grade-level science standards. Or, when studying area and perimeter in mathematics, the teacher could introduce a problem-based task and have students calculate how much carpeting he or she would need to purchase to update the classroom. Finally, it's a good idea to integrate art, music, and drama into curriculum content whenever possible—especially if these subjects have been on the chopping block.

▽ **English language arts strands:** Another way to increase the success of any curriculum plan is to integrate the strands of English language arts (Reading, Writing, Speaking and Listening, and Language) wherever possible. A strong curriculum plan at Tier 1 will have language arts integrated throughout. Per the Common Core, "The Standards insist that instruction in reading, writing, speaking, listening, and language be a shared responsibility within the school" (NGA & CCSSO, 2010a, p. 4). All teachers, even if they are not designated language arts teachers, should routinely integrate instruction and practice using language arts into their instruction. Every opportunity that students can get to practice literacy skills is valuable. When teachers take collective responsibility for literacy development, the students will have the support, encouragement, and opportunities to apply their skills in context.

These suggested enhancements to the core curriculum are easy-to-implement techniques that may be familiar to many educators. Now, let's take a more detailed look at a couple powerful ways to boost the effectiveness and relevance of any Tier 1 core curriculum through exploring big ideas and abandoning less valuable opportunities.

Exploring Big Ideas

As teachers interpret the standards, verify that commercial curricula or existing courses are in line with the standards, and attempt to integrate 21st century skills into their own core instruction, they must also look for how the many concepts within the curriculum might be connected. How can these educators help students see links between seemingly isolated facts? We recommend that teachers seek out an overarching *big idea*—a thematic plan or question that they can use as a content organizer. Students will be more likely to engage with a well-organized curriculum that focuses on a single bigger picture or outcome. Big ideas help us make sense of things. Determining a big idea and using it as an umbrella will help students create a mental schema to connect and make sense out of what is being taught. Examples of big ideas include:

▽ Energy can make things move.

▽ You are what you eat.

▽ Living things grow and change over time.

The big idea could also be expressed as an *essential question*. According to Jay McTighe and Grant Wiggins (2013), a good essential question is open ended and thought provoking and calls for higher-order thinking skills. Similar to the open-ended questions we described in problem-based learning (page 100), good essential questions foster more questions and are not answerable in a brief sentence—sometimes, they're not answerable at all. Curriculum designed around good essential questions can spark meaningful connections and promote the transfer of ideas.

Examples of essential questions include:

▽ Why do people move to another house or a different city?

▽ How does the weather in our area affect our daily lives?

▽ Where do artists get their ideas?

▽ What is a food chain—who eats who?

Here are some considerations to keep in mind when organizing curriculum with an essential question.

▽ Is it clever enough to hook students' interest?

▽ Does the question lend itself to real-world applications?

▽ Does the question (and response) integrate several subjects?

▽ Does the question initiate creative and critical thinking?

▽ Could there be multiple answers—or no definitive answer?

As we noted previously, adding new dimensions to content areas and approaches isn't the only way to enhance core curriculum. Now, let's explore how educators can achieve that enhancement by eliminating less productive strategies, tasks, and content.

Evaluating Less Valuable Opportunities: Selective Abandonment

When evaluating the strength of a Tier 1 core curriculum, it's important to assess the amount of time that the curriculum plan might address nonessential learning tasks. This is where selective abandonment comes into play. Many times, elementary classrooms create morning gathering routines that continue all year—routines that often repeat the same information every day. Consider, for example, some of the circle times, meetings, and routines that take place in many elementary school classrooms. Could you modify or reduce the time you spend on repetitive morning meetings, calendar scheduling, sharing, and so on? Perhaps as the year progresses, some of the routine tasks may no longer deserve repeating *every* day. In addition, some holiday activities or school traditions (such as Spring Festivals or Winter Showcases) can take on a life of their own. Every year, new activities can slip into the schedule and begin to consume valuable time. Elementary schools are often bombarded with such "opportunities": second-grade Dairy Council poster contest, fourth-grade symphony performances, and first-grade apple farm visits. Many times these terrific opportunities end up taking a lot of additional preparation and participation during valuable class time.

In all cases, classroom time needs to be used wisely, so educators seeking to enhance their own core curriculum are wise to evaluate the necessity and benefit of all activities and tasks it includes. Teachers and teacher teams can carefully review existing traditions to determine whether some have evolved to include way too many tasks over several weeks. Perhaps some activities should be selectively (thoughtfully) abandoned or modified. When new possibilities are suggested, teacher teams might review and consider them, and then respectfully just say, "No!"

Taking time to examine the curriculum's content and design for potential enhancement is a powerful strategy to abandon or prevent less valuable opportunities, which will benefit all students. A series of lessons that simply addresses the standards but fails to engage the students will be much less effective than a set of interdisciplinary, relevant, and thoughtfully organized learning opportunities. Teacher teams can determine what big ideas and essential questions will be the most effective to organize the standards into an engaging and effective curriculum. When teachers design a framework collaboratively, they can work together to plan its specific instructional tasks, activities, and projects. Creating a pacing calendar or a curriculum map can help maintain a timeline of implementation. The nonprofit organization Great Minds (http://greatminds.net/curriculum-tools) and the Rogers Public Schools in Arizona (http://rogersstaff.ss5.sharpschool.com) have rich resources and suggestions to help K–12 teams organize and plan a Tier 1 curriculum map. See figure 4.9 for a fourth-grade example.

Fourth-Grade Year at a Glance					
First Quarter	**Second Quarter**		**Third Quarter**		**Fourth Quarter**
Math Unit 1 Nine weeks Addition, subtraction, and multiplication with multidigit whole numbers	**Math Unit 2** Nine weeks Connecting understanding of multidigit whole-number operations to fractions		**Math Unit 3** Nine weeks Connecting whole-number operations to addition and subtraction of mixed numbers and multiplicative comparison		**Math Unit 4** Nine weeks Connecting geometric measurement and decimals to fractions and whole numbers
Science Nine weeks Body systems Water cycle Trends and patterns	**Science** Nine weeks Animal classifications Adaptations Interdependence of organisms Electricity		**Science** Nine weeks Force and mass Properties and changes in matters		**Science** Nine weeks Arkansas divisions and natural resources Changes to Earth's surface
ELA Unit 1 Five weeks Tales of the Heart	**ELA Unit 2** Six weeks Literature settings: Weather or not	**ELA Unit 3** Six weeks Animals are characters too: Characters who gallop, bark, and squeak	**ELA Unit 4** Eight weeks America in conflict	**ELA Unit 5** Five weeks Stories of the Earth and sky	**ELA Unit 6** Six weeks Literary heroes
Social Studies Civics	**Social Studies** Geographic representations		**Social Studies** History (Civil War)	**Social Studies** Human and environmental change over time	**Social Studies** Economics

Source: Adapted from Rogers Public Schools, 2015.

Figure 4.9: Sample curriculum map for fourth grade.

When teaching teams reach agreement on curriculum content, then all team members can be confident that they (and their teammates) are teaching the intended curriculum with fidelity within the proposed time frame. With a powerful core curriculum established, the next step is to explore how daily differentiated instruction will take place. Building up a repertoire of high-impact, research-based strategies allows a teacher to have ready resources and choices available to address the wide variety of learning needs in a diverse classroom.

Taking the Discussion Further

Following are some of the important ideas from this chapter that are worthy of further reflection and discussion. Educators in a PLC may want to read through this chapter with their collaborative teams and discuss each section, recording the issues related to each piece of information and considering classroom implications for students. Collaborative teams can reflect on the prompts to deepen understanding and set subsequent goals for improvement.

▽ Discuss the issues related to developing a core curriculum and the expectations for students at Tier 1. Consider the following concepts.

▶ Essential standards

▶ 21st century skills

▶ Problem-based learning and project-based learning

▶ Assessment

▽ Consider these three key criteria in selecting essential standards.

a. Endurance

b. Leverage

c. Readiness for further study

▽ Revisit figure 4.2 (page 82), and select essential standards to write in student-friendly language. Consider the important skills and strategies, key concepts, and selected learning activities and tasks.

▽ Review the concept of problem-based learning, and discuss the benefit of this approach.

▽ What steps can you take to create and plan a problem-based unit of study? Create a problem that students would find intriguing that is grounded in standards (knowledge and skills), then plan the resources, steps, and so on necessary to help students successfully pursue a solution to the problem.

▽ Discuss learning progressions and how they can be of value in providing appropriate challenges for students.

▽ Discuss proficiency scales. Does your team use them? How could they be used to greater ensure success?

▽ Consider any opportunities in upcoming units of study to make connections between and among the disciplines, including ELA, mathematics, science, and social studies.

▽ Review the material in this chapter on big ideas, then discuss and develop essential questions that would challenge and intrigue students in the next unit of study.

▽ What nonessential activities in your school take time from learning and achieving competencies? Identify those that you might selectively abandon.

Differentiating Instruction Through Pluralized Teaching Strategies

So far, we've set up how to create a brain-friendly classroom, how to reach each learner in that classroom, and the essential elements of a core curriculum. Now, we dive headfirst into daily differentiation. In this chapter, we are going to explore a range of teaching strategies that educators can use to expand their instructional repertoire and develop a toolbox of techniques for addressing a broad spectrum of student learning preferences. For every concept, skill, standard, and task you are planning to teach, consider how you might present it in several different ways—or think of the *pluralized* implications for each strategy. Pluralized instruction is the manifestation of a teacher's instructional intelligence. Dynamic, successful teachers recognize, and are sensitive to, the wide variety of diverse learners in every classroom, and they routinely orchestrate instructional variety as a way to promote learner engagement, interest, curiosity, and mastery. Pluralized teaching incorporates a broad spectrum of *multimodal* instructional strategies and a variety of novel learning experiences to teach every concept, skill, and standard. Daily differentiation asks teachers to routinely orchestrate instructional variety as a way to promote learner engagement, interest, and curiosity. Therefore, pluralized instruction offers many opportunities for teachers to consider every student's learning preferences, interests, multicultural backgrounds, developmental readiness, prior knowledge, and mindsets.

We begin this exploration with a short review of the shift from traditional to progressive instructional models and the role of pluralized strategies in that transition. This chapter also reviews some of the most powerful strategies for specific learning areas, including technology and vocabulary, and it outlines methods for using learning centers and stations as a strategy for boosting student engagement and interest. Finally, we take an extended look at how teachers can incorporate an explicit pluralized pedagogy in their instructional plan in order to build greater student learning. Some of the ideas that we reference in this chapter have been introduced and explained in previous chapters of the book, but here we offer a closer look at the role these ideas play as single elements within a broad and multifaceted strategic approach to daily differentiated instruction.

Moving From Traditional to Progressive Instructional Methods

In previous chapters of this book, we've described a number of instructional methods aimed at moving education from a *teacher-centered* activity to a *student-centered* activity. That shift emphasizes curriculum content and educational approaches designed to more fully engage students' interests and give them more ownership over their learning. Adopting those approaches is one step toward moving away from strictly traditional education to a more progressive educational model.

Traditional education is rooted in long-established norms—ideas, content, and instructional methods largely designed to support the teaching process. *Progressive* education, on the other hand, is the result of modern education reform efforts that promote a holistic approach focused on supporting each student's needs and self-expression. Traditional and progressive education coexist in modern society. Many educators believe traditional teacher-centered methods that foster rote learning and memorization should be replaced with student-centered and task-based approaches (Hattie, 2009).

Traditional education differs radically from progressive education in many ways. Traditional education relies on the transmission of facts, skills, and moral and social standards that society deems necessary for success in the future from one generation to the next. Students are expected to obediently receive and believe this fixed set of information as teachers communicate it from stand-and-deliver modes. Educational progressivist John Dewey (1938) describes this transfer of knowledge as being outside the learner and transmitted from the teacher, which as we've seen is not effective for modern learners.

Historically, the primary education strategy was simple oral monologue (Beck, 1956). Teachers stood in front of the class and communicated a fixed set of educational "truths." Traditional education continues this model. It supports a passive role for learners, in which students try their best to look and listen and answer when called on. The teacher's role is to deliver information and assign activities, which the students then study and memorize for the tests. That test usually is given at the end of a unit, and the process—assignment-study-recitation-test—is then repeated. Teachers who focus on teaching for the test cause the following adverse classroom conditions (Center for Public Education, 2006; Yeh, 2005).

▽ A limited curriculum, as they do not include criteria not on the test

▽ A narrowed learning experience involving receiving and memorizing information with little dialogue or application

▽ Too much time on test prep, rather than learning

This approach emphasizes rote memorization (often with little student understanding of meaning), and disconnected, unrelated assignments. These assignments are often busywork, with no relationship to anything in the real world. All in all, the process is rather disrespectful of both the teacher's and the student's time. Everyone learns everything as a single group. If students don't learn on time, they fail. This approach has been prevalent in American education, and many classrooms still use it today.

Active Learning

Given what we have discussed in previous chapters about the neuroscience of how the brain learns, and in light of the abundance of research available about best practices in instruction, it becomes evident that we can improve on the traditional education model.

We begin that process by understanding that teaching and learning are two different processes: the teacher teaches, and the learner learns. In 21st century classrooms, the shift to a more progressive model of education does not necessarily involve revising the teacher's role from a provider of information to a facilitator of learning. Instead, this shift redefines teachers as activators of student thinking. To prepare to succeed in today's environment of global entrepreneurism, multiculturalism, rapidly advancing technology, and shifting economic and political systems, students have to adopt a whole new range of skills, knowledge, and understanding. Progressive education addresses this need by demanding that students do less listening and more talking in order to construct their own meaning and understanding around curriculum content.

Constructivism

As we've seen, neuroscience continues to teach us more about the brain, and one of the most important neurological findings for educators involves dendrites. As we learned in chapter 2, the human brain continues to grow dendrites—connections between and among cells—throughout life, based on experiences and new learning. This neuroplasticity of the brain enables learning throughout life. This neurological process fits with the concept of *constructivism*. Constructivism's main premise is that humans construct new learning based on present information stored in the brain and interactions with new information that becomes available over time. The learner in a constructivist educational setting, therefore, is active not passive. The traditional classroom, on the other hand, is based on transmittal, and thus it doesn't necessarily facilitate the construction of new learning.

Learners begin with what they know, and because students have had different prior experiences, each has his or her own unique fundamental knowledge set. That fundamental knowledge will influence how they construct new knowledge. In classes where students are passive, uncovering the inaccuracies, inadequacies, and misconceptions contained in their fundamental knowledge set can be quite difficult. Students need to be active in order to reveal their existing constructs or approach to concept development. Throughout this active learning process, they apply current understandings, note relevant elements in new learning experiences, judge the consistency of prior and emerging knowledge, and—based on that judgment—modify knowledge.

Constructivism, therefore, has three important implications for teaching.

1. Information is not the transmission of knowledge from the enlightened educator to the unenlightened learner. Constructivist teachers are not the sage on the stage. They should, instead, serve as a guide on the side, or an activator of learning.

2. If learning is based on prior knowledge, then teachers must discover what fundamental knowledge students already possess. Then, they can devise a plan to shore up the background information or correct misconceptions within that knowledge set. Teachers cannot assume that all learners share the same understanding of anything. Students, therefore, may require different learning experiences to reach a greater level of understanding.

3. Teachers also need to create learning experiences that respond to the interests, ideas, and activities that are important to the learners. Giving students some scope and choice in the projects and problems they tackle and, whenever possible, having students work with partners or in small groups enables students to be more engaged in the learning process, build on one another's thinking, and construct new understanding through dialogue.

Students require time in order to build knowledge—to reflect on new information and current understandings and their view of the world. Therefore, classroom time should be devoted to constructing knowledge with appropriate tasks and opportunities. Rushing to cover the curriculum rarely works for anything other than surface learning.

Constructivism, although not new, is progressive in that it helps students develop understanding and not just trivia for test taking. Understanding and building knowledge greater ensures long-term memory and students' ability to use knowledge in their lives.

In this chapter, we explore the best practices for shifting to a progressive classroom model. Another critical aspect of progressive classrooms is the inclusion of technology, which engages, enhances, and enriches student learning.

Maximizing the Power of Technology

Many elementary classrooms are now filled with *digital natives* who bring with them prior knowledge and experience with technology that may be well outside their teachers' experiences. The days are gone when educators could view technology as a mere distraction. The time has come to reframe that thinking and understand that any powerful core curriculum has to leverage students' skills and interests in technology and enhance and expand those skills. In any case, technology offers educators a set of powerful strategies for advancing learners' skills and knowledge.

Of course, educational leaders have been trying to implement technology since the 1980s, with limited success. Lack of funding for hardware and professional training and teachers trying to keep up with rapidly evolving technology are major hurdles in achieving that success. Many students have portable technology that they happily would bring to school, but their school system may identify technology as a distracting gadget and ban it from the premises. Finding interesting and useful ways to incorporate common and increasingly essential technologies into daily differentiated instruction and core curricula is a much more valuable—and difficult—solution. Teachers have to be creative in finding ways to encourage students to learn new tasks and create new solutions with technology.

Meeting these challenges involves more than just replacing books with online reading or asking students to use Google or Bing to do basic research or use their electronic tablets as writing instruments. Instead, teachers need to find more engaging ways to use technology to trigger students' higher-order thinking and creativity. Educators need to rethink the way they use technology in classroom instruction. Too often, technology alone doesn't really contribute much to the instructional process or the students' cognitive skills. Rather, teachers use technology as a substitute for work that is not rigorous to begin with. PowerPoint and word processing programs, for example, often are mere replacements for traditional presentations, worksheets, or pencil-and-paper writings. SMART Boards and document cameras may simply replace chalkboards. Student response systems, such as clickers, can be motivating for students, but these systems only assess students' knowledge at the basic recall levels—an assessment that a teacher could conduct through multiple-choice paper tests (Rodgers, 2011). An excess of such rote use of technology and, in some cases, information overload may keep students (digital natives) from developing the ability to think deeply about complex ideas, develop patience, control impulses, and develop social skills. Students need to use technology to research, access information, compare and contrast sources, and verify truth in dealing with real-world problems and projects.

Triggering the Creative Use of Technology

Technology is a creativity generator and a powerful motivator. Teachers can choose from among multiple strategies to enhance student motivation and creativity, including digital storybooks, infographics, cartooning, blogs, mind-mapping tools, video and auditory production, global communication, and even games. As students spend time with a variety of technology tools, they build their skills, confidence, and imagination.

Several ideas for leveraging and teaching technology in the classroom come from the Center for Applied Research in Educational Technology (CARET), a project of the International Society for Technology in Education in partnership with Education Support Systems and the Sacramento County Office of Education. CARET suggests the following guidelines for using technology to improve student learning (Smith & Throne, 2007).

▽ Technology must be integral to the curriculum, rather than a mere add-on. Ideas for integrating technology include using word processing tools, online encyclopedias, and creativity applications and using it to provide remediation or offer a challenge as an enrichment or extension activity.

▽ Technology should encourage collaboration through social interaction and dialogue between learning partners or within small groups. As groups work collaboratively with each other, group members can teach each other new skills and understandings.

▽ Technology tasks must address students' varying abilities, prior knowledge, and experience in order to engage all students in the learning process. While many young learners are more technologically adept than their teachers, others have less background in technology.

▽ Technology improves learning when it is integrated throughout the day, not just in isolated lab learning. Technology should be readily accessible in the classroom so it is available as a go-to strategy.

▽ Technology improves learning when students use it to create projects. Such projects may include using multimedia or video streaming to creatively enhance or extend thinking and application.

▽ Technology improves learning when educators support its use. The support of school administrators is essential, as well, through the provision of just-in-time staff development.

Educators can draw from multiple resources in discovering best practices for integrating technology in their classroom and curriculum. See the two resources *Using Technology to Differentiate Instruction* (Honaker, n.d.; Tenkely, 2015) for a plethora of websites that support the use of technology in the classroom to help educators differentiate technology instruction. Visit **go.solution-tree.com/RTIatWork** to access materials related to this book. These and other sites reference multiple strategies for using technology to engage student learning.

Using Flipped Lessons

One powerful strategy for integrating technology into a creative approach for learning is the flipped lesson. A *flipped lesson* is one that inverts the typical cycle of content acquisition and application, in which students receive topic instruction in class, and then apply the knowledge later when they do homework. In the flipped lesson, students watch prerecorded, online teacher presentations before class, using whatever technology is available to them at home or in a library. Students who don't have technology available to them can preview presentations on a classroom or resource center computer, or they can view the material with a classmate. Students can view the material several times if necessary for clarification. After previewing the presentations, students then can use time in class to discuss the relevant topic, ask questions, and pursue projects or complete exercises. When applying their learning, therefore, they have the teacher, learning partners, or small-group members to help them work through any questions or problems they encounter.

The flipped lesson allows more time in class for discussion, questions, and projects based on the content presented. The process benefits students, but it also helps teachers by enabling them to get off the stage and interact with students individually and in groups related to the viewed content. Teachers guide students as they actively and interactively apply their knowledge. Students may find this approach to learning far more engaging than that achieved in regular *sit and get* classrooms, and the visuals and auditory elements of teacher presentations are usually stimulating. More students have the background knowledge they need to go deeper with the learning and apply the concepts shared in the video presentation. Early studies show that student success increases, as does engagement and ultimately students' interest in school (Marlowe, 2012).

Teachers must exercise caution as they initiate the flipped-lesson strategy. Learning to prepare and record the presentations can take time, although the process becomes easier with practice. Teachers are wise, therefore, to use already-prepared material in composing flipped-lesson presentations. They also must be sure to plan the activities for in-class tasks, as they won't be spending as much time in stand-and-deliver mode. We recommend that teachers also collaborate with other teachers online, in their school, or in their collaborative teams to share ideas and materials. In all cases, teachers should think big and start small when learning to create and use flipped lessons.

Many websites, such as the Khan Academy (www.khanacademy.org) and TED (www.ted.com/talks), offer teachers presentations related to a variety of topics. Here are some resources that can help teachers further their understanding of the flipped-lesson strategy.

▽ **"The Flipped Classroom"**: www.youtube.com/watch?v=2H4RkudFzlc

▽ **"Why I Flipped My Classroom"**: www.youtube.com/watch?v=9aGu LuipTwg

Letting Students Take the Lead

Often we think that lack of resources, training, and teacher expertise will inhibit success with technology, but many teachers and school systems have overcome these issues to achieve real success in implementing technology strategies. Sometimes the secret to adopting such new techniques is simply a matter of getting out of the way. As we've noted, even if teachers aren't proficient with technology, some of their students are. In fact, educational researcher and professor of educational technology at Newcastle University in England Sugata Mitra (2013b) suggests that in the 21st century "knowing is obsolete," even though many schools and educators fail to understand this truth. He writes:

> Schools still operate as if all knowledge is contained in books, and as if the salient points in books must be stored in each human brain—to be used when needed. The political and financial powers controlling schools decide what these salient points are. (Mitra, 2013b)

To illustrate how adept students can be at self-guided technology learning, in 1999, Mitra put a computer with Internet access in a New Delhi slum, and then he left a hidden camera to record the scene. Before long, the computer drew the attention of young children, who played with the computer, learned how to go online, access information, and then help teach others the same skills. Although English was the language displayed on the computer, these children neither spoke nor wrote English. In spite of that, they learned many things navigating the technology through trial and error. Their innate curiosity, enthusiastic motivation, and sense of wonder propelled the students to persevere and figure things out with both their curiosity and seeking system in high gear. Mitra's (2013b) inspiration for his School in the Cloud came from this experiment. (See *Build a School in the Cloud*, Mitra, 2013a.) The School in the Cloud (https://www.theschoolinthecloud.org) organizes students in collaborative groups where they choose a big question (self-selected) that integrates several subject areas and use the Internet to talk to experts and volunteer mentors in various fields.

Educators sometimes need to take a leap of faith, however, and have confidence that experimentation and exploration can yield results—for themselves and their students. Mitra's (2013a, 2013b) work, for example, demonstrates that students will uncover and make sense of new ideas and concepts and get them into their long-term memory if they have the opportunity to seek out information for themselves and construct their own meaning. As he reminds us, modern technology makes most of what we need to know accessible, replacing the need to memorize with the need to be comfortable with and capable of adapting to rapidly evolving technologies. Technology is at the heart of the 21st century skills students will need in order to participate in and create the future. That's why finding effective strategies for integrating technology in every possible aspect of the daily differentiated instruction of a powerful core curriculum is a necessity for all educators.

Using Multiple Approaches to Develop Student Vocabulary

Vocabulary can be an excellent indicator of intellectual ability and a strong predictor of school success (Elley, 1992). The vocabulary of kindergarten and first-grade students, for example, significantly predicts their reading comprehension in the middle and secondary grades (Chall & Dale, 1995; Cunningham, 2005; Cunningham & Stanovich, 1997; Denton et al., 2011). Finding the most powerful strategies to build student vocabulary, therefore, should be an explicit goal for all teachers, regardless of grade or subject discipline.

In the classroom, three types of vocabulary increase students' ability to comprehend new information in a variety of subject disciplines: (1) everyday words, (2) general-academic words, and (3) domain-specific words. Based on the work of Isabel Beck, Margaret McKeown, and Linda Kucan (2008, 2013), the Common Core for English language arts (NGA & CCSSO, 2010a) categorizes these vocabulary types in three tiers, which include the following.

▽ **Tier one:** This tier includes everyday words most students learn in conversations. These words include basic, concrete terms most students know at a particular grade level. Examples include *clock*, *baby*, *house*, *family*, *run*, *stove*, and *angry*.

▽ **Tier two:** This tier includes abstract, general-academic words, which students encounter across the curriculum. Tier two words have high utility across instructional areas. Examples include *additional*, *similar*, *stumble*, *solution*, *examine*, and *predict*.

▽ **Tier three:** This tier contains domain-specific academic vocabulary made up of highly specialized, subject-specific words that lack generalization and occur infrequently in texts. Examples for second-grade mathematics include *Venn*, *acute*, *plane*, *prism*, and *face*.

A limited vocabulary can create a major barrier to success in the classroom. Everyday language often suffices up to third grade, but once academic words and domain-specific terminology become common in the classroom, some students fall behind. One contributor to this barrier is the lack of prior knowledge and experience related to the disciplines.

Determining Important Words

Students learn new words through a variety of instructional strategies (Beck et al., 2013; Stahl & Fairbanks, 1986). So educators should explicitly teach words critical to understanding assigned text, general words that they are likely to use many times across the disciplines, and difficult (metaphorical or abstract) words that need interpretation.

While all tiers of vocabulary are important to student learning and achievement, tier two's academic vocabulary is especially important. Lack of academic vocabulary may be a roadblock to doing assignments and responding on tests across the curriculum in many disciplines. For example, students can use cross-curricular tier two words for third grade like *develop*, *credit*, or *typical* in science, social sciences, English language arts, art, and music. Command of tier two academic vocabulary is one of the most prevalent indicators of how and if students will learn subject-area content in school (NGA & CCSSO, n.d.a; Stahl & Nagy, 2006). Tier two vocabulary is:

▽ Essential to understanding academic texts

▽ Learned with deliberate effort, unlike tier one words

▽ More likely to be found in written texts than in everyday speech

▽ Used to express otherwise relatively simple things in subtle or precise ways

▽ Rarely scaffolded the way tier three words are

As a student's vocabulary grows, newly learned words serve as a catalyst and foundation for learning more words. Prior knowledge helps the learner make new connections more easily. Here are some important facts that can guide educators as they implement strategies to expand tier two academic and tier three domain-specific vocabulary (Chall, 1996).

▽ Students can reasonably be taught a deep understanding of about three hundred words each year.

▽ Divided over the content areas (literature, mathematics, science, and history), of these three hundred words, teachers should teach students roughly sixty words in each subject area each year.

▽ Each subject-area teacher can expect to teach thoroughly about eight to ten words per week.

To make the best use of classroom time, teachers should devote instruction to teaching *fewer* words. Educators, therefore, should focus on important cross-curricular tier two words for students to know, remember, and use. At the same time, teachers can simply provide and define the more domain-specific tier three words. Before each unit or new topic, the teacher can make decisions about which words to teach, after first identifying the standards the lesson is targeting. Then, the teacher can list the key words necessary for reading and understanding the lesson's key concepts.

Here is a series of steps teachers can use to help students work with tier two academic vocabulary words (Beck et al., 2013).

1. Read a story or text.

2. Contextualize each tier two word in the text.

3. Have students say the tier two words.

4. Provide student-friendly definitions for the words.

5. Engage learners in interacting with the words through discussions and dialogue.

   ▸ Respond with actions or gestures to illustrate the meaning.

   ▸ Answer questions, and give reasons to support word usage and definitions.

   ▸ Identify examples of what the words mean, as well as nonexamples of what the words *don't* mean.

6. Have students repeat the words again.

7. Review, and use the new words.

One way to preassess student vocabulary and to get students thinking about academic vocabulary is to have them fill in a chart, such as the one in figure 5.1, that explores their familiarity with specific terms. Teachers fill in appropriate words in the first column. If students know the definition of a word in the first column, they write the definition in the second column. If they can't define a word but have seen or heard it before, students put a checkmark in the third column; if they are completely unfamiliar with the word, they check the last column. Notice the last column is labeled *I haven't learned it yet*—a good message to students that contributes to their growth mindset by telling them they aren't deficient, they simply are still building their vocabulary.

Word	I can define it.	I have seen or heard it.	I haven't learned it yet.

Figure 5.1: Vocabulary preassessment chart.

*Visit **go.solution-tree.com/RTIatWork** for a reproducible version of this figure.*

Another method students can use to interact with new vocabulary is the Frayer method (Frayer, Fredrick, & Klausmeier, 1969; figure 5.2). In the first quadrant, students write examples of the new word. Then, they write nonexamples, or words or phrases that the new term is *not* about. Third, they draw a nonlinguistic representation. In the fourth quadrant, they use the word in a sentence. Lastly, they write their own definition.

Examples	Nonexamples
Nonlinguistic representation	Use it or apply it . . .
Now write your own definition.	

Figure 5.2: Frayer method vocabulary chart.

Getting Started With Teaching New Terms

In *Building Academic Vocabulary*, Marzano and Pickering (2005) outline eight research-based findings regarding effective vocabulary instruction. These findings shed light on some common practices for teaching vocabulary, as well as pointing the way toward strategies that educators should adopt.

1. Definitions *alone* are not an efficient or effective form of vocabulary instruction.

2. Students must use linguistic and nonlinguistic ways to represent their knowledge.

3. Effective vocabulary instruction involves providing word meanings through multiple repetitions and exposures to gradually shape student knowledge.

4. Teaching word parts (prefixes, suffixes, and so on) helps enhance students' understanding of terms.

5. There is not one way to teach students vocabulary, as different types of words require different types of instruction.

6. To become fully familiar with new vocabulary, students should discuss the terms through cooperative group learning.

7. Students should have ample opportunity to play and interact with words using vocabulary games.

8. Instruction should focus on terms that have a high probability of increasing student success.

In light of these findings, here are six steps teachers can use to teach new terms (Marzano & Pickering, 2005).

▽ **Step 1:** Provide a description, explanation, or example of the new term.

▽ **Step 2:** Ask students to restate the description, explanation, or example in their own words.

▽ **Step 3:** Ask students to construct a picture, symbol, or graphic representing the term or phrase.

▽ **Step 4:** Engage students periodically in activities that help them add to their knowledge of the terms in their notebooks.

▽ **Step 5:** Periodically ask students to discuss the terms with one another.

▽ **Step 6:** Involve students periodically in games that allow them to play with terms.

As we have seen, in introducing any new topic, vocabulary development is key. Without a full understanding of the terms involved in instruction, students cannot deeply understand the new information. With an established vocabulary, the process of learning can more effectively take place through active learning and processing tasks that the teacher orchestrates. As teachers work to implement strategies for building student vocabulary, they may want to remember this important idea:

> Words are not just words. They are the nexus—the interface—between communication and thought. When we read, it is through words that we build, refine, and modify our knowledge. What makes vocabulary valuable and important is not the words themselves so much as the understandings they afford. (Adams, 2009, p. 180)

Differentiating Instruction Through Learning Centers

As we've seen, differentiated instruction allows teachers to engage and empower students by attending to their learning preferences and interests. A *learning center* is an area in the classroom set aside for independent or small-group work. The area has a variety of materials, resources, and media for students to refer to. Learning centers offer multiple strategies for instructional differentiation by providing students many ways to develop concepts. By offering students a menu of learning tools and opportunities from which to choose, these centers increase student ownership of their learning process, boost student engagement, and enhance learning objectives, concepts, themes, and skills. These areas also may help students consolidate, expand, or enrich their learning, and they allow for both student and teacher creativity.

Teachers can design centers to have a greater or lesser level of complexity to reflect student readiness levels, using a multiplicity of resources. The centers' organization can reflect students' skill level or interests, including remedial or enrichment resources. Learning centers take a number of different forms, but most fall within one of three different types: (1) skill centers, (2) interest or exploratory centers, and (3) enrichment centers.

In *skill centers*, students can reinforce learned concepts and practice skills, such as working with mathematics factors, geometry shapes, phonics, word families, or other tasks that require repetition. This practice is useful after the students' initial learning experience. Teachers assign students to skill centers to address readiness, rather than allowing students to work there by free choice.

Interest or exploratory centers differ from skill centers in that students choose to work in them in order to meet their needs and satisfy their learning preferences. Interest centers provide hands-on tasks that apply student knowledge and allow students to practice skills that can be accomplished in a variety of ways. These centers may remain ready for use in the classroom, so students can go to them when their other work is finished as a sponge activity that will occupy their time in a constructive way. Students also may sign up to work in interest centers during the week. These centers may be set up with the multiple intelligences in mind, so that all students can find their flow and zone of proximal development (see chapter 3, page 72, for a full discussion of flow).

Enrichment centers give more capable or advanced learners opportunities to enhance or extend their understanding of topics beyond grade-level tasks. For example, after a unit on pond life, students may use an enrichment center to:

▽ Construct an aquarium with pond plants and rocks

▽ Investigate ponds in different parts of the country

▽ Examine the value of pond life for the community

▽ Write about the issues of pond pollution

▽ Observe and summarize a virtual podcast about pond life

▽ Paint and label a mural on pond life

Whatever their use and form, well-planned and constructed enrichment centers offer an effective strategy for encouraging students to create and follow an individualized approach to learning.

Organizing Learning Centers

When designing learning centers, here are some features to consider.

▽ **Furniture and space:** Space in the learning center should be convenient and comfortable with tables arranged appropriately for work.

▽ **Storage:** Storing materials in plastic tubs will keep the center orderly.

▽ **Materials:** The centers should offer all necessary materials to save on task time and avoid off-task behavior.

▽ **Responsibilities:** Teachers should assign jobs in the center on a chart so students know what to do and how to clean up.

▽ **Instructions:** Teachers can post instructions for using the center on a chart, and list them in order of completion, so students can be self-sufficient. These instructions should include a procedure students are to follow when they need help in the center.

▽ **Assignment:** The teacher can decide whether students will choose to work in the center, or if he or she will assign them to work there.

▽ **Duration:** Teachers must decide how long the center will be available to meet program goals and hold students' interest. For example, sometimes teachers might set up an interest center for a week, whereas another center might be available for an entire unit of study to ensure all students get a chance to experience it.

▽ **Assessment:** Teachers can use rubrics or student self-reflections to assess tasks students complete within the learning center.

When they accommodate all of these features, learning centers can support powerful opportunities for learning in core subject areas. Elementary classrooms can benefit, for example, from a spelling center, reading center, art center, science center, writing center, or mathematics center. A helpful way to assign students to learning centers is to organize them in groups and post the lists to let students know their assignment (for example, see figure 5.3).

Green Group	Blue Group	Red Group
Student 1	Student 1	Student 1
Student 2	Student 2	Student 2
Student 3	Student 3	Student 3
Student 4	Student 4	Student 4
Orange Group	**Purple Group**	**Yellow Group**
Student 5	Student 5	Student 5
Student 6	Student 6	Student 6
Student 7	Student 7	Student 7
Student 8	Student 8	Student 8

Figure 5.3: Organizing centers.

Additionally, giving students a schedule, like the one in figure 5.4, lets them clearly know the time and place where they will be working.

	Monday	Computer Station	Spelling and Vocabulary	Choice Centers	Writing Workshop	Guided Reading
A	10:05–10:35	Orange	Purple	Green	Blue	Red and Yellow
B	10:40–11:10	Purple	Yellow	Blue	Red	Green and Orange
C	11:15–11:45	Yellow	Orange	Red	Green	Purple and Blue

Figure 5.4: Sample center schedule.

Providing Learning Center Menus and Choice Boards

Allowing students to choose activities from menus and choice boards gives students autonomy to learn concepts in ways they choose and enjoy, thus offering another powerful strategy for enhancing student engagement and learning. Choice boards often include multiple boxed areas offering specific activities. Students can choose freely among the listed activities. A *wild card* area in a choice board remains blank, so students can add their own activity ideas. Choice board activities should focus on standards, content, and skills that students need to know and be able to do. Figure 5.5 is an example of a choice board for English language arts.

Compose a song that tells the story.	Write questions that you would ask the main character in an interview.	Draw a map of the setting of the story.
Compare this story with the last one you read using a Venn diagram.	Wild Card!	Choose something in the story that has a connection to your life, and explain it.
Collect some props that could be used if the story were a play.	With a partner, create a storyboard for the story.	Create a role play with dialogue for a different ending.

Figure 5.5: Sample choice board for English language arts.

Figure 5.6 is a choice board that appeals to the multiple intelligences (see chapter 3, page 59).

Verbal-Linguistic	Musical-Rhythmic	Visual-Spatial
Write a play or essay. Prepare a report. Give a speech. Plan a presentation. Create a poem or recitation. Create a word web. Listen to a podcast or watch a DVD.	Create a rap, song, or ballad. Write a poem. Write a jingle. Create rhymes. Select music to match a scene.	Create a mural. Illustrate an event. Make a diagram. Create a storyboard. Create a poster. Create a collage.
Bodily-Kinesthetic Write and perform a role play. Construct a model. Create a tableau. Manipulate materials to . . . Create a simulation. Design actions for . . . Develop a mime.	**Wild Card!**	**Logical-Mathematical** Design a sequence or process. Develop a rationale. Create a pattern. Analyze a scenario. Write a sequel. Critique. Classify, rank, or compare _____. Provide evidence to support a hypothesis. Label and classify. Predict _____. Design a game show related to_____.
Naturalist Categorize materials or ideas. Adapt materials to a new use. Discover or experiment. Connect ideas to nature. Examine materials to make connections. Draw conclusions based on evidence. Look for ideas from nature.	**Intrapersonal** Reflect and plan. Enter thoughts in a journal. Keep track of _____, and comment on it. Review or visualize. Reflect on the character and express his or her feelings. Use your empathy to explain.	**Interpersonal** Discuss and come to a consensus. Solve a problem together. Work with a partner or group. Conduct a survey. Interview others. Dialogue about a topic. Use cooperative group to complete a group task. Project a character's point of view.

Figure 5.6: Sample choice board for multiple intelligences.

Using learning centers and providing choices are excellent ways to offer active and self-directed learning opportunities for students. They provide pluralized learning, attend to a student's learning preferences, and provide students with multiple rehearsals to develop understanding, mastery, and long-term memory. Using a mixed-modality, pluralized pedagogy including the best instructional practices also contributes to greater student learning.

Implementing a Mixed-Modality, Pluralized Pedagogy

Pedagogies that encompass a variety of best practices provide pluralized strategies that can engage *all* learning preferences, rather than catering to just a few. Based on a meta-analysis of available research, Marzano et al. (2001) offer nine instructional strategies that produce expected increases in percentile gains for student learning ranging from 22 to 45. Percentile gains translate to a point gain (or loss) for a student at the 50th percentile in the normal distribution of achievement scores. For example, for a strategy with a 34 percentile gain, a student would be expected to be in the 84th percentile. Consider the following yields for Marzano et al.'s (2001) nine instructional strategies.

1. Setting objectives and providing feedback (a 23 percentile gain)

2. Reinforcing effort and providing recognition (a 29 percentile gain)

3. Designing cooperative learning tasks (a 27 percentile gain)

4. Using cues, questions, and advance organizers (a 22 percentile gain)

5. Offering nonlinguistic representations (a 27 percentile gain)

6. Promoting summarizing and note taking (a 34 percentile gain)

7. Rehearsing learning through homework and practice (a 28 percentile gain)

8. Identifying similarities and differences (a 45 percentile gain)

9. Generating and testing hypotheses (a 23 percentile gain)

In later research, teachers using these nine strategies discovered new evidence-based findings about implementation challenges and techniques that contributed to their success (Dean, Hubbell, Pitler, & Stone, 2012). After field testing this implementation for ten years, Dean et al. (2012) regrouped the strategies into three categories based on the strategies' benefits and how educators could best use the strategies in the classroom. The categories are:

1. **Creating climate**—Including strategies 1 through 3

2. **Helping students develop understanding**—Including strategies 4 through 7

3. **Helping students extend and apply knowledge**—Including strategies 8 and 9

Figure 5.7 illustrates these categories and how they relate to the nine strategies.

Each of the nine strategies within these categories aligns with the neuroscientific evidence we examined in chapters 2 and 3. As such, it's not surprising that these strategies have a powerful influence on student achievement. Now, let's explore the

Creating Climate

1. *Setting objectives and providing feedback*

Clear instructional goals help students focus when the goals are in general terms that each student can personalize. Continuous feedback from the student, teachers, and peers is important.

2. *Reinforcing effort and providing recognition*

The ability to relate effort and hard work to success helps develop a growth mindset.

3. *Designing cooperative learning tasks*

One of the most effective and well-documented instructional strategies is the formation of heterogeneous groups to accomplish academic tasks. This strategy uses higher-order thinking skills and develops social skills.

Helping Students Develop Understanding

4. *Using cues, questions, and advance organizers*

Cues, questions, and advance organizers help students open mental files to access prior knowledge before new learning takes place. This process helps students and educators preassess the students' standard-related knowledge and skills and gives a context for the learning experience to come.

5. *Offering nonlinguistic representations*

A variety of methods, such as graphics, models, mental pictures, drawing, and movement, can elaborate on and rehearse new learning.

6. *Promoting summarizing and note taking*

Learning to summarize, delete, distill, and analyze information helps students gain skill in selecting what is important or relevant for learning.

7. *Rehearsing learning through homework and practice*

Homework and practice provide additional learning experiences that will help students further rehearse concepts and skills. Students do not necessarily do more of the same classwork or just finish work.

Helping Students Extend and Apply Knowledge

8. *Identifying similarities and differences*

Classifying information, ideas, objects, and so on in groups based on like attributes, theme, or patterns helps students learn to compare and contrast.

9. *Generating and testing hypotheses*

Students articulate hypotheses, evaluate their accuracy, and further develop their inductive and deductive processes.

Source: Dean et al., 2012.

Figure 5.7: Effective instructional strategies for differentiation.

three categories of these high-impact strategies in more detail and how they support multiple intelligences, learning preferences, and modalities.

Creating Climate

We know that the brain needs a safe, risk-free, and supportive classroom in order to learn; otherwise, the survival brain takes over and no learning takes place (for more information on survival mode, see chapter 2, page 25). The first category of instructional strategies, *creating climate*, addresses this need through setting objectives and providing feedback, reinforcing effort and providing recognition, and designing cooperative learning tasks. Let's look more closely at these strategy types and how each promotes student understanding.

Setting Objectives and Providing Feedback

The first element within this category, *setting objectives and providing feedback*, is crucial to learning success. The brain responds to challenges best in a safe, supportive environment, and setting goals promotes that environment by letting the brain know where it's going and what the destination looks like (see chapter 2). Positive, correct feedback keeps the brain interested, as it responds to its built-in seeking system. Offering students an overview of the learning outcomes or standards targeted for the lesson or unit of study gives them some indication of why, what, and how they are going to learn. When students restate those outcomes in their own words, they demonstrate that they are clear about the expectations. Allowing students some input as to how they will demonstrate their understanding or competence will also increase their chances of success.

Reinforcing Effort and Providing Recognition

The second strategy in this category, *reinforcing effort and providing recognition*, contributes to the students' growth mindset, which is critical for creating a sense of capability and continued engagement. This strategy is in line with Dweck's (2006) recommendations regarding the importance of a student mindset and the notion that effort matters more than IQ in the long run (see chapter 2, page 33).

Recognition in the form of praise is a strong tool for building a classroom atmosphere of support and safety. Marzano et al. (2001) note five general categories for effective praise.

1. **Contingent:** Praise directly related to completing a task that comments on effort, improvement (compared to self and past performance), and success or progress toward it

2. **Specific:** Praise that directly states the accomplishment, rather than offering generalities and vague supportive comments, for example, "You followed the directions well and have made good progress" rather than "Good job!"

3. **Sincere:** Genuine comments that reflect true praise, rather than obligatory words of encouragement; students easily detect sincerity and respond only to genuine comments

4. **Varied:** Praise that uniquely addresses individual incidents and accomplishments, rather than a canned "That's awesome!" comment for every situation

5. **Credible:** Praise that is accurate, positive but realistic, and if directed toward future performance, addresses something that's likely to happen

Designing Cooperative Learning Tasks

Designing cooperative learning tasks, the third strategy in this category, will give the brain what it needs in terms of social interaction and sense of belonging and also will construct knowledge through dialogue and interaction (see Dean et al., 2012; and chapter 2, page 35). Creating the climate for learning by including brain-friendly strategies of sharing expectations, providing feedback, and building a collaborative learning environment is crucial for student success. No matter students' learning preferences, transparency and social support are necessary for a nurturing, supportive environment where brains can learn and grow.

Helping Students Develop Understanding

The second category of instructional strategies, *helping students develop understanding*, shapes the interactions and rehearsals and learning tasks with which students engage to make sense of new knowledge and skills. Students need multiple rehearsals or interactions with content to develop the strong and lasting neural connections that enable students to recall and use surface learning in new situations. Teachers draw on these strategies to offer multiple tasks that engage students' visual, auditory, and kinesthetic modes and tap into their multiple intelligences. This category of instructional strategies includes using cues, questions (including probes and prompts), and advance organizers; offering nonlinguistic representations; promoting summarizing and note taking; and rehearsing learning through homework and practice. Let's look more closely at these strategy types and how each promotes student understanding.

Using Cues, Questions, and Advance Organizers

Cues, questions, and advance organizers are the first set of key strategies within this category. They help the student's brain open its mental files in order to prepare for new learning and to check new input against existing knowledge. These strategies also help teachers understand what students already know or uncover any misconceptions they may have.

Cues are verbal and nonverbal prompts from the teacher that help learners make connections and facilitate responses (Walsh & Sattes, 2005). For example, the teacher might help students understand prefixes by relating bi- and tri- to the words *bicycle* and *tricycle* and then help students understand what the prefixes mean. Color coding is a cue that can help students remember the words for colors in a foreign language, such as printing the French word for *red, rouge,* in red ink.

Probes and prompts help students go deeper with their thinking, as in these examples.

▽ "Tell me more about that idea."

▽ "How did you come to that conclusion?"

▽ "So what would you suggest?"

▽ "What would you do about that?"

▽ "Who has a different perspective?"

Questions such as those in the preceding list are foundational in teaching and in differentiating instruction. Questions promote discussion and interaction, provide assessment and a check for understanding, and—most importantly—engage students in thinking.

When using questions as an instructional strategy, teachers should follow these guidelines.

▽ Ask questions at all levels of thinking taxonomies (see chapter 7, page 182).

▽ Redirect questions to all students. Ask the question, and then choose a student to answer the question.

▽ Incorporate think-pair-share tactics with student pairs and small groups to increase thinking for everyone (refer to chapter 2, page 45, for a full discussion of think-pair-share).

▽ After asking a question, allow time for students to access long-term memory and consolidate their answer (Rowe, 1986). Don't be afraid of quiet; it facilitates thinking and reduces panic and rash answers.

▽ Use open-ended questions to increase thinking and possibilities rather than one-word or yes-no answers.

The last guideline is of particular importance in developing students' understanding of learned information. Often teachers ask questions that are factual and have only one correct answer. While such questions are appropriate in some learning situations, students answering these questions are, essentially, playing Trivial Pursuit. Asking questions that have multiple answers with nuanced meanings causes students to go deeper in their thinking to find evidence that justifies and rationalizes their answers.

So, questions that work within this instructional strategy may include those that rely on factual information with evidence, as well as hypothetical questions that ask "What if?" Tweaking questions by changing conditions is another effective way to implement this instructional strategy, as is the use of inferential questions that ask "What led you to believe that?" or "How did you come to that conclusion?" Such questions allow students to think about what influenced their ideas—the type of deep thinking that drives each student's brain to build more connections and expand learning.

Developing essential questions for the unit helps students focus on the purpose and expectations for the unit. Additionally, having students add questions of their own will increase the relevance and meaning for their brain.

Survey, question, read, recite, review, also known as SQ3R, is another active processing strategy that teachers can use to help students deepen their understanding of text and give them a format to organize their thinking (Anderson & Armbruster, 1984).

The SQ3R strategy involves the following five steps (see figure 5.8 for a chart teachers could display on the classroom wall for student reference). Using multiple strategies to engage students helps teachers reach all learners and ensure they're learning the core curriculum.

	SQ3R	
	Survey	Look over the assignment.
	Question	Make up questions for each heading.
3	Read	Read for information.
	Recite	Tell the answers.
	Review	Make notes to answer the questions.

Figure 5.8: SQ3R.

1. **Survey:** Students skim the material, notice the headings within the text, and form an idea of the content. This overview helps students access any prior knowledge they have related to the content.

2. **Question:** Students generate a question for each section of the material, which then gives them a personal purpose for reading. The heading may give them a prompt for creating the question.

3. **Read:** Each student individually reads each section and responds to the question he or she wrote for that section.

4. **Recite:** After the reading, students cite the information that they have learned from the text that provided the answer. The question may be answered orally or in writing.

5. **Review:** After they have finished reciting, students review the questions and recall the answers from memory. Students may take notes during this step, if they haven't done so previously. The teacher may provide a SQ3R note-taking or summarizing organizer like figure 5.8 to facilitate note taking.

The final strategy within this set, *advance organizers*, offers supports for students to organize their learning. Advance organizers may take the form of a short reading, video, or flipped presentation to prime the pump for learning (see also chapter 2, page 31). Such learning tools help open students' mental files and fill in some gaps that may be missing before the new learning activities take place.

David Ausubel (1968), an American psychologist, was the first to introduce these learning aids to help students organize and understand new information. We know students learn best when they can hook new information to prior knowledge. Sometimes, however, students *have* no previous knowledge that relates to new learning, and in those situations, teachers can use advance organizers to provide the hook. In addition to content, advance organizers provide schemas or patterns necessary for learning new material in a process often referred to as jumpstarting, backfilling, or intellectual scaffolding (Ausubel, 1968). Using advance organizers can be a key strategy for building the understanding of new material for ELs, whose culture may not have included the prerequisites for learning. (See chapter 6, page 149, for pre-assessment tools to use as advance organizers.) Additionally, using a short reading, video, or flipped presentation as an advanced organizer may access prior knowledge and provide context and information to get students ready for learning.

Offering Nonlinguistic Representations

Offering nonlinguistic representations, such as visuals, graphics, or physical representations or actions, is another powerful strategy for differentiating student understanding. Nonlinguistic representations support the brain as a parallel processor and a sensory-driven organ, because visual and kinesthetic learning can be, in some cases, more powerful than auditory learning. Most classroom learning has a verbal-linguistic and logical-mathematical focus, which ignores the visual-spatial and bodily-kinesthetic learning modes that some students prefer. Consider the following nonlinguistic representations.

▽ **Graphic organizers:** Using graphic organizers for note taking and summarizing helps students learn how to note key information and content. Graphic organizers that are partially completed are more motivating than when students have to start from scratch or create one of their own. Over time, students may self-select an appropriate organizer that suits their purpose. Many graphic organizers also support various thinking skills, such as cause and effect, compare and contrast, sequencing, and concept development. For example, the W5 chart in figure 5.9 helps students get key information in an advance reading. Teachers can have students explore the *who, what, when, where,* and *why* of an event or a chapter in a story. The Education

Who?	
What?	
Where?	
When?	
Why?	
So What?	

Figure 5.9: W5 chart.

Place (www.eduplace.com/graphicorganizer/) offers a variety of graphic organizers.

▽ **Concept maps:** Many powerful strategies for writing, like concept mapping and webbing, combine words and pictures to develop learning (Daniels & Bizar, 2005). We talk more about concept maps later in this chapter (page 137).

▽ **Pictographs:** Using pictographs—graphic symbols to represent terms, quantities, ideas, and so on—is a powerful strategy for helping students learn new information. These symbols may be computer clip art, hieroglyphs, or other graphic representations. The quality of art is not as important as the ideas the symbols represent. The potato symbols in figure 5.10, for example, offer students a big-picture representation of a farm's total potato production over five years, as well as the opportunity to compare and contrast production by year. Students can generate hypotheses related to the potato yield and also make predictions.

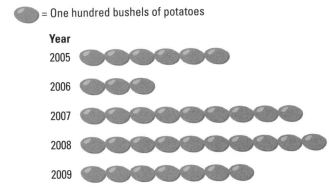

Figure 5.10: Sample pictographic representation.

▽ **Constructed models:** These are concrete representations of ideas rather than visual or verbal representations. For example, students may create 3-D models, such as dioramas or trioramas, of land regions.

▽ **Kinesthetic representations:** This nonlinguistic learning aid involves creating hand movements that represent ideas or body movements that act out processes, role playing, and playing games like charades to help students develop muscle and episodic memory.

Promoting Summarizing and Note Taking

Summarizing and note taking train students to pay attention to important, meaningful, relevant information and to expand the brain's natural ability to delete nonessential data. *Summarizing* is a rehearsal strategy that helps student brains make connections by prompting them to think deeply about new information and then make decisions about what information to delete, substitute, and keep.

Summarizing converts information into a synthesized form. Students can summarize information by using either of the following two tactics.

1. **Rule-based summarizing:** This type of summarizing involves minimizing text by deleting trivia and redundant material. Marzano et al. (2001) suggest that educators teach students to delete trivial and redundant material and substitute superordinate categories for lists—such as using *countries* to substitute for the names of several individual countries.

2. **Summary frames:** Students can use a number of frames depending on the situation.

   ▸ *Narrative frame*—Students use this frame to identify the *who*, *what*, *when*, *where*, and *why* of the story (the main characters, setting, initiating event and response, goal, consequence, and resolution).

   ▸ *Definition frame*—Students use this frame to define a concept or topic in their own words. In their summary, they consider what they're defining, the category it fits in, and the characteristics that define it.

   ▸ *Argumentative frame*—Students present an opinion based on evidence and consider what they're claiming, what led them to their assumption, how to support the assumption, and the possible counter position.

For many students, visual note taking is a creative way to synthesize and remember key information more clearly. Mike Rohde (2013), author of *The Sketchnote Handbook*, shares useful note-taking ideas on the following websites. Visit **go.solution-tree.com/RTIatWork** to access live links.

▽ **RohDesign, *The Sketchnote Handbook*:** http://rohdesign.com/handbook

▽ **Pencils, "How to Take Better Notes":** http://howtotakebetternotes
.com

Marzano et al. (2001) suggest that the more notes students take, the better their learning will be, but that verbatim notes—which merely repeat taught information word for word—are the least effective notes for learning. Copying notes from a whiteboard, overhead, PowerPoint, or other form of presentations or receiving a prepared summary do not represent a thinking process and, therefore, does little to differentiate student learning and memory. Students need to interact with material to make sense, interrupt meaning, and develop understanding. The learner must manage the task, comprehend what he or she is reading or hearing, identify important information, and then personally create notes (Piolat, Olive, & Kellogg, 2005).

Providing a concept map or lecture outline (see figure 5.11) can help guide students in their note taking.

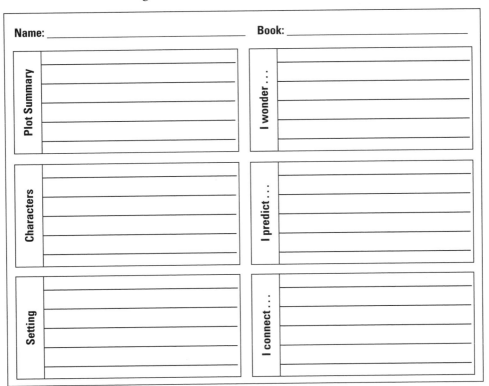

Source: Adapted from Lamb & Johnson, 2007.

Figure 5.11: Visual note taking.

Rehearsing Learning Through Homework and Practice

Homework and practice are among the multiple forms of rehearsals the brain needs to deepen skills and knowledge. As we've seen in previous chapters, multiple repetitions help strengthen neural connections. To ensure that practice makes perfect, however, homework and practice must conform to the following guidelines.

▽ Homework should be aligned with standards or outcomes rather than just representing busywork.

▽ Students should receive constructive feedback for their work.

▽ Students also should receive any necessary coaching or monitoring from someone who cares.

▽ The quality of assigned homework has more influence on student learning than does its quantity.

It stands to reason that the more practice students have with information they are learning, the better their skill development and retention of material will be. Sometimes students need guided practice before being gradually released to independent practice. Homework may be differentiated to accommodate the student's level of expertise. More complex tasks or application of skills might be necessary to challenge more capable learners, and teachers may give less complex tasks or practice assignments to students who are struggling with the concepts or skills. Hattie's (2009) meta-analysis suggests that when used poorly, homework has little if any effect (and could be destructive) on elementary students' learning with only an ES of 0.15 in comparison to the ES of 0.64 for high school students. Although teachers or parents do not monitor short practice and rote-rehearsal homework tasks, this type of homework may have a debilitating effect on a student's self-concept as an independent capable learner. Alternatively, tackling projects and complex tasks and practicing reading encourage lifelong learners. These tasks also provide students with opportunities to work with other family members to reinforce skills and obtain background information for science or social studies using informational texts.

Helping Students Extend and Apply Knowledge

This final category includes two instructional strategies: (1) identifying similarities and differences and (2) generating and testing hypotheses. These strategies help students extend their thinking and transition their surface learning (recall) to deeper understanding. The following sections explore these types of strategies and offer examples of them in practice.

Identifying Similarities and Differences

Identifying similarities and differences is one of the ways the brain makes sense of new information by comparing it to what the brain already knows. The brain looks for patterns and connections by comparing and contrasting multiple sets or pieces of information. Analogies, for example, are powerful thinking tools that help students understand a new concept by comparing it to something they know well.

With an effect size of 1.61, this strategy of identifying similarities and differences has the greatest potential to enhance student achievement (Hattie, 2009). This strategy fosters deep learning and includes the following tactics.

▽ Comparing

▽ Classifying

▽ Creating metaphors

▽ Creating analogies

Educators can use these tactics in all subject disciplines, with activities as varied as comparing folktales, fishing villages on the East and West Coasts of North America, species in science, or explorers in social studies. Using a Venn diagram (two overlapping circles), students can compare and contrast two elements. Characteristics that are the same between the two elements go in the middle, and aspects that are different go in the respective circles. Educators can give students criteria to use for comparison purposes or generate their own. For example, criteria for the comparison of cars and bikes might be purpose, structure, and features (see figure 5.12).

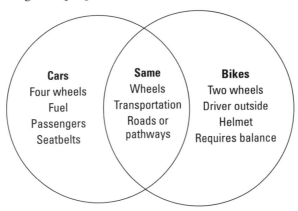

Figure 5.12: Comparing bikes and cars.

*Visit **go.solution-tree.com/RTIatWork** for a reproducible version of this figure.*

Criteria to compare two countries could be geography, continent, currency, culture, and sports (see figure 5.13).

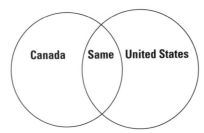

Figure 5.13: Comparing two countries.

*Visit **go.solution-tree.com/RTIatWork** for a reproducible version of this figure.*

Using a triple Venn diagram to compare types of habitats, criteria might be climate, materials, and location (see figure 5.14).

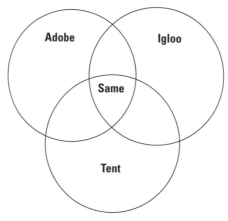

Figure 5.14: Comparing types of habitats.

*Visit **go.solution-tree.com/RTIatWork** for a reproducible version of this figure.*

Cross-classification is another tactic for comparing and contrasting two or three elements based on stated criteria. Using a chart, students can list criteria down the left column and three items across the top. (See figure 5.15.)

Criteria	1 Three Billy Goats Gruff	2 Three Little Pigs	3 Little Red Riding Hood
Characters			
Setting			
Plot			
Theme			

Figure 5.15: Cross-classification chart.

*Visit **go.solution-tree.com/RTIatWork** for a reproducible version of this figure.*

Asking students to classify deepens their thinking by directing them to determine what similarities enable items to be grouped together. As we discussed, graphic organizers can help with the process of classification. When student pairs or small groups use graphic organizers to classify information, they are, in effect, leveraging three strategies to enhance learning and retention.

A *metaphor* is a powerful tactic to compare and contrast a known concept with a new idea or concept. Using metaphors deepens student understanding by leading them to analyze and then reconnect specific characteristics of each item (such as a *blanket of snow* covered the playground, or too much TV was making him or her a *couch potato*) As Bernice McCarthy (2000), author of *About Teaching*, says, "Thinking in metaphors engages the imagination in ways that go both to the inside of things (their essence) and to the outside of things (their impact on the world)" (p. 102).

Similarly, analogies look for commonalities or relationships between two concepts, such as "How is learning like a taking a trip on the highway?" Standardized testing includes many analogies. Another tactic for using analogies to extend and apply knowledge includes relating analogous thinking through patterns, for example, through incomplete statements such as, "Beagle is to dog as _____ is to fish." See also *Analogies: Sampler for Grades K–12* (Ridgewood Public Schools, 2003) for more examples.

Generating and Testing Hypotheses

Generating and testing a hypothesis is a powerful way to extend and apply learning, because as we know, the brain is curious and has a great need to seek patterns and apply what it knows to new situations. A *hypothesis* is a testable explanation or supposition created on the basis of background research to begin further investigation. In a lesson on hibernation, for example, students may learn about animals that hibernate, migrate, or adapt during the winter. They might first ask, "If animals, like bears, hibernate in winter to escape the cold, what might birds do?" Then, they'll form their hypothesis, for example, "If I observe birds in the summer, those same birds will be gone in the winter."

Project- and problem-based learning, as we described in chapter 4 (pages 97–103), are essential elements of a powerful core curriculum. These approaches also offer a differentiated instructional strategy for extending student learning by encouraging students to form and test hypotheses. Students may have an opportunity to study systems such as ecosystems, computer networks, government, or weather. In one example, students could create an invention, suggest how it might work, and then develop and test their invention. Alternatively, students can observe and generate predictions and then test them, engage in problem solving by creating and testing probable solutions, or use their understanding of a particular situation or event to come to a generalization and then make a prediction in a new situation based on this knowledge.

Making the Most Effective Use of Promising Practices

After a decade of gathering data about how teachers implement these nine strategies, Dean et al. (2012) note that teachers basically move through four levels of implementation in regular classroom use. The four levels move from awareness of the strategy to routine and refined use of the strategy over time with practice and reflection (see table 5.1, page 142).

Table 5.1: Four Stages of Implementation

Stage	Characteristics
Beginning	The teacher uses the strategy with little finesse in a straightforward manner. Errors occur, and simplistic or inappropriate expectations are involved.
Developing	The teacher uses the strategy with precision and fewer errors. He or she shows an ease of use and includes appropriate complexity for students.
Applying	The teacher shows relative ease of use with no errors. He or she monitors students' reactions and probes and refines student thinking.
Innovating	The teacher is able to adapt the strategy for student needs and extensions with ease and expertise.

Teachers need time, feedback, and collaboration to develop expertise in learning to use these strategies. In fact, people in general need practice, feedback, and collaboration to successfully develop new skills. It may take many practice trials and rehearsals to refine the skills we've outlined in this chapter. Educators and students alike must persist to get through the discomfort zone or implementation dip of change and growth.

The preceding ideas and instructional strategies offer a huge repertoire of research-based practices that will not only increase student achievement but also provide enough variety to meet learners' preferences and make the classroom engaging and stimulating. Students may need multiple rehearsals to develop skills and understandings, so being instructionally intelligent is an important skill for educators attempting to use these strategies in providing daily differentiated instruction. Educators demonstrate that skill by selecting the appropriate strategy for the task at hand, as well as for the student's level of competence.

Using multimodal pluralized instructional strategies daily will engage more learners and provide students with multiple ways of developing understanding and long-term memory. In the next chapter, we will discuss strategies to build cognitive rigor, depth, and complexity.

Taking the Discussion Further

Following are some of the important ideas from this chapter that are worthy of further reflection and discussion. Educators in a PLC may want to read through this chapter with their collaborative teams and discuss each section, recording the issues related to each piece of information and considering classroom implications for students. Collaborative teams can reflect on the prompts to deepen understanding and set subsequent goals for improvement.

▽ Revisit the discussion on traditional versus progressive education and use figure 5.16 to create a T-chart listing their characteristics. Where is your PLC in relationship to these characteristics, and what steps might take your team closer to its goals?

Traditional Education	Progressive Education

Figure 5.16: Traditional education versus progressive education.

▽ As a team, discuss the concept of constructivism and how it impacts the type of learning activities the team provides for students.

▽ Discuss how technology is a creativity generator and a powerful motivator. Examine the websites on pages 116–117 for ideas and resources.

▽ Review the flipped-classroom strategy, and view the suggested YouTube videos. What is the benefit of this strategy? Has any collaborative team member tried it? What steps might your team take to implement it?

▽ Consider the differences in the three types of vocabulary—everyday, academic, and domain specific—and discuss how teachers on the team are currently dealing with vocabulary. What in their practice is working and what do they need to improve?

▽ Discuss the benefits of the different types of learning stations and centers—skill centers, interest centers, and enrichment centers—and how to manage them.

Continued →

▽ Discuss menus and choice boards, and create one for a unit of study that will help students develop knowledge and skills.

▽ Discuss the concept of *mixed modality*, and review the suggestions for implementing the three categories.

    a. Creating climate

    b. Helping students develop understanding

    c. Helping students extend and apply knowledge

▽ Discuss questioning, including the SQ3R method (Anderson & Armbruster, 1984), and questioning's influence on student learning.

▽ Examine and discuss ideas for nonlinguistic representations. Consider the graphic organizers from Education Place (www.eduplace.com/graphic organizer/).

▽ Examine and discuss ideas for guiding students in summarizing, note taking, homework, and practice.

▽ Discuss ideas for identifying similarities and differences using:

    ▸ Comparing

    ▸ Classifying

    ▸ Creating metaphors

    ▸ Creating analogies

Using Data to Inform Instruction

Assessment is a critical component of a multitiered system of intervention. *Convergent assessment* is an ongoing process of collectively analyzing evidence to determine each student's specific learning needs and the effectiveness of the instruction as they develop over time. While ongoing assessment is an integral piece of Tiers 2 and 3, this process is also at the heart of the Tier 1 teaching and assessment cycle.

The early elementary school years represent a crucial period in brain development and early learning. Big achievement gaps may have developed among students during the years prior to kindergarten. Instruction and assessment of student learning during this critical early period must recognize and consider each student's developmental needs. To optimize student learning, teachers need to utilize an instruction and assessment process that identifies each student's strengths and areas for growth. This powerful cycle of assessment data for learning must take into account the whole child, including the learner's culture, family, health, and early childhood experiences. Gathering and using these data, therefore, is integral to the instruction and learning process at Tier 1. This type of assessment and data collection occurs *during* the learning process and shouldn't be confused with *summative* evaluations at the end of a learning cycle.

In this chapter, we are going to review this critical process of ongoing, accurate assessment. We begin by overviewing the data-gathering process—what kinds of data educators can and should gather and the five opportunities for doing so. Next, we review each of these five assessment processes, how teachers can best organize and conduct the assessments, and how they can use the data to inform and adapt their instructional modalities. By examining how assessment data can influence instructional tools and approaches, and by exploring multiple methods for providing students with the most effective and informed feedback, this chapter offers a broad range of ideas for gathering and using assessment data to shape the most powerful daily differentiated instructional plan and promote student achievement.

As shown in figure 6.1, teachers have five opportunities to collect student data, which they then can use to plan for student success.

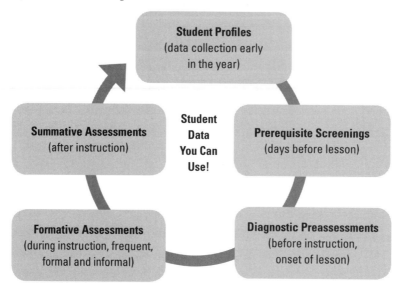

Figure 6.1: Student data you can use.

Those opportunities include the following.

1. **Student profiles:** Educators create these early in the student's academic career to provide information essential for understanding the student's unique individual mindset, learning preferences, interests, and more.

2. **Prerequisite screenings:** Educators typically conduct prerequisite screenings to determine essential skills days before teaching a lesson.

3. **Diagnostic preassessments:** Educators typically conduct preassessments at the onset of an associated lesson.

4. **Formative assessments:** Formative assessments gauge instructional effectiveness and student progress, which take place throughout the lesson or instructional block.

5. **Summative assessments:** Summative assessments gauge student progress and occur at the end of a lesson or instructional block.

Carol Ann Tomlinson (2003) insists that to do a proper job of ongoing differentiation, teachers need to become *assessment junkies*. With that approach, everything that students say and do can become a potential source of assessment data.

Understanding all five student data-gathering elements takes time. Teachers must learn how each aspect contributes to their ability to use the data to inform their instructional plan. Just as a teacher develops his or her instructional intelligence, learning how these five assessment opportunities work together will help teachers better plan for student success and mastery learning.

Student Profiles

As you learned in chapter 3, a student profile is a valuable tool to help teachers get to know their learners. Student profiles include data on student attitudes (mindsets), learning preferences, interests, needs, and strengths. Early in the year (or semester), educators collect these data to document how each student learns best, so they can anticipate needs *before* a student struggles and requires intervention. A good student profile is a dynamic living document that reflects how the learner evolves and grows. It is crucial to gather data about the youngest students as they enter the halls of learning. Many schools and districts routinely create kindergarten student profiles within the first sixty days of the school year. While some of the information in the student profile may need to be collected through a *test* or *screening*, the majority of the data can come from multiple formative assessments such as observations, student work examples, conversations, and embedded instructional tasks, with additional input coming from parents and families, school support staff, early childhood programs, and even health care providers.

These initial assessments gather data related to five areas of the student's current development. These areas include:

1. Approaches to learning

2. Cognitive development

3. Emotional social development

4. Health and physical development

5. Language development and communication skills

This data-collection process engages teachers and students and helps set the stage for an effective learning relationship. As the data-gathering continues beyond the initial stage, it becomes an integral part of the instructional and learning process (K–3 North Carolina Assessment Think Tank, 2013). Teachers can take time early in the school year to find out key details that might really make a difference in how they plan for each student. They can use the data from the student profile to support students' learning preferences, working preferences (independently or collaboratively), requirements for engagement (frequent movement breaks), learning styles (step-by-step instructions or a big-picture overview), and home-life implications (stress or other impacts on concentration and learning).

Prerequisite Screenings

In instructional planning, the best intervention is prevention. Effective curriculum plans have clearly defined grade-level targets that lay the groundwork for the second form of assessment—screening for the prerequisite skills students must have in order to master upcoming instruction and work independently on upcoming concepts. Teachers can identify these prerequisite skills and concepts several days before instruction begins and then create a preassessment tool to determine each student's command of them. This tool can take a form of a checklist. For example, before beginning a series of lessons on standard units of measurement, a teacher might identify the following prerequisite skills and concepts.

▽ Count and identify numbers.

▽ Understand one-to-one correspondence.

▽ Understand parts to whole.

If the lesson is going to include calculating area and perimeter of rectangles, students must also have a basic grasp of addition and multiplication. Knowing that a student is still developing a prerequisite skill wouldn't keep a teacher from teaching the new concept, but it will assist him or her in making decisions about how to design the activity. Often teachers can embed the prerequisite skill within the task and students can build understanding along the way.

Determining if a student has the necessary prerequisite skills can take place anywhere from a month to several days before the associated instruction is scheduled to begin.

Screening students' readiness can take a variety of forms, including that of the previous unit's summative assessment. Reviewing a standard's learning progression can be helpful when trying to identify what teachers should expect students to know and be able to do (see chapter 4, page 86, for the discussion on learning progressions). When educators pose the question "Where are we now?" they also want to reflect on the specific knowledge or skills that could help students master the next standard.

While teachers may find it difficult to resist filling in all of a student's gaps in learning, they are unlikely to be able to do so. When screening for necessary prerequisite skills, therefore, we recommend that teachers target only the specific skills and concepts that will make the greatest difference in a student's chance for success. Consider the following strategies.

▽ **Backfill:** If the teacher can determine that a student hasn't developed some prerequisite knowledge and skills, then he or she could benefit from targeted lessons to equip the tools, resources, skills, and information he or she will need to be successful. This could be a quick reteaching, minilesson, or a specific task that helps build the foundation for what's to come. This may come in the form of a discussion that helps students recall previous lessons or prior knowledge.

▽ **Acceleration:** In *Learning in the Fast Lane: 8 Ways to Put All Students on the Road to Academic Success*, Suzy Rollins (2014) suggests that rather than considering screening as *remedial* instruction, by teaching students the skills they will need to be successful ahead of the instruction, they are, in essence, being *accelerated*: "Accelerating students is not pre-teaching; that risks tedium. Rather, it is an enriching experience designed to stimulate thinking, develop concrete models, introduce vocabulary, scaffold critical missing pieces, and introduce new concepts just prior to acquisition of new learning" (p. 10).

▽ **Preadjustments:** Depending on the data they gathered ahead of time, teachers may decide to adjust the upcoming instructional strategies. Based on the readiness and skill levels of students, teachers may decide to group students in a different way. (See Adjusting Assignments, page 166.)

When teachers take the time to determine if the students have the necessary foundational concepts and skills, they are working with a *prevention* mindset rather than forging on ahead and finding it necessary to implement an *intervention* later on.

Diagnostic Preassessments

Diagnostic preassessments regarding the learning target should occur at the beginning of a learning sequence, such as the day before the sequence begins or as part of the first instructional strategy. Using a preassessment as a diagnostic tool can help educators gain valuable information that they can use to adjust their instructional strategies. With a cleverly designed preassessment tool, teachers should be able to determine a reasonable understanding of:

▽ What each student already knows—the student's declarative knowledge

▽ What each student is able to do—the student's procedural knowledge

▽ What skills and information specific students are missing that they will need in order to reach the desired level of understanding and proficiency

▽ What mastery a student may already have about the skill or concept

Although teachers can assume that a student's prior knowledge generally increases with age, this growth may also be accompanied by errors that become incorporated into the student's knowledge database. Students acquire incorrect information in a variety of ways—through interactions with peers and siblings, exposure to the media, or early instruction that may have been superficial or incorrect. Preassessments must look, therefore, not only for what the student knows but also for inconsistencies, inaccuracies, and gaps in his or her understandings (K–3 North Carolina Assessment Think Tank, 2013).

Depending on the upcoming unit or task, teachers can create diagnostic preassessments to accomplish several goals, including:

▽ Gathering information about each student's readiness to learn a targeted skill or concept

▽ Learning what prior experiences each student has had with the skill or topic

▽ Discovering information about each student's mindset, interest, or attitude about the upcoming area of study

▽ Generating initial questions about or concerns a student might have about the learning

▽ Identifying incorrect understandings and misinformation

Teachers in elementary classrooms rely on the following five main types of diagnostic preassessments.

1. Pretests, observations, or quizzes determine what knowledge and understandings a student already has regarding the topic.

2. Surveys about the topic can provide information about a student's prior knowledge or understanding of the target concept. Rather than yes-or-no responses, a five-point gradient allows students to plot a range of answers.

3. For older elementary students, exit tickets from the day before or entrance cards on the day of instruction provide a way for students to write down what they already know and understand about the topic. (Chapter 3 introduces the use of exit tickets as a tool for building student metacognition.)

4. Commercial curriculum or program preassessments typically take the form of a teacher-administered screening that includes the teacher's observations.

5. Small-group and class discussions, as well as miniconferences with each student, offer information about student understanding.

The purpose of diagnostic preassessments is to get an idea of who knows what. That's why preassessment needs to elicit responses from students about their prior knowledge and experiences. We do not recommend that teachers use formal *post-tests* (tests to determine learning *after* a lesson) as preassessments to determine readiness and to identify what students don't know—their *deficits*—before beginning a unit. This deficit model is an all-too-common practice that accomplishes nothing more than having students start a new unit by failing an assessment on curriculum they have never been taught—hardly a great way to build confidence and self-efficacy. We find little to no research to support this practice or evidence that it leads to significant gains in student achievement. Preassessments also must be ungraded. Teachers must ensure, therefore, that students know the importance of showing what they know and take it seriously.

Diagnostic preassessments offer many benefits, but educators can only realize those benefits when they use the data to inform their instruction. Without using the information that comes from a preassessment to adjust instruction and document students' learning growth, teachers may have older students who begin to doubt the worthiness of the task.

Good teachers are responsive. The standard one-size-fits-all lesson may, in reality, only fit with some learners; teachers will need to adapt their approach to benefit the broad range of students in their classroom. Later in this chapter, we review a variety of methods for adjusting learner tasks, groups, and workflow to reflect the results of assessment data.

Formative Assessments

Educational research scientist Caroline Wylie (2008) defines *formative assessment* as "a process used by teachers and students during instruction that provides feedback to adjust ongoing teaching and learning to improve students' achievement of intended instructional outcomes" (p. 3). Effective teachers are constantly engaged in the process of formative assessment. In a more traditional classroom, such assessment may involve the teacher offering an additional explanation based on a question a student asks. Or, it may be in the form of asking a student to reread a paragraph (this time aloud) to help determine fluency and understanding. An ungraded pop quiz to determine how learning is coming along is another type of formative assessment.

As the National Council of Teachers of English (2013) writes:

> Formative assessment is the lived, daily embodiment of a teacher's desire to refine practice based on a keener understanding of current levels of student performance, undergirded by the teacher's knowledge of possible paths of student development within the discipline and of pedagogies that support such development.

When teachers differentiate instruction, the real-time opportunities for formative assessments multiply. Collecting data informally or formally and using that information to adjust the next steps is what good teachers do when they are providing appropriate instruction at Tier 1 for all students.

Due to the critical role it plays in both the instructional and learning processes, formative assessment truly is assessment *for* learning. A position paper from the Third

International Conference on Assessment for Learning (The National Center for Fair and Open Testing, 2009) states, "Assessment for Learning is part of everyday practice by students, teachers and peers that seeks, reflects upon and responds to information from dialogue, demonstration and observation in ways that enhance ongoing learning." Teachers must develop a level of expertise that enables them, when students respond to planned or informal prompts, to quickly assimilate the information and be ready to make decisions about the next steps in the learning progression. The process focuses directly on the learner's developing capabilities.

Educators collect data on student progress for multiple reasons, and formative assessments produce data educators can use in multiple ways. As illustrated in figure 6.2, teachers can use the data to assess the instructional effectiveness of the associated task or other learning and then make informed decisions about the next steps for instruction or reteaching. The data teachers gather from the formative assessment also provide guidance as to what modifications may be helpful for student learning.

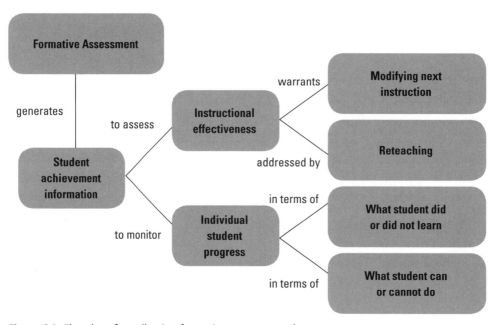

Figure 6.2: Flowchart for collecting formative assessment data.

Formative assessments also produce data on *student achievement*, which informs students where they are on the learning continuum—what they do know and what they do not yet understand. The data also point students toward their own next steps in learning.

Developing Effective Formative Assessments

As we've noted, formative assessment can be brief and informal or more structured and detailed. There are five critical attributes of formative assessment that have the most influence on learning (Wylie, 2008).

1. **Learning progressions:** Teachers must identify and understand the various subgoals leading up to the ultimate learning target. By examining the standards for the prior grade level and reviewing the standards for the next grade level, teachers can identify the steps in between and can help students make the necessary progress for their current grade level.

2. **Learning goals and criteria for success:** Teachers must clearly identify and communicate the standards and learning goals, along with the criteria for mastery, to students in learner-friendly terms. "I can" statements are a helpful tool.

3. **Descriptive feedback:** Teachers should provide specific, "just in time" evidence-based feedback to students that is clearly linked to the instructional standards, learning targets, and criteria for success.

4. **Self- and peer-assessment:** Students should have explicit instruction for how to think metacognitively about their learning. Self-assessment opportunities should be readily available. Students should routinely have a chance to get—and give—constructive feedback to and from peers.

5. **Collaboration:** The climate and culture in the classroom should be conducive to collaboration. Teachers and students should have an established partnership around learning. In addition—teacher teams use their collaboration to develop formative assessments.

Not every formative assessment will leverage all five of these suggested elements, but they form a solid foundation for building up a repertoire of formative assessment strategies, as shown in figure 6.3.

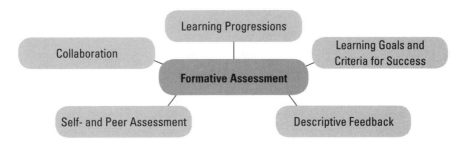

Figure 6.3: Formative assessment attributes.

Implementing Formative Assessments

Integrating frequent formative assessments needs to become a habit for teachers. Building up a broad repertoire of simple, easy-to-implement strategies can help teachers be ready to routinely check for understanding. Here are some examples of tried-and-true formative assessments to add to your toolbox.

▽ **Thumbs-up, thumbs-down:** Students use a thumbs-up or thumbs-down to indicate whether they agree or disagree with the teacher's statement. Variations include *response cards* that are green (for agree) and red (for disagree) or a happy face and frowny face.

▽ **Jigsaw activities with whole-group sharing:** In small groups, students determine an answer to a question, summarize a text, form an opinion, create a solution, or so on, and then each group reports its work to the whole class. The class might then determine which response was the most feasible or accurate. You can observe how various student groups approach the task.

▽ **Exit tickets:** At the end of a lesson or work time, ask students for feedback about their learning experience. Students write their feedback on an index card and hand it in on the way out the door. Consider the following forms of exit tickets.

  ▸ *Catchphrase*—Sum up the day's lesson or key point in a few words or a catchy phrase. (K–2 students may choose from a catchphrase bank.)

  ▸ *Are You Smarter Than a _____ Grader?* Write three good questions (include the answers) that might appear on a quiz related to the day's lesson.

  ▸ *I have a question!* Write a question that you have about the day's lesson.

  ▸ *Twexit cards*—Summarize what you learned in only 140 characters (the maximum length of a tweet).

  ▸ *Padlet*—Post a comment on the electronic posting board from your computer before you go.

  ▸ *Quick-writes*—In one to five minutes, write down your opinions, a summary, a reflection, or so on. Students can hand them in or share them with others.

  ▸ *Two roses and a thorn*—Write down two things you liked and one thing you didn't like about the lesson.

  ▸ *3-2-1*—Write down three things you learned, two interesting things, and one question you still have about the lesson.

▽ **Student-made quiz:** Students write higher-order questions about the text or task, and choose two to answer.

▽ **Teacher observation checklists:** Observe students in action and record progress.

▽ **Define key vocabulary:** Students select domain-specific (key) vocabulary words from the text and provide definitions in their own words.

▽ **Compare and contrast (similarities and differences):** Students identify the theory or idea the author is presenting. Then, they identify an opposite theory. What are the similarities and differences between these ideas?

▽ **Examples and nonexamples:** Students list (or draw or show) three elements that fit the criteria and three elements that are similar but are not examples.

▽ **Four corners:** Each corner of the room has a designation (A, B, C, or D) or choices. Students *vote with their bodies* by moving to and standing at their preference.

▽ **Tableaux, living diorama:** Create a living diorama by directing several students to pose in a scene from the story or text.

▽ **Illustration:** Students demonstrate understanding by creating a visual representation of a scene from the story.

▽ **Study guide:** Students create a study guide that summarizes the main ideas and provides page numbers for citations.

▽ **Mind maps for key points:** Students create a mind map that represents a concept using a digital diagram-making tool (like Inspiration or Gliffy) and share the link to the mind map with their teacher and classmates.

▽ **Simile summary:** Students complete the sentence, "What we learned today is like . . ."

▽ **One-minute write and draw:** Without stopping, students write about what most confuses them or their favorite part of the associated unit or lesson.

▽ **Talk a mile a minute:** In one minute, students summarize the text as fast as they can using both words and gestures.

▽ **Storyboard (comic strip):** Students create at least a three-panel storyboard or comic strip about what they have learned.

▽ **Response gradient 1–5:** Students mark on a gradient how confident they feel or the level of agreement they have about the topic, with 5 equaling "Very confident" or "Completely agree." (The scale could also be in fingers, from fist to five.)

▽ **Response metaphor:** Students use a metaphor to describe how they are feeling after the lesson. For example, a speed metaphor might include:

  ▸ Racing

  ▸ At speed limit

  ▸ Chugging along

  ▸ Stalled out

▽ **Clickers response system:** Using the Poll Everywhere app or something similar, students use classroom clickers or smartphones to respond to a question.

▽ **Interview questions:** Students write three interview questions for the main character or historical figure.

▽ **Google Forms and Flubaroo:** Students use Google Forms to create a miniquiz. You can use the add-on from Flubaroo (www.flubaroo.com) to get feedback on student responses.

▽ **Miniconference:** Conduct a brief three- to four-question miniconference to find out how a student is doing.

▽ **Outline:** Students create an outline of main ideas and supporting details using a graphic organizer or digital outlining tool.

▽ **Character or plot summary using diamante poems:** Students create a seven-line poem in the shape of a diamond using the following characteristics.

  ▸ *Line 1*—One-word topic (a noun)

  ▸ *Line 2*—Two adjectives

  ▸ *Line 3*—Three verbs

  ▸ *Line 4*—A four-word phrase

  ▸ *Line 5*—Three verbs

  ▸ *Line 6*—Two adjectives

  ▸ *Line 7*—A renaming noun for the topic

▽ **Write and draw:** Students use two columns in a notebook (or two facing pages) to reflect on the reading.

  ▸ *Column 1*—Words, phrases, sentences, or notes

  ▸ *Column 2*—Drawings and illustrations

▽ **Placemat chart:** Students in groups of four each write or draw his or her understanding in one section of the placemat, and then the group agrees on common understandings and writes those in the center. (See figure 6.4 for sample student work.)

▽ **Digital Socratic seminar:** Students respond to questions posed online via a program such as Socrative (www.socrative.com) or MasteryConnect (www.masteryconnect.com).

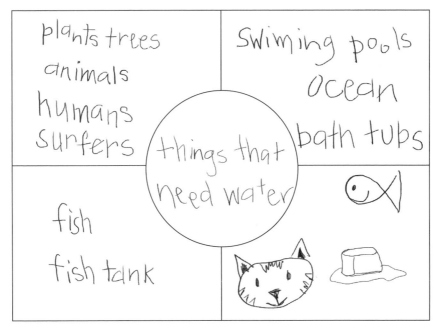

Figure 6.4: Sample placemat.

Using Common Formative Assessments

As discussed in chapter 1, using common formative assessments is one of the most proven, powerful instructional practices available to educators (Ainsworth, 2007; Fullan, 2007; Hattie, 2009; Odden & Archibald, 2009; Reeves, 2002; Schmoker, 2004) and the linchpin in the PLC at Work process (DuFour et al., 2010). Far more than merely administrating the same test, an assessment is common when a team of teachers have the intention of using the results to (DuFour et al., 2010):

▽ Improve individual practice

▽ Build the team's capacity to achieve its goals

▽ Intervene and enrich on behalf of its students

To achieve these outcomes, a team can take the following five steps.

1. **In a particular unit of study, identify the essential learning outcomes that all students must master:** Common assessments take time to create, evaluate, and most importantly, collectively analyze the results and plan next instruction. It is unrealistic, and in some ways

undesirable, to expect every standard and assessment to be a common assessment. Therefore, teachers should commit to giving at least one common assessment for each specific learning standard that is absolutely essential to future student success (see chapter 4 for more on essential standards).

2. **Determine how students will demonstrate their learning:** Teachers could create a specific assessment or rubric to measure student learning of the essential content, while still providing students with flexibility regarding how they can demonstrate their learning. If the common formative assessment is a multifaceted authentic task or includes a performance or product, teams must be careful to embed specific benchmarks or elements that they can identify and evaluate independently.

3. **Begin instruction:** Each teacher can determine the instructional practices and differentiation methods to best meet each student's needs, including classroom activities, targeted practice, formative assessments opportunities, and corrective feedback to help students prepare for the common assessment.

4. **Administer the assessment:** The team should determine when to give the assessment during the unit. When using a common rubric, it's critical for team members to collectively grade at least a few projects to ensure they are applying it consistently.

5. **Collectively analyze results:** There are five powerful outcomes from using common assessments.

   a. *Identify which students did not demonstrate mastery of essential standards*—Because common assessments measure student mastery of essential standards, common assessments identify students who need additional help and support—and specify which standards each student did not master.

   b. *Validate effective instructional practices*—Because teachers have autonomy in *how* they teach essential standards, common assessment data help validate effective practices. To ensure this, teachers can share and compare student results with other teachers who teach the same course.

   c. *Determine patterns in student mistakes*—Besides identifying best instructional practices, teachers should use these data to determine ineffective instructional practices. When analyzing students' mistakes, patterns emerge that can point to weaknesses or gaps in the initial instruction.

   d. *Measure the accuracy of the assessment*—If the common formative assessment is a quiz or test, through a careful item analysis of the assessment, a team can determine each question's validity. Over time, this will build a team's capacity to improve and create better assessments.

   e. *Plan and target interventions and extensions*—The ultimate goal is to ensure high levels of learning for all students. By identifying students in need of additional help, determining effective and ineffective instructional practices, and measuring the assessment's validity, the team has the necessary information to plan and implement targeted interventions.

The true power of common assessments occurs during collective reflection. Reflective teaching must be based on evidence of student learning, and this reflection is most powerful when it is done collectively (Hattie, 2009). Visit **go.solution-tree .com/RTIatWork** for the reproducible "Common Assessment Team Protocol" to guide team conversations toward these key outcomes.

Providing Students With Feedback

Feedback provides information about how we are doing in our efforts to reach a goal and is an essential element of formative assessment. A player hits a tennis ball with the goal of keeping it in the court, and the player gets immediate feedback by seeing where the ball lands—in or out. Someone tells a joke with the goal of making people laugh, and the joke-teller observes the audience's feedback in its reaction to the joke. During a lesson delivery, a teacher gets feedback on student engagement when he or she sees that the students are riveted or nodding off (Wiggins, 2012).

The goal when providing feedback about a student's progress or achievement is to offer information that may help the student as he or she tries again and improves on the effort. Such feedback takes many forms. Hattie's (2009) research states that giving students feedback is a highly effective strategy for differentiated instruction, resulting in an effect size of 0.75.

Educators must be clear about what appropriate feedback looks and sounds like. Wiggins (2012) describes it this way: "Helpful feedback is goal-referenced; tangible and transparent; actionable; user-friendly (specific and personalized); timely; ongoing; and consistent" (p. 11). *Tangible feedback* has clear, evident results or outcomes. If the science experiment reacted (or didn't) in the way one predicted, the results offer tangible feedback in the form of clear evidence. In the classroom, *initial feedback* usually comes to a student from the teacher or a peer. Ideally, this feedback is not advice, and the student is not evaluated. Feedback might be information about the final quality of the work, such as a summative (benchmark) assessment, in which students may not have an opportunity to redo the task. The feedback they receive in this situation lets them know how they did in the form of a grade, points, and so on. In every case, the feedback should help the learner understand where he or she is on the learning continuum toward a goal and provide helpful information on what still needs to happen to reach mastery.

Feedback is one of the essential tools for using assessment data to inform the instructional process. The frequent and ongoing types of assessment in this chapter offer multiple opportunities to collect important data and share them with the student through feedback. When students have opportunities to get frequent, accurate feedback, they can adjust their next efforts accordingly. Many refer to this as *feed forward*, as opposed to *feedback*, because it includes information in the form of prompts that provides students with ideas and tools for doing better on a similar problem or task in the future. If students will have such future opportunities, or if mastery of the content is critical for other future work, giving the students feed-forward is essential. Here are three common feed-forward prompts.

1. **Reminder prompt:** Remind students of the directions, materials, procedures, where to get help, and so on.

2. **Scaffold prompt:** Provide students with a graphic organizer, a short-ened version of the task, an additional resource, an opportunity to complete the work on a computer, a suggestion for where to begin, or similar scaffolded instruction.

3. **Example prompt:** Show the student an example of the task or problem to solve. This could be a quick reteach, a chance to watch a video clip, an opportunity to work with another student who is on track, and so on.

When providing feedback to students during the learning process, educators should remember the acronym SPATE, which stands for *specific, personal, actionable, task,* and *effort*.

▽ **Specific:** Comments should focus on specific observations. Educators should focus a student's attention on just one or two items within the task where he or she might target his or her next steps or improvement.

▽ **Personal:** Feedback should target the student and his or her efforts and achievements. Educators should avoid comparing the work to others or referring to the student's abilities.

▽ **Actionable:** The feedback should provide clear direction for next steps. Feedback must include data the student can use to improve.

▽ **Task:** Feedback comments should only address the task at hand. Educators should speak in the present about what the student is working on right now.

▽ **Effort:** Powerful feedback should include observations about what the student has already done correctly, the student's progress and growth, and the time, precision, and perseverance that the student has put into the task. This element of feedback is a critical piece for developing a growth mindset (revisit chapter 2, page 33, for more on the growth mindset).

When students receive ongoing feedback that measures their performance against a concrete, achievable goal, they also need opportunities to redo the task so that they can *use* the feedback to modify their next efforts. Specific accurate comments about the student's effort and then a chance to improve the results will continue to build a student's growth mindset. Ongoing formative assessment guides learners toward showing mastery on the next type of assessment—summative assessment.

Summative Assessments

At the end of a learning experience or unit, teachers should administer a summative assessment to evaluate each student's progress toward, and achievement of, the learning target or targets. The summative assessment or evaluation provides an opportunity for students to demonstrate the level of mastery they have acquired. Teachers can then assign a grade or record the proficiency level related to the competency or expectation.

It's important that students understand that at some point the learning process will culminate and the teacher will note a benchmark or snapshot of their progress toward mastery. For the purpose of this book, we are focusing on the best practices for daily differentiation. Designing appropriate summative assessment tools, using the proficiency scales, grading, and recording progress are all important next steps.

Adjustments to Student Tasks, Groups, and Processes in Response to Assessment Data

As we have noted, formative assessment is an essential method for gathering data about both the effectiveness of instruction and the students' individual progress and achievement. If educators fail to use data to inform instruction, the time spent in assessment is merely wasted. Educators can adjust their instruction as necessary to better meet students' capabilities and needs. Here are just some of the ways teachers can implement those adjustments.

▽ By adjusting the task or assignment to better meet each learner's readiness level

▽ By regrouping students into leveled clusters for short-term reteaching or extension opportunities

▽ By making decisions about the type of lesson and its scope, including selectively abandoning parts of it altogether, if necessary

Depending on the type of assessment, these adjustments must address a variety of results. If a preassessment demonstrates that a student has already mastered the skill in an upcoming unit, for example, the teacher must be ready to modify that student's experience by implementing an option that adds depth and complexity to the task. (Chapter 7, page 177, offers a more detailed description of such options.) If a student already knows the content in an upcoming lesson, the teacher should be ready to extend that student's learning experience. The following sections discuss a number of ideas for adjusting tasks and workflow, groups, and assignments in response to assessment data.

Adjusting Tasks and Workflow

After assessing student work, teachers often need to determine a way to organize educational tasks and workflow to optimize learning. Three common techniques for implementing such adjustments include scaffolding, jumpstarting, and compacting. Let's look at each of these techniques individually.

Scaffolding

Educators implement scaffolded instruction to provide a struggling student or English learner with sufficient support tailored to the student's needs to achieve his or her learning goals. The teacher gradually removes these supports as the student develops mastery and transitions to performing the skill independently—a form of the *gradual release of responsibility model*. In keeping with Vygotsky's (1978) theory of the zone of proximal development, during the learning process, the responsibility for the learner's achievement or the task's accomplishment moves from the teacher (a *more knowledgeable other*, or MKO) to the learner. This instructional model requires the teacher to orchestrate the learner's experiences so that there is a fluid transition from the teacher introducing the concept or skill and helping students understand or accomplish the learning to the student independently demonstrating mastery of the concept or skill on his or her own. This transition is referred to as a gradual release of responsibility (see figure 6.5).

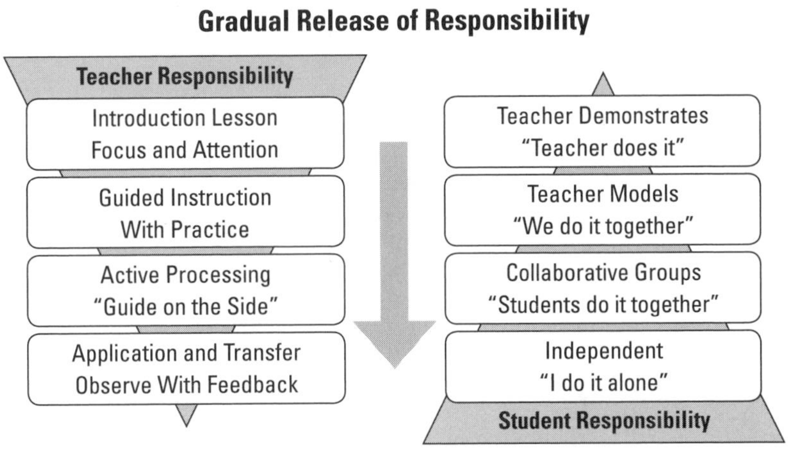

Gradual Release of Responsibility

Figure 6.5: Gradual release of responsibility.

Fisher and Frey (2008) have developed a gradual release of responsibility model to help teachers envision instruction that moves from explicit modeling and instruction, to guided practice, and then to collaborative activities that can help students develop into independent learners by accepting total responsibility for the task. There are many versions of the gradual release of responsibility model, but Fisher and Frey's (2008) version is a good representative that includes these four phases.

1. **Focus lesson:** "I do it"

2. **Guided instruction:** "We do it"

3. **Collaborative learning:** "You do it together"

4. **Independent work:** "You do it alone"

In the gradual release of responsibility model, the MKO is the teacher during the "I do it" and "We do it" phases. The MKO resurfaces again in the collaborative process where peers may assist each other. In 21st century classrooms, computer-assisted learning may be the MKO during a learning task.

Teachers can implement scaffolded instruction informally with any student at any time. Ideas for implementation might include:

▽ Structured directions, including step-by-step guidance, icons, or illustrations

▽ A graphic organizer to provide a nonlinguistic representation (see chapter 5 for an in-depth look at the use of graphic organizers as learning tools)

▽ A study buddy to help work on some part of the task

▽ Technology to assist with the task

▽ Adjusted scope of a reading passage or a more appropriate leveled version

▽ A video clip that illustrates the lesson

▽ An audiobook presentation

▽ Frequent designated check-in times to determine progress

▽ Adjustments to task or lesson pacing and completion times or dates

As we noted, scaffolding is an especially important instructional tool for educators who are asking students to work in their zone of proximal development. The tasks involved in that process may be extra challenging, and the students may need some support and organizational help in order to remain engaged and avoid becoming discouraged. Students identified with an IEP may need scaffolding on a regular basis as they begin to learn new skills and concepts. When students with special needs work within the regular classroom, teachers should refer to the student's IEP for suggested scaffolding strategies.

Students can get frustrated, intimidated, and discouraged when taking on new learning challenges, especially if they experience multiple failures over time. Scaffolding can help avoid this negative spiral and move the student toward independent achievement. In Vygotsky's (1987) words, "What the child is able to do in collaboration today he will be able to do independently tomorrow" (p. 211).

Jumpstarting

When students show a lack of enthusiasm for a task, confusion as to how to begin, or reluctance to proceed, a teacher may want to provide a *jumpstart* to get the task moving. Also referred to as *front-loading*, jumpstarts are effective ways to streamline the beginning of an activity. Jumpstarts can take multiple forms, such as the following.

▽ Reading aloud the first few pages or chapters of a book to help students become familiar with an author's style and vocabulary

▽ Letting students begin with only half of the problems or assignment

▽ Posting a word bank for students to draw from

▽ Providing students with definitions of key vocabulary terms for the task

▽ Highlighting key text (using highlighting tape in textbooks)

▽ Bookmarking key websites to use for a specific task

▽ Providing a graphic organizer with key words or phrases

Compacting

Sometimes, teachers must edit planned content to eliminate material a student has already mastered, and that editing process is known as *compacting*. If a student exhibits mastery of a task or topic (by achieving scores of 85 percent and higher) in a preassessment or initial survey of background knowledge, then teachers must consider what parts of the planned lessons to skip or eliminate so students remain challenged. Helping teachers understand how they might compact the curriculum for high-ability learners has been a goal of Joseph Renzulli and Sally Reis (n.d.) at the Neag Center for Gifted Education and Talent Development at the University of Connecticut (www.gifted.uconn.edu). Consider the following simple strategies to compact lesson content in response to assessment data.

▽ Students can work on different aspects of the task during different time blocks (prearranged).

▽ Skip some lessons and have students work on an alternate task that is related to the concept and skills.

▽ Create an extension activity that would be an alternative to the basic lesson.

▽ Orchestrate ways for the student to utilize a technology enhancement to work at a more challenging pace.

Adjusting Groups

When teachers collect formative assessment data, one fairly common response is to temporarily group students into two or three learning groups. These flexible groups gather students together who need reteaching, additional time, or extended learning. (See also chapter 2, page 43, for more on flexible groupings.) Form temporary or flexible student work groups for a specific activity or task. For example:

▽ Regroup based on readiness or student interest.

▽ Use prearranged partners and groups.

▽ Form learning clubs (temporary reteaching groups) to gather students for a reteaching opportunity.

▽ Create some groups that might utilize technology for part of the lesson.

Groups may also be made up of students with:

▽ A mixed preference profile

▽ Various readiness levels

▽ Mixed readiness levels (heterogeneous)

▽ Particular interests

▽ Mixed interests

▽ Mixed cultures and languages

▽ Student choices

When adjusting student work groups in response to assessment data, however, teachers must also be cognizant of strategies that are detrimental to student success. Specifically, as we've discussed, the practice of long-term tracking persists in many schools, despite the negative effects on students (Oakes, 1985). Tracking, or grouping students based on ability, "is especially harmful to poor and minority students because these students are more likely to end up in the low tracks" (Cole, 2008, p. 4).

Within a classroom with a risk-free climate and a positive culture, frequent regrouping will be the norm at Tier 1. Within the daily schedule, students may work independently for a short time, gather for whole-group instruction for a couple of short lessons, rotate through stations with an assigned group, and meet with temporary groups for further instruction. When flexible student groupings and partnerships are a naturally occurring part of daily learning, students feel included and supported.

Adjusting Assignments

Educators can adjust assignments by designing two or three variations to better meet students' needs in a diverse classroom. Adjusted assignments, or tiered lessons, can reflect various levels of complexity, processes, products, or readiness.

One way to accomplish such an adjustment is to create three-level assignments, with the levels targeted toward students whose proficiency is on level with their current grade, students below proficiency, and students above proficiency. The process for developing three-level assignments might have the following progression (see figure 6.6).

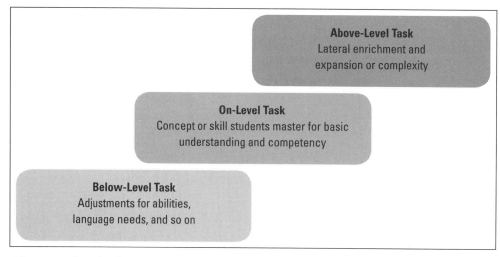

Figure 6.6: Three-level assignment.

1. **On-level tasks:** First, determine what the *on-level* task will be. Design a lesson sequence to teach a concept or skill students master for basic understanding and competency. Some scaffolding support may be included as students work in their zone of proximal development.

2. **Below-level tasks:** Next, determine what a *below-level* task might be. Adjust the lesson as needed for abilities, language needs, and so on. Add scaffolding to support students as they construct their understandings. (Note: Completing this modified task could only be ranked as a 2.0 score on a proficiency scale, see page 89.)

3. **Above-level tasks:** Finally, determine what an *above-level* task might be. Use compacting strategies and integrate the depth and complexity model (we describe this model fully in chapter 7, page 192).

Students working below grade level might lack some prerequisites for completing assignments and, therefore, need various adjustments to the task. These students typically have difficulties with any one or a combination of the following.

▽ Basic reading skills

▽ Listening comprehension

▽ Oral expression

▽ Written expression, spelling, or both

▽ Mathematical calculation, reasoning, or both

▽ Concentration for extended periods of time

▽ Perseverance

▽ Complicated, multistep directions

▽ Emotional control, verbal outbursts, or both

These students may or may not have a formally identified learning disability, or they simply may lack the past experiences or opportunities to build the skills needed for the task. Without prior experiences with new learning concepts, they will need scaffolding, backfilling, extra time, or a jumpstart in order to catch up with the students working at grade level. Students with IEPs, as well as hearing, visual, or physical impairments, may need actual accommodations of the task in order to achieve success. Students lacking English language development may not be able to complete the task at the basic level without some additional accommodations.

Students preassessed to work at the on-level task—those who work at their basic grade level—typically fit one or more of these descriptions.

▽ They have some prior experience with the content or process.

▽ They have some experience with the requisite skills necessary to complete the task.

▽ They are working within a zone of proximal development for this task.

▽ They are developing the social skills necessary for any group or partner work.

▽ They usually can work independently if required or, with some additional help and guidance, can continue to persevere.

▽ With a little scaffolded instruction and help from an MKO, they probably will be able to meet the standard and master the concept.

Students capable of working at an above-level task (above basic or advanced) typically fit one or more of these descriptions.

▽ They have demonstrated proficiency or near mastery of the standard.

▽ They have evidence of prior experiences with the relevant topics or skills or with similar topics or skills.

▽ They often demonstrate a high level of curiosity and show interest and excitement about new concepts.

▽ They usually can work successfully, whether independently or with partners and groups.

▽ They can follow directions and attempt to solve problems as they arise.

▽ They have above-basic levels of reading, writing, or mathematics skills for the grade level.

Students identified as above-level learners will need adjusted tasks or challenges that will expand the basic lesson. Teachers may compact the original lesson to abandon content these students don't need to cover and use the freed-up time to emphasize lateral enrichment and add depth and complexity.

Teachers must also consider behavior issues, but they should not limit a student's chance to work on above-level tasks. Behavioral supports to provide include clear procedures about allotted time, where one can work, with whom one can work, and expected results.

Workstations or learning centers, which we discussed in chapter 5 (page 123), make adjusted assignments easier to administer. Students could be in heterogeneous groups, but the appropriate adjusted assignment might be in each student's folder at the different learning centers.

Alternatively, stations could be arranged with various adjusted versions of the assignment, and teachers could group students by readiness, with students assigned to the most appropriate task.

Using a template like figure 6.7 (pages 170–171) can help with creating adjusted assignments. This example is for a Common Core Reading assignment.

Now, let's review some specific examples of adjusted assignments in a variety of subjects.

Adjusting a Mathematics Task

The following example illustrates an adjusted grade 2 assignment for studying polygons (Flynn, n.d.).

All students will:

▽ Go on a hunt for polygons around the school

▽ Use a graphic organizer to record the polygons

▽ Complete the assigned graphic organizer, making sure to include at least one example of each polygon (triangle, quadrilateral, pentagon, hexagon, and octagon)

Here is the assignment's on-level form.

> Students will be given a graphic organizer with the names of the polygons listed. Students will illustrate and provide the number of sides of each polygon type and find at least two examples of polygons on their scavenger hunt.

Here is the assignment's below-basic adjustment.

> Students will be given a graphic organizer with the five types of polygons with the number of sides noted. Students will find one example of each polygon type on their scavenger hunt and record it.

Here is the assignment's above-level adjustment.

> Students will create their own graphic organizers. Students will illustrate an example, list the names, and provide the number of sides of each polygon type. An extra challenge is to graph the number of each type of polygon found on the scavenger hunt.

Adjusting a Reading Task

The following example illustrates a grade 5 adjusted reading task for reading informational text.

All students will:

▽ Read a current event article on Newsela (www.newsela.com), such as "Groups Say Monarch Butterfly Needs Protecting" (*St. Louis*

Lesson Goal: Core Essential Standard—Text Types and Purposes

W.1.3 — Write narratives to develop real or imagined experiences or events using effective technique, well-chosen details, and well-structured event sequences.

Big Idea, Essential Questions, or Learning Target

▷ Students will be able to write a personal narrative about a small event in their lives on four pages of a picture book.
▷ Students will be able to read their stories in a small-group setting.

Prerequisite Skills

▷ Identify parts of a book: cover, title, pages.
▷ Write simple words with inventive spelling.

Preassessments

▷ Question-and-answer task about parts of books
▷ Whole-class discussion
▷ Prior observation of writing words

First Task, Introductory Activity, or Hook: Whole-Class Activity

▷ Teacher reads a picture book to the class that has lots of details in both the pictures and the words. Share a small moment with the class.
▷ Discuss how the story is told through the pictures and words of the book and how important these details are.
▷ Distribute a blank four-page booklet to each student.
▷ Ask students to think of a small moment from their lives.

Student Groupings

▷ Students share their stories with their partners while touching each page of their booklets. Partners do not have to be on the same level.
▷ Students work independently at table groups; OK to get help from others.

Adjusted Tasks or Activities

Below Grade Level	At Grade Level	Above Grade Level
▷ Students write their small moment across the other three pages of their booklet. The writing can be in the form of pictures and a few words. ▷ Students add details so that viewers can see, and students can read the story when they finish. Students label their pictures. ▷ Students use pictures and a few words (at least one word per page) to tell a cohesive story with a clear beginning, middle, and ending. ▷ English learners (newcomers) can dictate words to be translated. Teachers provide language support.	▷ Students write their small moment across the other three pages of their booklet. ▷ Each page should have at least one picture and one sentence at the bottom of the page that tells what is happening in the picture. ▷ Students write a cohesive story with a beginning, middle, and ending. Books include a picture and a single sentence at the bottom of each page telling what is happening. Sentences should have details that explain each picture. ▷ ELs use language supports such as dictation, a peer cowriter, word bank, or a graphic organizer.	▷ Students write their small moment across the three pages of their booklet with a picture and two or more detailed sentences at the bottom of each page. ▷ Students use descriptive words in their story and make sure sentences match what is happening in the picture. Students are sure to have a closure at the end of their story. ▷ Students write a cohesive story with a beginning, middle, and ending. Students sketch their pictures and write complete sentences at the bottom of each page telling the story. Students write two or more sentences per page adding needed details. ▷ ELs use language supports as necessary.

Differentiation (Check all that apply.)

X	Content	X	Process	X	Product		Technology support
X	Readiness	X	Interests		Learning preference	X	Language support
	Choice		Resources		Challenge		Environment or setting

Strategies (Check all that apply.)

X	Pluralized (variety in choices)		Adjusted lessons		Varied writing or journal prompts
	Supplementary materials		Centers or stations		Group investigation or research
X	Highlighted or modified texts		Adjusted products		Small-group instruction
X	Varying activities		Graphic organizers		Independent study
	Varied texts		Interest centers		Learning contracts
	Jigsaw		Compacting		RAFT writing
	Think-pair-share		Literature circles	X	Study buddies
	Choice boards		Discussions		Other: _____

21st Century Skills for Added Value

Collaboration	Communication	Critical Thinking	Creativity
Sharing stories with partners; reading aloud to a small group	Telling a story through pictures and words	Targeting a small moment, using descriptive details to enhance learning	Adding pictures to illustrate the story; decorating the book

Assessments and Evaluation

Formative Assessments (Check all that apply.)

X	Preassessment aligned with learning targets		Journals or learning logs
	Anecdotal records	X	Conferences and interviews
X	Self-assessment and reflection		Open response
	Class discussions		Other: _____

Summative Assessments (Check all that apply.)

	Multiple-choice and selected response
	Writing portfolio tasks
X	Performance tasks
	Oral examination

Next Learning Targets

▷ Students write and illustrate another book. They should add more words and more descriptive words than used in the first book.

▷ Students use a storytelling app on the computer to create a five-page book.

Figure 6.7: Sample adjustable lesson.

*Visit **go.solution-tree.com/RTIatWork** for a reproducible version of this figure.*

Post-Dispatch, 2014), choosing from three different Lexile versions of the article: 660L, 850L, and 1150L (Students might select which level is best for them, or the teacher may have selected which Lexile level would be the most challenging for each student.)

▽ Participate in a class discussion about content of the article

▽ Complete one of the related tasks differentiated by complexity

Here is the assignment's on-level form.

> Write and record a thirty-second radio news broadcast describing the issues brought up in the article. Provide at least two solutions that should be considered. An extra challenge is to create a TV news broadcast and select two images to be shown.

Here is the assignment's below-basic adjustment.

> Write a one- or two-paragraph public service announcement describing the issues highlighted in the article, or create a poster illustrating those issues; the article or poster also must offer at least one possible solution to the problem suggested specifically in the text.

Here is the assignment's above-level adjustment.

> Write an editorial piece (one page), or record an editorial report on the information provided in the text. Take a side regarding the issue and support your opinion with evidence from at least one other source.

Adjusting a Writing Task

The following example illustrates a grade 3 adjusted writing task.

All students will:

▽ Learn the five parts of a friendly letter

▽ Practice their writing skills

▽ Reread their letter and correct spelling, punctuation, and capitalization

▽ Review published books, letters, thank-you notes, cards, and post-cards to prepare their writing

Here is the assignment's on-level form.

> Write a friendly letter to someone (without prompts). Tell about something you have been studying. Include a heading, salutation, body, closing, and signature. You may use a computer or the fancy paper and calligraphy pens.

Here is the assignment's below-basic adjustment.

> Write a short informal letter to a friend using a computer program set up with prompts. Include a heading, greeting, body (message), closing, and signature. You can use the model at ABCya.com (www.abcya.com/friendly_letter_maker.htm).

Here is the assignment's above-level adjustment.

> Write a friendly letter to someone and provide detailed information about something you are interested in. Decide on three aspects and write a paragraph on each one. Include all parts of a friendly letter. Use a computer or paper and pen.

As noted, to better meet students' capabilities and needs, teachers can adjust tasks and workflow, groups, and assignments in response to assessment data. Frequent adjustments to instruction are essential to optimize student learning in Tier 1.

A Commonsense Approach to Assessment

Creating a great lesson based on a targeted standard with clear goals is most important. As we have described in this chapter, collecting data about students and developing student profiles that indicate learning preferences, interests, strengths, and challenges helps educators anticipate what students will need to be successful in their academic process. However, sometimes learners struggle with even well-planned lessons that the teacher has targeted specifically toward the students' strengths and challenges. In these situations, teachers may need to rely on their own common sense to find the most effective intervention. When parents ready their children to go to the park, they take a few minutes to determine the necessary prerequisites to avert a possible problem and meltdown later. Does the child have shoes on? Does he have a sweater? Did she go to the bathroom? Does he need a drink or snack before going? Does she have a ball or a favorite toy to bring along? Is he in need of a nap soon? Common sense is the guiding factor as parents help children be prepared for any upcoming experience. In much the same way, determining the prerequisite skills and concepts a student will need in order to be most successful during the upcoming lessons is what instructionally intelligent teachers must do as a prevention strategy.

Throughout this chapter, we've outlined a number of commonsense core instructional strategies educators can use in response to data they gather from assessments. The following list represents some of these, along with some other ideas that represent best practices for initial interventions.

1. **Check basic needs:** Is the student hungry? Thirsty? Hot? Cold? Tired? Needing to move around? Needing to be by a window?

2. **Consider a short-term study buddy:** Ask another student to work with the struggling student, or make sure the student knows who to go to if he or she needs additional help.

3. **Implement a scaffolding strategy:** Chunk the task into manageable pieces, set time frames, reduce the size of the task, or offer a graphic organizer.

4. **Insert technology:** Use any available technology to reteach or increase engagement and student motivation and help the student with learning or completing the task.

5. **Boost the lesson with a creative twist:** Add music, role plays, art, games, and minicompetitions.

6. **Offer a choice:** Propose an alternative assignment or task. Students can choose between two versions of a task or from multiple choices on a choice board.

As we have outlined in this chapter, ongoing assessments are essential tools for gauging the effectiveness of instructional plans as well as students' progress. From creating student profiles early in their academic career, to screening for prerequisite skills or learning associated with specific tasks, to conducting diagnostic preassessments, formative assessments, and final summative assessments that reflect students' level of learning at the end of a lesson, unit, or sequence, assessments offer critical data for planning interventions for struggling students and shaping daily differentiated instruction. Educators can share the commonsense approaches to intervention we've offered here with parents and instructional aides. For all of these individuals and the students they serve, these strategies form a powerful first response, as well as a strong strategy for heading off future student struggles.

As teachers develop their instructional intelligence, they will begin to use frequent formative assessment strategies—often quite low prep and informal—to gather data about students' progress and the effectiveness of instruction. This constant monitoring allows for adaptations and differentiation to occur in a timely fashion. Students will get the help they deserve right when they need it. Likewise, high-ability students will be noticed and provided with challenges that keep them moving forward. This cycle helps promote student engagement.

Taking the Discussion Further

Following are some of the important ideas from this chapter that are worthy of further reflection and discussion. Educators in a PLC may want to read through this chapter with their collaborative teams and discuss each section, recording the issues related to each piece of information and considering classroom implications for students. Collaborative teams can reflect on the prompts to deepen understanding and set subsequent goals for improvement.

▽ Discuss the five opportunities to collect student data. What are the bene-fits of each?

▽ Discuss the value of preassessments and how you use them in your classroom.

▽ Examine the formative assessments strategies suggested in this chapter. Which have you tried? Which might you use?

▽ Review figure 6.2 (page 152) and figure 6.3 (page 153), and discuss the five critical attributes of formative assessment.

▽ Discuss the value of providing students with feedback, and consider SPATE as a strategy for improving the quality of feedback.

▽ How can adjusted tasks, groups, and assignments benefit your instruction?

▽ Discuss the concept of scaffolding and the types of supports educators can implement and remove as students develop more independence.

▽ Discuss compacting and flexible grouping and their uses in Tier 1 differen-tiated instruction.

▽ Collaboratively design an adjusted assignment related to a specific ele-mentary standard.

▽ Consider the commonsense approaches for assessment and determine which may apply to your students.

Building Cognitive Rigor, Depth, and Complexity

When students have the opportunity to initiate and explore ideas without fear of failure and work cooperatively with other students with whom they can discuss, hypothesize, agree, disagree, and so on, they are using the brain's natural drive to find meaning. As a result, students make stronger connections in their learning—connections that eventually may transfer new knowledge and skills to long-term memory. It takes an environment that supports a risk-free expression of ideas and intellectual exploration to encourage rigorous, complex thinking, as well as tasks and interactions designed to spark it. In addition, students need a variety of product and performance opportunities to demonstrate learning at high levels. When students have opportunities to actively process their learning, teachers can begin to consider ways to increase their students' cognitive rigor.

Heather Bower and Joelle Powers (2009) define rigor through their research as "how the standard curriculum is delivered within the classroom to ensure students are not only successful on standardized assessments but also able to apply this knowledge to new situations both within the classroom and in the real world" (p. 4). They also identify higher-order thinking and real-world application as two critical aspects of rigor, suggesting that it is not enough for students to know how to memorize information and perform on multiple-choice and short-answer tests. Students must have deep and rich content knowledge, along with the ability to apply that knowledge in authentic ways.

In *Making Connections: Teaching and the Human Brain*, Renate and Geoffrey Caine (1994) put forth three elements that should be present during instruction to maximize student learning.

1. **Relaxed alertness:** As we explained in chapter 2, a classroom climate that is challenging but maintains low threat offers students a safe and secure learning environment. When the brain shifts into survival

mode, it becomes less flexible and open to new ideas. In a supportive environment, students can remain relaxed, yet alert, so their brains are better able to learn.

2. **Orchestrated immersion in complex experiences:** Students learn not only from teachers but also from engaging in interesting real-world tasks, ongoing activities, and a variety of social interactions—in short, from the entire educational experience and its physical context. This immersion in a complex and inter-related mix of experiences develops a student's understanding and—ultimately—real-world competence.

3. **Continuous active processing of experiences to consolidate learning:** *Active processing* refers to student tasks and opportunities that involve offering input, generating ideas, reorganizing information, self-explaining, exploring through trial and error, collaborating, reflecting and self-assessing, or otherwise going beyond the simple memorization of presented material. In a brain-friendly classroom, students have multiple opportunities for active processing.

In effect, each element is also an essential requirement for helping students build cognitive rigor, depth, and complexity. Increasing cognitive rigor is about *dynamic instructional effectiveness*. In most cases, providing a rigorous learning experience demands that educators adjust their instructional approach and tactics, increase their expectations, and provide each student with the opportunity to grow in ways they cannot imagine (Williamson & Blackburn, 2010). To accomplish that goal, teachers must be sure that the rigorous tasks they design are truly more advanced and complex, not simply more work for students. In the words of Terry Heick (2013), "Rigor matters because it imposes cognitive load on students, forcing them to confront misconceptions, reconsider positions, separate the implicit from the explicit, and other critical thinking practices that distinguish shaky familiarity from true understanding."

What should rigorous curriculum and instruction look like at Tier 1 in elementary classrooms? With new initiatives and standards—including the Common Core State Standards—educators are being challenged to create more rigorous instructional tasks for *all* of their young students. The first step in meeting this challenge is to reduce the volume of curriculum content, especially content that involves little more than heavy factual information. Then, educators can focus more closely on developing the students' depth of understanding and complexity of thinking around fewer, more important concepts. Challenging tasks that demand problem-solving skills, research, questioning, and experimentation help students develop this essential cognitive depth and complexity, as well as the important 21st century skills of communication, collaboration, creativity, and critical thinking that we introduced in chapter 4. While developing literacy is a main educational focus in the early years, providing active processing opportunities for students to think, problem solve, imagine, and create are all part of developing rigorous thinking at all stages in the educational process.

Of course, elementary educators need to raise the bar for all students, and that means being prepared to provide essential scaffolding and support for all those who need it. Curriculum designers and classroom teachers, therefore, must extend or enrich the curriculum for those students who already have developed proficiency or who master the new concepts quickly. That way, rigorous learning is part of every student's experience—even highly capable learners. John F. Kennedy once said, "A rising tide lifts all boats." In education, an environment that provides a rigorous learning experience in a supportive classroom helps *every* student develop the cognitive depth and complexity necessary to rise to levels of achievement they might have never imagined attaining.

In this chapter, we are going to explore multiple ideas, methods, and strategies for developing curricula and instructional plans that will help students build cognitive rigor, depth, and complexity. After a brief review of the benefits of a learning environment that supports risk as well as achievement, we examine methods for helping students develop higher-order thinking skills and go beyond "sit and spit" regurgitation of new information. We also take a close look at using proficiency scales to guide educators, without allowing them to limit their expectations or instructional approach. Practical, specific strategies for improving cognitive rigor by adding depth and complexity, including the 4Cs of 21st century skills, and leveraging technology integration can contribute to any instructional plan. We end the chapter with a review of some basic lessons in multiple forms, adjusted to offer differentiated instruction for students at all levels of capability and need. The ideas, strategies, and techniques outlined in this chapter provide educators with the instructional momentum necessary to help lift all students on the rising tide of intellectual rigor, depth, and complexity.

Creating Rigorous Learning Environments and Tasks

How might the classroom environment encourage rigorous learning? As we explained in chapter 2, classroom teachers must first work on creating a safe and secure, brain-friendly classroom in which there is an expectation that every student will work and learn at high levels. Rigorous learning is not just about the quality of the curriculum being taught or the level of the classes that students take. It is all about the teacher's (and the student's) expectations of learning. At the elementary grades, teachers must orchestrate the classroom climate and environment in ways that encourage students to take risks, make mistakes, and develop a growth mindset. Every student must feel supported and know that they can make mistakes, fail, and have opportunities to redo tasks. They know that learning is a *process* and that their own learning may not happen at the same pace as others'. This understanding is key to a healthy growth mindset in early learners.

To develop that mindset, students need an environment of supported risk, so that they will feel willing to take chances. Knowing how to respond to failure and handle adversity is integral to a student's mental and emotional health. An unbroken string of successes in school may not prepare students for the pitfalls they inevitably will encounter in the real world. Providing students with rigorous tasks engages them in a healthy struggle to succeed. As they lead students through these supported risks, elementary teachers will need to include processing opportunities to encourage discussions about frustrations, failures, and how to learn from mistakes (Blackburn, 2008).

One way to help students understand the essential nature of making mistakes is to encourage them to understand that, rather than failure stopping them dead in their tracks, they just need to try again to succeed. In other words, teachers must encourage students to engage in do-overs. Here are some simple techniques for offering that encouragement.

▽ Using the phrases "Not yet" and "Almost there" frequently with students implies that they will be able to complete the task successfully—and soon. It also lets students know that they are on their way to completing a task correctly.

▽ Celebrating the opportunity to redo a task or assignment lets students see that one can always improve his or her efforts.

▽ Asking students "What will you do differently this next time?" or "How could you improve your work or effort if you did it again?" helps students process the experience and analyze the product.

▽ Providing a rubric for a more accurate self-assessment during a task or assignment helps students see what they're accomplishing along the way to completing the task, rather than placing all of the learning emphasis on the end product.

▽ Letting students know that mistakes are really just learning opportunities helps alleviate some of the sting of setbacks, and it can encourage students to try again.

▽ Sharing their own first-time stumbles or failures helps students understand that everyone has to redo something during the course of learning.

Beyond creating a risk-supportive classroom climate and environment, educators also contribute to students' development of cognitive rigor and depth by providing tasks that challenge them to think more deeply and stretch their current level of complex, higher-order thinking. As educator and author Larry Ainsworth (2011) notes, "A rigorous curriculum serves as both the detailed road map and the high quality delivery system for ensuring that all students achieve the desired end: the attainment of their designated grade- or course-specific standards within a particular content area." To develop a plan for creating a rigorous curriculum and instructional plan, educators may first need to abandon some of the prevailing myths that surround such rigor. Here are four of the most common myths.

1. **Lots of homework is a sign of a rigorous curriculum:** More isn't always better. Rigor shouldn't be equated with the amount of work but rather the task's quality and complexity and its appropriateness for each student.

2. **Rigorous instruction means demanding that students do more:** Rigor is not the amount of time one spends doing a task—it's the level of complexity. Teachers should find out each student's zone of proximal development and design tasks that push students to work hard for reachable goals.

3. **Rigor is not for everyone:** All students can learn at higher levels with the right supports. The brain loves challenge, and every student— regardless of his or her unique needs—can be motivated to work hard and think deeply about meaningful tasks.

4. **Support makes the learning experience less rigorous:** Providing scaffolding and encouraging students to work collaboratively are clever ways to make tasks more rigorous. Students often work at a higher level if they know support is on the way.

In previous chapters of this book, we have offered a number of ideas educators can use to adjust classroom learning and skills to differentiate instruction for students at varying levels of experience and knowledge. We offer seven ideas specifically targeted toward helping teachers add rigor to *any* level of classroom task.

1. Make sure that tasks are within the student's zone of proximal development (Vygotsky, 1987; see chapter 6).

2. Design tasks and projects that have multiple, developmentally appropriate steps and require students to use a variety of resources.

3. Select more complex texts and explicitly teach students close-reading skills (we talk about these skills in detail later in this chapter).

4. Ask students to form an opinion and defend it. Require evidence, for example, by asking "How do you know?"

5. Design projects that students must complete over time and that demonstrate transfer of knowledge through problem-based learning appropriate to the grade level (see chapter 4, page 97).

6. Use technology more rigorously by challenging students to go beyond basic skills and applications.

7. Create opportunities for students to collaborate and build negotiation and cooperation skills.

Teachers also can encourage parents to be supportive of their child's development of cognitive rigor at home by not being so quick to intervene when the child is attempting, even failing at, challenging tasks—something many *helicopter parents* may not be comfortable with at first. Letting young students struggle to complete a task can be painful for teachers and parents, and yet it is an important process for young brains to go through.

Now, let's review some specific techniques and tools for incorporating rigor-building tasks and processes into the curriculum and instructional plan.

Developing Students' Higher-Level Thinking Skills

Challenging students to develop higher-level thinking skills—the terms *critical thinking*, *higher-level thinking*, and *problem solving* are often interchangeable—isn't a new idea in education. The definition for higher-level thinking usually includes the understanding that a person will take new learning and combine it with information stored in his or her memory. The consolidation of the new and old rearranges and extends this information to eventually achieve a purpose or find possible answers for perplexing situations. Higher-level thinking, according to Newmann (1990), "challenges the student to interpret, analyze, or manipulate information" (p. 44). Students need opportunities to use their higher-level thinking skills—to question everyday assumptions and then learn how to create new solutions that might positively impact the quality of their lives and even contribute to the greater good of the planet.

Higher-level thinking, such as critical, logical, reflective, metacognitive, and creative thinking, can be taught and then applied to complex real-world situations. Early learning theorist John Dewey (1933) suggests that problems, questions, confusion, and doubt evoke higher-level thinking. Learning critical-thinking and problem-solving processes must involve active inquiry and discovery.

The simple act of asking open-ended questions that don't have one right answer is a good place to begin the effort of building students' higher-level thinking skills. Grappling with such questions gives students a chance to respond to challenges in creative ways without being afraid of being wrong, and it helps their brains connect the new learning to their prior experiences. After reading a book aloud, for example, rather than asking students something like "What was the main character's name?" a teacher might ask, "If you were that character, how would you have done _____?" When the student responds, the teacher takes the cognitive process further by asking, "Why do you think that?"

Here are some other examples of questions teachers might ask in order to generate higher-level thinking.

▽ "What do you think might happen next?"

▽ "Does this remind you of anything from your life?"

▽ "Why did he or she act that way?"

▽ "How is _____ similar to or different from _____?"

▽ "Can you explain or show me that in another way?"

▽ "How do you imagine _____ would look?"

▽ "What do you think a solution might be?"

▽ "Why did you decide to choose _____ over _____?"

Another simple way to generate higher-level cognitive processes involved in applying, analyzing, evaluating, and creating information is to increase *cognitive dissonance*, the phenomenon that occurs in one's thinking when one encounters something that does not align with a previously held truth or belief. Cognitive dissonance can be an uncomfortable feeling. At first, many learners may be resistant to new information that disrupts their current knowledge and try to prove it as incorrect. But dissonance can be a very powerful motivator—we have an innate desire to seek to uncover the truth or solve a mystery. In classrooms, teachers can promote such investigations and build a sense of curiosity by presenting alternative viewpoints, seemingly incongruous ideas, arguments, or suppositions that cause students to rethink, investigate, and provide evidence.

When students use their brains to make connections and arguments, they are strengthening their neural pathways. Statements and questions such as the following encourage that kind of brain work, as they create cognitive dissonance for students and promote their critical thinking.

▽ Did you know that an adult is about 60 percent water? Explain how that is possible.

▽ Roz Savage is a British woman who rowed a boat solo across all three major oceans. Predict what she would have to do to have accomplished that.

▽ There is a place in the United States where you can be in four different states at the same time. Do you think that is possible? Brainstorm how you could find out where that might be.

▽ If you live two thousand years ago, which would be the best to own: a horse, a cow, or a dozen chickens? Why?

▽ What is the difference between *wanting* something and *needing* something?

Developing higher-level thinking in elementary students demands that educators expose learners to real problems and questions and then give them opportunities to explore possible solutions and actions. Few of the most important problems or questions we deal with in the real world have simple black-and-white answers. By teaching students to look further and dig deeper, and by giving them the time to do so, educators help them develop the habit of deep and complex thinking they will need to succeed in school and adult life.

Beyond the use of open-ended questioning, there are several models that teachers can use both to understand and to integrate higher-level thinking into everyday standards-based instructional strategies. One such model, Bloom's Revised Taxonomy, describes a hierarchy of thinking process categories that defines lower-order thinking skills as the foundation for higher-level thinking. Webb's Depth of Knowledge model categorizes standards and tasks according to the demands they place on students' cognitive skills—a categorization that enables educators to assess the cognitive expectations of instructional strategies and processes. Now, let's examine these models in more detail to identify how they can help teachers build more cognitive rigor into their students' daily learning activities.

Using Bloom's Revised Taxonomy

Bloom's Taxonomy of the Cognitive Domain, originally developed in the 1950s, divides cognitive processes into six categories, which together form the *cognitive domain*, or the lowest and highest levels of abilities and thinking skills. The revised version uses process verbs to better describe the levels of thinking (Anderson & Krathwohl, 2001)—for example, *remember* rather than *knowledge, understand* instead of *comprehension*, and *create* in place of *synthesis* (see table 7.1). By reviewing the continuum of thinking levels, teachers can easily determine if the learning task will only demand a minimum of cognitive load or if, in fact, the task will be quite rigorous and demand higher levels of thinking and processing.

A majority of standards-based instruction is often limited to the two lowest levels of thinking: *remembering* and *understanding*. Tasks and activities that focus on the two lowest levels may not be as engaging as working at the higher levels of thinking (*creating* and *evaluating*). Using Bloom's Revised Taxonomy to help you stretch your instructional strategies to more complex learning will intrigue and interest students. In turn, by developing sophisticated thinking skills in students, they will be better prepared for the 21st century workforce.

Table 7.1: Bloom's Revised Taxonomy

Category	Cognitive Processes	Definition	Alternate Verbs
Remember	▽ Recognize ▽ Recall	Retrieve relevant knowledge from long-term memory.	▽ Identify ▽ Retrieve ▽ Recall
Understand	▽ Interpret ▽ Summarize ▽ Explain	Construct meaning from instructional messages, including oral, written, and graphic communication.	▽ Paraphrase ▽ Generalize ▽ Conclude ▽ Predict ▽ Explain
Apply	▽ Execute ▽ Implement	Carry out or use a procedure in a given situation.	▽ Use ▽ Carry out ▽ Apply
Analyze	▽ Differentiate ▽ Organize ▽ Attribute	Break material into its constituent parts and determine how parts relate to one another and to an overall structure or purpose.	▽ Discriminate ▽ Select ▽ Distinguish ▽ Determine
Evaluate	▽ Check ▽ Critique	Make judgments based on criteria and standards.	▽ Test ▽ Judge ▽ Monitor ▽ Detect
Create	▽ Generate ▽ Plan ▽ Produce	Put elements together to form a coherent or functional whole; reorganize elements into a new pattern or structure.	▽ Hypothesize ▽ Design ▽ Construct ▽ Invent

Source: Adapted from Anderson & Krathwohl, 2001.

Using Webb's Depth of Knowledge

As schools began to focus more on teaching core standards, Norman Webb (1997) developed a process and criteria for systematically analyzing the alignment between standards and standardized assessments. His Depth of Knowledge model helps teachers understand and analyze the cognitive expectation from standards, curricular activities, and assessment tasks (Webb, 1997).

The DOK model is based on the idea that instructional tasks can be categorized according to their *cognitive demand*—the cognitive expectation or depth of knowledge required to produce an acceptable resolution to the task. As Tracie Hummel (2014) notes:

> Depth of Knowledge categorizes the cognitive complexity of an activity, as evidenced by the amount of planning, discussing, fact-checking, and researching employed to accumulate the knowledge needed to complete the activity. In essence, it looks at the structure and complexity required to work with the activity.

Each of the four levels reflects a different depth of knowledge level (here, the term *knowledge* is intended to broadly encompass all forms of knowledge, such as procedural knowledge, declarative knowledge, and so on). Table 7.2 reflects an adapted version of Webb's (1997) model.

Table 7.2: Webb's Depth of Knowledge Levels

DOK Level	Title
1	Recall and Reproduction
2	Skills and Concepts
3	Short-Term Strategic Thinking
4	Extended Thinking

Source: Adapted from Webb, 1997.

As we have seen, Bloom's Revised Taxonomy can help teachers identify the cognitive skills necessary for students to perform a task and describe the thinking processes necessary to answer a question or complete an activity. DOK levels, on the other hand, give educators a means of identifying the depth of content understanding and the scope of a learning activity, as well as cognitive skills like planning, researching, conducting an experiment, drawing conclusions, and so on required to complete the task from beginning to end.

Putting the Models to Work

When designing rigorous lessons and tasks, teachers can begin by using the DOK model to establish *expectations* for the level of understanding they want students to be able to demonstrate by the end of the lesson, as well as the complexity of thinking required to successfully complete the task. Teachers can then review the levels of thinking in Bloom's Revised Taxonomy to select the most effective thinking strategies and related instructional methods for covering the lesson in a way that will stretch the students' cognitive skills. See table 7.3 for a comparison.

Table 7.3: Webb's Depth of Knowledge and Bloom's Revised Taxonomy

Webb's Depth of Knowledge Model	Bloom's Revised Taxonomy					
	Remember Retrieve knowledge from memory. Recall, list, recognize, state, and identify	**Understand** Grasp the meaning. Summarize, describe, explain, interpret, and paraphrase	**Apply** Carry out and use new learning. Demonstrate, use, implement, produce, and organize	**Analyze** Break into parts to understand the structure. Compare, contrast, examine, and select	**Evaluate** Make judgments based on criteria. Choose, defend, criticize, and challenge	**Create** Reorganize several known elements into something new. Invent, create, synthesize, and construct
DOK 1 Recall and Reproduction Focus on specific facts, details, or procedures. One correct answer	**ELA** Recall basic facts, details, and events explicit in the text. Read words fluently and accurately. **Mathematics or Science** Recall and identify properties, formulas, and patterns.	**ELA** Describe and explain characters and details using who, what, when, where, and why. **Mathematics or Science** Solve a one-step problem. Represent mathematics relationships in words, pictures, and symbols.	**ELA** Apply rules to edit spelling, grammar, punctuation, and so on. Use word relationships to determine meaning. **Mathematics or Science** Solve a linear equation. Apply an algorithm or a formula to calculate.	**ELA** Identify information represented in charts, graphs, maps, tables, and so on. **Mathematics or Science** Retrieve useful information from a chart or graph to answer a question.		**ELA, Mathematics, or Science** Brainstorm ideas, concepts, or solutions to a topic, problem, or concept.
DOK 2 Skills and Concepts Focus on applying skills and concepts—explain how and why. One correct answer		**ELA** Explain cause-and-effect relationships. Make inferences. **Mathematics or Science** Summarize results. Make predictions from data or observations.	**ELA** Use context to identify meaning of words and phrases. Apply simple conventions to a piece of writing. **Mathematics or Science** Solve routine problems using multiple steps. Represent data in a table or graph.	**ELA** Identify use of literary devices. Distinguish fact from opinion. **Mathematics or Science** Compare and contrast data or figures. Categorize and classify data based on characteristics.		**ELA, Mathematics, or Science** Generate hypotheses based on observations or experiences.

Continued →

DOK 3 **Strategic Thinking and Reasoning** Focus on reasoning and planning, complex thinking, and defending with evidence. Multiple answers or approaches	*(shaded)*	**ELA** Explain and connect ideas using supporting evidence. Write a longer composition for a specific purpose and audience. Describe how word choice affects the interpretation. **Mathematics or Science** Use concepts to solve nonroutine problems. Provide evidence to justify theories and results.	**ELA** Revise final draft for progression and consistency of ideas. Apply word choice, point of view, and tone to influence readers' interpretation. **Mathematics or Science** Design and conduct an investigation. Use reasoning and evidence to solve problems. Translate problems and results into symbolic notations and data.	**ELA** Analyze or interpret the author's literary devices and viewpoint. Use reasoning and provide evidence to support inferences. **Mathematics or Science** Analyze and draw conclusions from data; cite evidence. Interpret data from complex graphs. Identify a pattern.	**ELA** Develop a logical argument and cite evidence. Compare and contrast the solution methods. Critique or justify a presented conclusion. **Mathematics or Science** Develop a logical argument and cite evidence. Verify the reasonableness of results.	**ELA** Develop an alternative story ending. Design a complex model for a given situation. **Mathematics or Science** Develop a scientific or mathematical model for a complex situation. Synthesize information from one data set, source, or text. Formulate an original problem.
DOK 4 **Extended Thinking** Focus on complex reasoning. Make real-world applications in new situations. Multiple answers possible Requires extended time with many steps	*(shaded)*	**ELA** Develop generalizations of the results and apply them to new situations. **Mathematics or Science** Relate mathematical or scientific concepts to other content areas or other concepts.	**ELA** Investigate how multiple themes (historical, social) may be related. Research a novel problem and select a possible solution. **Mathematics or Science** Conduct an extended project that identifies a problem and discovers a solution.	**ELA** Analyze multiple works by the same author or themes. Analyze various writing styles from multiple sources. **Mathematics or Science** Analyze multiple sources of evidence. Gather, analyze, and begin evaluation based on criteria.	**ELA** Evaluate accuracy and completeness of information from multiple sources. Provide justification of your selection. **Mathematics or Science** Conduct an investigation—gather, analyze, and evaluate results to draw conclusions.	**ELA** Synthesize information from multiple sources or texts. Propose a new theory or perspective. **Mathematics or Science** Design a scientific or mathematical model to solve a practical situation.

Source: Adapted from Hess, 2009, and Webb, 1997. Used with permission from Martha Kaufeldt © 2015. All rights reserved.

Tasks with a DOK level 1 expectation, *recall and reproduction*, are likely to engage students only in Bloom's two lowest-level categories of thinking, *remembering* and *understanding*. Students need not engage in much cognitive rigor to simply define, compute, copy, and identify. A student responding to a DOK level 1 item either knows the answer or does not. The answer does not need to be figured out or solved.

Tasks with a DOK level 2 expectation for cognitive depth, *skills and concepts*, will engage students in some mental processing that goes beyond simply recalling or reproducing information. Successfully completing tasks at this DOK level requires both comprehension and additional processing. A wider range of Bloom's thinking levels may be used to complete tasks that have more than one mental step, such as comparing, organizing, summarizing, predicting, and estimating. In assigning DOK level 2 tasks, teachers ask learners to *apply* learned knowledge by making use of information in a context different from the one in which they learned it. A DOK level 2 task asking students to describe or explain skills and concepts, for example, would have students go beyond a simple description or explanation of recalled information to, instead, describe or explain a result produced by the information or the information's *how* or *why* elements.

When working at a DOK level 3 expectation, *short-term strategic thinking*, students must use reasoning, engage in detailed planning, and provide evidence for their answers. Learning at this level involves understanding deeper knowledge; tasks may have multiple valid solutions and students must justify their choices. Educators can integrate a wide range of Bloom's processing levels within DOK level 3 tasks. The expectation for tasks at this level often requires coordination and integration of knowledge and skills from multiple subject areas to carry out processes and reach a solution in a project-based setting. Examples include summarizing and analyzing information from multiple sources, designing and conducting an experiment, or examining characteristics of various types of books and stories.

The most complex cognitive expectations occur in tasks at DOK level 4, *extended thinking*. The extended thinking expected at a DOK level 4 might include several different levels of processing from Bloom's Revised Taxonomy. The hallmarks of solving problems or completing tasks targeted at this level of thinking include using multiple sources, working on a project over an extended period of time, and transferring knowledge to another domain to solve problems. Bloom's highest levels of processing—*analyze*, *evaluate*, and *create*—are all engaged during various stages of the extended-thinking task. In completing these tasks, students engage in conducting extended investigations that involve multiple decisions to solve real-world problems with unpredictable outcomes. For example, when studying standard and metric measurements, fourth-grade students might also weigh grocery items using pounds, ounces, and kilograms. This type of problem allows students to apply new knowledge about weight when shopping with parents or others. Teachers can also create an activity involving a relay race, where students race to grab items from the grocery store (a table filled with items like canned goods) and weigh them. Students can then make a shopping list with items to reach a particular weight goal. Real-world activities like this one allow students to work at the highest level of Bloom's Taxonomy and Webb's DOK level 4.

Using information from Bloom's Revised Taxonomy and Webb's DOK levels, educators can craft tasks that address standards while challenging students to build cognitive depth and complexity at multiple levels. Here are a series of examples that demonstrate differentiated tasks for a lesson on the water cycle, designed to build students' cognitive skills at all four of Webb's levels of cognitive thinking.

> **Standard:** Grade 2 Next Generation Science Standard on earth science—The Roles of Water in Earth's Surface Processes, How do the properties and movements of water shape Earth's surface and affect its systems? (ESS2.C; NGSS Lead States, 2013)

▽ **Task at DOK level 1, *recall and reproduction*:** Write a definition for these key features of the water cycle: *evaporation, condensation, precipitation*, and *accumulation*. Label them on a chart.

▽ **Task at DOK level 2, *skills and concepts*:** Design and make a model of a watershed, and label these elements: *stream, river, erosion, delta*, and *ocean*. Locate these elements on a map of a local watershed.

▽ **Task at DOK level 3, *strategic thinking*:** Using the National Drought Mitigation Center's (http://droughtmonitor.unl.edu) drought maps, analyze and compare the development of drought conditions in California in 2012, 2013, and 2014. Determine which regions of California are in the most critical situation and which regions are not doing too badly. Create a bar graph to represent the development of the drought (three years) for at least three regions of your choice.

▽ **Task at DOK level 4, *extended thinking*:** Collect precipitation amounts for your own region and at least one region of California for a two-week period. Use a rain gauge, if possible, to gather precipitation amounts. Look online for accurate precipitation amounts for the California region you have chosen. Consider using the U.S. Department of Agriculture Natural Resources Conservation Service for California (www.nrcs.usda.gov/wps/portal/nrcs/main/national /water/snowsurvey). Then, look at a ten-day weather forecast for the two regions. Report in a paragraph or two what you predict will be happening during the ten days regarding precipitation for the two areas, and tell why you are making that prediction.

When students look further and dig deeper, they develop the habit of deep and complex thinking necessary to succeed in school and life. In the next section, we'll look at ways they can go even further—to surpass proficiency.

Going Beyond Proficiency

Often, general education classroom teachers have difficulty developing challenging extension tasks to meet high-ability students' needs and enable them to go *beyond* proficiency. But what, exactly, does going *beyond* proficiency look like? If we look back at the proficiency scales we presented in chapter 4 (page 89), we can see that, in general, demonstrating a 4.0 score would demand a much more rigorous and complex task than would demonstrating a 3.0 score. In effect, helping students attain level 4 in the DOK model, through extended thinking, also would help students demonstrate proficiency with additional depth, complexity, and critical thinking.

The Flip Book (Kaplan, Gould, & Siegel, 1995) offers a solid description of what it means to create and build depth and complexity within a lesson. In *The Flip Book*, the authors define *depth* as digging deeper in the lesson, extending the study, venturing further, going from concrete to abstract, and elaborating. Students develop cognitive depth by identifying patterns, trends, and big ideas. The authors use *complexity* to describe a greater breadth of understanding. Students develop cognitive complexity by exploring multiple perspectives, changes over time, and so on (Kaplan et al., 1995). When educators combine both types of learning in a single task, the task becomes more rigorous (Gregory & Kaufeldt, 2012). To create depth, teachers can consider eight areas: (1) language of the discipline, (2) details, (3) patterns, (4) unanswered questions, (5) rules, (6) trends, (7) ethics, and (8) big ideas. Three additional areas build complexity: (1) cross-curricular applications, (2) changes over time, and (3) multiple perspectives. Each of the eleven areas has a simple representational icon to create an easy visual reference. (See table 7.4, page 192.)

The eleven icons of the depth and complexity model provide teachers with relatively easy prompts to generate more rigorous questions and tasks. Once students have been introduced to the different dimensions of rigor, teachers can apply them more frequently. Many teachers include the icons as visual prompts. For example, when students see the glasses icon for *different perspectives* they know they will be asked to look at how point of view is important to the task. This low-prep model establishes for students that they will always be looking for ways to think more deeply about their learning. J Taylor Education (www.jtaylor education.com) offers a wide variety of helpful downloadable tools and products for depth and complexity.

Table 7.4: Depth and Complexity Chart

Area of Focus	Icon	Definition	Examples
Language of the discipline		What vocabulary terms are specific to the content or discipline?	Tools, jargon, icons, acronyms, special phrases, terms, slang, and abbreviations
Details		What are the defining features or characteristics? Find examples and evidence to support opinions and ideas.	Parts, factors, attributes, variables, and distinguishing traits
Patterns		What elements reoccur? What is the sequence or order of events? Make predictions based on past events.	Predictability and repetition
Unanswered questions		What information is unclear, missing, or unavailable? What evidence do you need? What has not yet been proven?	Missing parts, incomplete ideas, discrepancies, unresolved issues, and ambiguity
Rules		What structure underlies this subject? What guidelines or regulations affect it? What hierarchy or ordering principle is at work?	Structure, order, reasons, organization, explanation, classification, and "because . . ."
Trends		What factors (socioeconomic, political, or geographical) cause events to occur? Identify patterns of change over time.	Influence, forced direction, course of action, compare, contrast, and forecast
Ethics		What moral principles are involved in this subject? What controversies exist? What arguments could emerge from a study of this topic?	Values, morals, pro-and-con bias, discrimination, prejudice, judgments, differing opinions, points of view, right and wrong, and wisdom
Big ideas		What theory or general statement applies to these ideas? How do these ideas relate to broad concepts such as change, systems, chaos versus order, and so on? What is the main idea?	Conclusions based on evidence, generalizations, summarizations, theory, principle, and main idea
Cross-curricular study		Relate the area of study to other subjects within, between, and across disciplines. How might this task be integrated and examined through art, music, drama, science, and so on?	Connect, associate, integrate, and link ideas

Area of Focus	Icon	Definition	Examples
Changes over time		How are elements related in terms of the past, present, and future? How and why do things change? What doesn't change? How might we consider this concept or task if we looked to the past or projected what might be different in the future?	Connecting points in time, examining a time period, and comparing and contrasting
Different perspectives		How would others see the situation differently? How might we view this text, task, or concept from a different point of view?	Different roles and knowledge and opposing viewpoints

Source: Adapted from Gregory & Kaufeldt, 2012; Adapted from Kaplan et al., 1995. Used with permission from J Taylor Education.

Using Complex Texts and Text-Dependent Questions to Increase Instructional Rigor

Based on numerous research studies, including the 2006 report *Reading Between the Lines* (ACT testing organization), the CCSS (NGA & CCSSO, n.d.b) determine:

▽ Since the 1960s, K–12 reading texts have actually trended downward in difficulty and sophistication.

▽ Barely half of the students taking the ACT in 2006 were able to meet the benchmark in reading.

▽ K–12 students have not developed adequate skills in reading informational texts independently.

▽ The consequences of insufficiently high text demands in K–12 classrooms are severe for everyone, but they are critical for at-risk student populations.

As a result, the CCSS emphasize text complexity and *text-dependent questions* (questions requiring readers to use evidence from the text to present analyses, defend claims, and clarify) as ways educators can add more rigor to instruction (NGA & CCSSO, 2010a). In a move toward increased text complexity—a *staircase of complexity*—the CCSS require that students read grade-level appropriate texts that vary in complexity from *readily accessible* to *very complex*. Consider the challenging-text exemplars in appendix B of the CCSS, "Text Exemplars and Sample Performance Tasks for English Language Arts and Literacy in History/Social Studies, Science, and Technical Subjects" (NGA & CCSSO, n.d.b). Teachers can use reading strategies and text-dependent questions to help students develop the necessary skills to read text at the chosen level of complexity with greater understanding. *Close reading* is one strategy teachers can use to help students comprehend the varied complexities of such text. In close reading, teachers and students focus on small sections to fully derive their meaning and impact on the whole text. Rather than reading complex text selections in their entirety, therefore, teachers can identify key passages and read, reread, interpret, and discuss those portions more closely with students. With younger students or nonreaders, teachers can use *close observation* in place of close reading to lead students in investigating illustrations, photos, and video clips, and examining them for details that reveal their meaning. Patricia Polacco's books (such as *Thank You, Mr. Falker, Thunder Cake, The Keeping Quilt, Mr. Lincoln's Way*, and *My Rotten Redheaded Older Brother*) are particularly suited for close observing. These books are rich with feelings, complex problems, and beautiful images than can help generate discussion.

Teachers may have already incorporated many elements of close reading into their lessons. To challenge students to critically analyze a complex text, focus on specific details, and develop deep, precise understanding of the passage's meaning, consider the following.

▽ Select a text with sufficient complexity to challenge students' current understanding and skill set. (Not every text is appropriate for a close read.)

▽ Use shorter passages and excerpts, selecting text that is worth examining. Students may not need to read an entire piece. Chunk larger passages into manageable excerpts. The goal is to experience an in-depth exploration.

▽ Examine the text with students thoroughly and methodically. Dive right in and limit prereading activities. Have students read text as independently as possible. Help students begin to notice things they find confusing or interesting by encouraging them to read with a pencil (or highlighter). Ask them to take notes or mark passages to revisit.

▽ Use a progression of text-dependent questions. Focus student reading on particular words, phrases, sentences, and paragraphs. Use question prompts to guide students to use the author's words and provide evidence.

▽ Read, reread, and read again. When guiding students through a *close reading*, the passage might be read three or more times.

  ▶ The first read can be done as independently as possible or as a read-aloud. Focus on the *key ideas and details* in the text, making sure that readers know the main idea and story elements. Follow with a think-pair-share (page 45).

  ▶ The second read should include several text-dependent question prompts to guide students to investigate the author's *craft and structure*. Students should have an opportunity to discuss their findings and provide evidence from the text.

▶ The third close read of a text should go even deeper and require students to synthesize and analyze information and perhaps compare the text with another selection or prior reading. Students might be encouraged to record their ideas and write responses in a journal.

A thorough close reading of a text may take place over several days. Texts should include enough complex ideas worthy of exploring and discussing to sustain one or more days of instruction without getting boring, repetitive, and tedious.

The following sections offer more details about selecting an appropriately complex text and ideas for designing text-dependent questions.

Selecting a Complex Text

There are a variety of formulas to determine the level of a text's complexity. The CCSS recommend that educators assess text complexity by considering three equally important criteria (NGA & CCSSO, 2010a).

1. The *quality* of the text, which involves its structure and knowledge demands

2. The *quantitative* factors of the text, which include word frequency, sentence length, and so on

3. The *reader and task considerations*, including the student's background knowledge, experiences, and motivation

Appendix B of the CCSS has an extensive list of prose, poetry, and informational-text selections for each grade level (NGA & CCSSO, n.d.b). Appendix A of the CCSS (NGA & CCSSO, n.d.a) introduces a *text-complexity staircase* that accelerates previous recommended Lexile levels (quantitative factors) beginning in grades 2–3. Books with a higher (more challenging) Lexile level are now categorized at a lower grade level than they were previously based on college and career (CCR) readiness expectations (see table 7.5).

Table 7.5: Text-Complexity Grade Bands and Associated Lexile Ranges

Text-Complexity Grade Band in the Standards	Old Lexile Ranges	Lexile Ranges Aligned to CCR Expectations
K–1	n/a	n/a
2–3	450–725	450–790
4–5	645–845	770–980
6–8	860–1010	955–1155
9–10	960–1115	1080–1305
11–CCR	1070–1220	1215–1355

Elfrieda Hiebert and Heidi Anne Mesmer (2013) raise concerns that setting the bar higher in primary grades may have unintended negative effects: widening the gap, decreasing the levels of fluency and automaticity, and lowering engagement and motivation to read. Their research indicates that perhaps raising the complexity levels at middle and high school will be beneficial but recommend that teachers use common sense when selecting complex texts in the primary grades. Elementary educators must consider these changes carefully in addition to considering students' interests and background knowledge about the subject when selecting a sufficiently complex text.

Using a Progression of Text-Dependent Questions

There is no set system of developing text-dependent questions for close reading. Good text-dependent questions guide students in examining and extracting the key meanings from a passage. Text-dependent questions for close reading usually begin by exploring specific words, details, and arguments within the text and then move on to examine the text as a whole. These questions often target the academic vocabulary and specific sentence structures within the text as critical focus points for understanding the author's meaning and the exact message.

Good text-dependent questions ask students to perform one or more of the following tasks.

▽ Determine the role that individual paragraphs, sentences, phrases, or words play.

▽ Analyze sentences on a word-by-word basis.

▽ Analyze paragraphs on a sentence-by-sentence basis.

▽ Analyze illustrations and the subjects and objects that are in text.

▽ Investigate how the reader can alter the overall meaning of the passage by changing key words.

▽ Determine why an author may have chosen one word over another.

▽ Probe each argument in a persuasive text.

▽ Probe each idea in informational texts.

▽ Probe each key detail in a literary text.

▽ Question why authors choose to begin and end when they do.

▽ Consider what the text leaves uncertain or unstated.

Additionally, consider the following four steps in creating text-dependent questions (Achieve the Core, 2015).

▽ **Step one:** Identify the text's core understandings and key ideas.

  ▸ Who was the most important character in this story?

  ▸ What message or lesson do you think the author was trying to tell us?

▽ **Step two:** Start small to build confidence; answers should appear in text.

  ▸ What two things happen before there is a problem?

  ▸ What do you think happened earlier in the day in which this story took place? What makes you think that?

▽ **Step three:** Target vocabulary, word choice, and text structure.

  ▸ What words or phrases really describe what the main character looks like?

  ▸ Why do you think the phrase _____ repeats so much?

▽ **Step four:** Have students tackle difficult sections of text head-on, which may involve readers mastering dense information or making inferences, because the text doesn't include the answers.

  ▸ What do you think the author means by this quote _____?

  ▸ How do the main characters transform or change during the story?

Douglas Fisher and Nancy Frey (2013) illustrate the progression of text-dependent questions as a pyramid (see figure 7.1, page 198). In this progression, the questions build in focus from a single word in the text to the text as a whole. See also "Text-Dependent Questions" and *Unstoppable Learning* (Fisher & Frey, 2012, 2015) for more on close reading.

Elementary teachers can increase instructional rigor for all students by carefully selecting appropriate complex text passages and guiding students to read closely. Celebrating that primary students are becoming independent readers isn't enough. Helping students learn how to thoughtfully examine complex texts will build rigorous thinking strategies.

Increasing Rigor Using 21st Century Skills

As we mentioned in chapter 4, a key element of a powerful core curriculum is the integration of the 4Cs of 21st century skills: communication, collaboration, critical

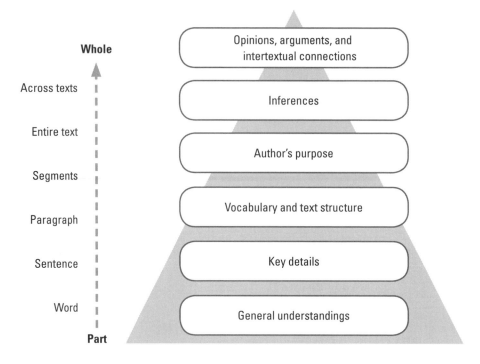

Source: Fisher & Frey, 2013.

Figure 7.1: Progression of text-dependent questions.

thinking, and creativity. The benefits of integrating these 21st century skills into the core curriculum go well beyond initiating students in a basic understanding of the skills and concepts included in the standards. The 4Cs are, in fact, survival (life) skills that will prepare students for an ever-changing digital world and help students think for themselves and eventually succeed in the workforce and in everyday life. Incorporating these skills into the curriculum, therefore, adds rigor to the instructional plan and develops students' cognitive depth and understanding.

As we explained in chapter 5, pluralized teaching and learning refers to the practice of integrating various skills and tasks to ensure every lesson has a high impact for every learner. In a standards-based curriculum, educators have multiple opportunities to go beyond the specific skill or concept they are teaching by incorporating 21st century skills into the lesson or unit. Rather than taking a single shot at a specific narrow target, we encourage teachers to consistently consider what other *add-ons* they might include in the lesson to broaden the learning opportunity. With those additions, the assignment gives students a chance to develop social skills, negotiation techniques, and cooperative learning strategies.

Table 7.6 lists multiple methods teachers can use to integrate the 4Cs of 21st century skills into any lesson, in order to add value through multiple layers of learning.

Table 7.6: Integrating the 4Cs Into Teaching

4Cs	Strategies
Communication	▽ Reading, writing, speaking, and listening ▽ Communicating digitally and networking
Collaboration	▽ Working in teams or partners ▽ Learning from and contributing to others' learning ▽ Using social-networking skills
Critical Thinking	▽ Thinking critically to design and manage projects; solving problems ▽ Making effective decisions using a variety of digital tools and resources
Creativity	▽ Considering and pursuing novel ideas ▽ Investigating economic and social entrepreneurialism ▽ Leading for action

Creating Added-Value Lessons

When planning instruction using state standards, educators can add value and rigor by including ways for students to collaborate, communicate, create with each other, and develop critical-thinking skills. We call these tasks *C1* to *C4* activities because they not only address the standards but also have the added value of embedding the 4Cs in them. (See table 7.7.)

Table 7.7: C1 to C4 Activities

Activity	Description
C	Task aligns with and targets a core standard. Task follows a basic lesson design involving knowledge acquisition and rote memorization and lacks 21st century skills.
C1	Task aligns with and targets a core standard and includes one of the 4Cs.
C2	Task aligns with and targets a core standard and includes at least two of the 4Cs.
C3	Task aligns with and targets a core standard and includes at least three of the 4Cs.
C4	Task aligns with and targets a core standard and includes all four of the 4Cs.

In this classification, as part of a brain-friendly environment, a *C* task is a standards-based lesson using the core curriculum. Such lessons may be quite targeted and include only basic interactions and instructional strategies. Teachers create a *C1* lesson by adding one of the 4Cs of 21st century skills to the tasks involved in the basic lesson; a *C2* lesson includes two of the 4Cs, and so on (see figure 7.2, page 200). By using this process to add value and rigor to each task, educators can multiply the effectiveness of the lesson, increase student engagement, and integrate 21st century skills on a regular basis.

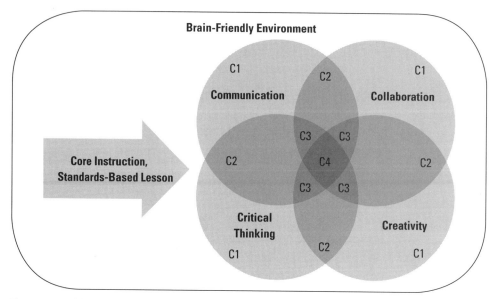

Figure 7.2: Added-value lesson.

Table 7.8 offers specific strategies to incorporate the 4Cs into instruction. (Revisit chapter 5, page 111, for detailed descriptions of the strategies.)

Table 7.8: C1 to C4 Activities Chart

Communication	Collaboration
RAFT writing (role, audience, format, and topic)	Think-pair-share
Oral presentations	Study buddies
Close reading	Elbow partners
Blogs	Appointment cards
Video journals	Group research reports
Interviews	Jigsaws
Debates	Tweets
	Academic controversy (debates)
Critical Thinking	**Creativity**
Project-based learning	Art (such as planning and creating a mural for the school)
Problem-based learning	
Community and social action (such as a campaign for the neighborhood or a design for an alternative solution to food waste in the cafeteria)	Fundraisers (such as organizing a cookie sale to raise money for a field trip)
	Music (such as composing music on a synthesizer to help someone relax)
Class consensus (such as a discussion on how everyone can share the recess equipment)	Economic and social entrepreneurialism (such as building awareness about excessive paper waste)

Teaching an Added-Value Lesson

Consider the following standards-based lesson using C, C1, C2, C3, and C4 activities for added value. In this lesson, fifth-grade students will be able to identify the major themes of the Bill of Rights—the first ten amendments to the U.S. Constitution—supporting several Common Core State Standards (NGA & CCSSO, 2010a).

▽ **C = Basic standards-based lesson:** Match each of the first ten amendments with the single word or short phrase that summarizes the main idea. Write your answers on the worksheet. Option: You can make a set of flashcards to study the themes of the Bill of Rights. (RI.5.2)

▽ **C1 = Standards-based lesson + collaboration:** Work with an elbow partner to create a succinct summarizing word or short phrase for each of the ten amendments, and write them on index cards. (SL.5.1)

▽ **C2 = Standards-based lesson + collaboration and critical thinking:** Work with a partner to create summary phrases for each of the first ten amendments, and write them on index cards. Place the amendments in what you believe is the order of their current level of importance. What amendment should be first? Second? Arrange your cards on a poster in the hierarchy you propose. (W.5.2; RI.5.3)

▽ **C3 = Standards-based lesson + collaboration, critical thinking, and communication:** Work with a partner to create summary phrases for each of the first ten amendments and write them on index cards. Place the amendments in what you believe is the order of their current level of importance. What amendment should be first? Second? Arrange your cards on a poster in the hierarchy you propose. Decide with your partner what your argument will be to defend your first four choices. Be prepared to share with the class and provide your rationale. (RI.5.5; RI.5.8)

▽ **C4 = Standards-based lesson + collaboration, critical thinking, communication, and creativity:** Complete the C3 activity, and choose one of the following creative ways to present your hierarchy. (RI.5.9)

  ▶ Create a colorful poster of your new arrangement of the Bill of Rights.

  ▶ Compose a song or rap to help remember the main themes of each of the first ten amendments.

  ▶ Create a Bill of Rights crossword puzzle with specific clues and an answer key. Visit A to Z Teacher Stuff (http://tools.atozteacher stuff.com) for a helpful template.

Developing 21st century skills in students plays an important role in extending instructional rigor while developing students' cognitive depth. As we've seen, the definition of rigor varies greatly in both research and practice.

The classroom must have a climate and an environment that support risk-free expression and intellectual exploration of ideas to encourage rigorous, complex thinking. Students make stronger connections in their learning and can transfer new knowledge and skills to long-term memory when they have multiple opportunities to engage in rigorous thinking.

Taking the Discussion Further

Following are some of the important ideas from this chapter that are worthy of further reflection and discussion. Educators in a PLC may want to read through this chapter with their collaborative teams and discuss each section, recording the issues related to each piece of information and considering classroom implications for students. Collaborative teams can reflect on the prompts to deepen understanding and set subsequent goals for improvement.

▽ Discuss the concept of *rigor*. Consider Heather Bower and Joelle Powers's (2009) and Terry Heick's (2013) quotes.

▽ Create your own definition of rigor based on the descriptions of rigorous instruction and the strategies in this chapter.

▽ Define what rigor is and isn't by exploring the four common myths.

▽ Discuss do-overs and how teachers can use them to help students succeed.

▽ Review Bloom's Revised Taxonomy and Webb's Depth of Knowledge model, and consider how you can apply them to an upcoming unit of study.

▽ How can your collaborative team use learning progressions in its planning?

▽ Develop some text-dependent questions related to an upcoming unit of study.

▽ How could your team increase rigor with technology?

▽ Discuss the 21st century skills and their implications for students and the curriculum. Using the 4Cs, create an added-value lesson for an upcoming unit of study.

Embracing the Journey

As we've seen, a teacher's job is a continuous journey—a cycle of reflection, adjustment, and action. Every lesson, unit, semester, year, and teaching opportunity with each student has its own ending, but the teaching journey is ongoing and, therefore, must reflect continuous progress. Ultimately, teachers must develop their own growth mindset and let it guide their philosophy of teaching. Educators must believe that—with continued effort, perseverance, and collaboration—they can get better at their craft, just as they must believe their students are capable of the same kind of growth and development. Furthermore, teachers must be prepared to tweak their instructional plans each year, as a new group of students with new strengths, needs, and preferences enters the classroom. That kind of adaptability and expectation of growth and change is a fundamental requirement for teachers as professionals in a demanding profession.

The Art of Teaching

Throughout this book, we've looked at a number of important ideas and strategic best practices for using daily differentiated instruction to provide a strong learning experience for *all* students at Tier 1. Over time, the notion of differentiation has been both a blessing and a curse. When the term first emerged in the late 1990s, it sounded ominous and almost insurmountably complex to many educators. Often, educational leaders presented differentiation with an abundance of strategies but with very little organization and even less clarity regarding how educators could actually implement the strategies. As a result, there was little agreement within the education community about what differentiation involved. Some thought of differentiation as catering to each student's learning styles and multiple intelligences. Some thought it was merely an updated form of tracking, which resulted in labeling each student as at, below, or above grade level. As we know now, and as we have outlined carefully in this book, differentiation actually is the abandonment of the one-size-fits-all myth in education. We all know that students don't look alike—they all have unique sets of genes, experiences, and environmental influences, and as a result, they all learn differently. Daily differentiation of instruction is an education approach that acknowledges these differences by finding and applying the best instructional practices to ensure that all students receive an effective and powerful education at Tier 1.

Essentially, differentiation is a predisposition to the belief that all students have potential and can be successful. Although we've outlined multiple strategies and tactics for using daily differentiation to help all students reach that potential, differentiated instruction is much more than just a set of strategies. It involves matching strategies to each student's readiness level, interests, and preferences and being instructionally intelligent (Bennett & Rolheiser, 2001). As we've seen, successful differentiated instruction demands that educators use ongoing assessment to identify the appropriate level and complexity of the tasks they offer.

Although some educators insist that they cannot differentiate instruction effectively, due to the age of high accountability and testing that prevails in education, these concepts are not mutually exclusive. Actually, students will do better on *all* tests if they have learned the content and skills they need to be successful in all areas of the core curriculum. However, promoting that kind of learning experience demands that teachers expand their repertoire beyond that of direct instruction from the sage on the stage. Instead, they must implement a variety of different brain-compatible instructional strategies that create a risk-supportive learning environment and that challenge all students in their zone of proximal development so that they move forward steadily in their learning. Differentiated instruction supports those changes, in addition to helping educators make better use of precious classroom time when under-challenging those who are ready and capable and over-challenging other students who need more background knowledge or scaffolded instruction related to the topic.

Some raise concerns that there is no research substantiating differentiated instruction. To some extent, that's true, because differentiated instruction is not a single *thing* but a multifaceted *process*. As we have outlined in this book, that process includes evidenced-based best practices. If educators use those best practices efficiently (as well as sensitively, responsively, and intelligently), their instruction will have an impact on student learning. In describing the content and methods of differentiated instruction, in other words, we have really been describing the art of teaching. That art includes understanding and responding to the needs of students, parents, and educators themselves.

As we have seen in this book, certain conditions need to exist for students to succeed. They require, for example, strong teacher-student relationships and strong classroom communities of supportive and empathic peers. Flexible groupings are just one of the ideas we've outlined in this book for building those relationships and communities, as well as for developing strong social skills, engaging in collaborative experience, and learning to think creatively. Students also need respectful tasks that will engage, excite, and challenge them, rather than leave them bored or frustrated. To achieve maximum learning, students need clear, targeted standards, so they can articulate and internalize information as they move through the learning experience. They also need scaffolded instruction that offers them a path toward independent implementation of even the most challenging ideas and activities. With an understanding of the big picture, and a series of structured and well-supported experiences to help them bring that picture into focus, students can apply its lessons in their own lives.

Helping parents and guardians understand differentiation is yet another facet of the art of teaching, which plays a key role in the implementation of differentiated instruction. Like all of us, parents understand innately that all people are unique. Most can articulate their own unique qualities as well as those of their children, yet they still tend to revert to the traditional one-size-fits-all thinking about what school *should* be like. Even in a world of rapid change and unpredictable technological developments, they cling to their own memories of the classroom experience. Educators have to find ways to ease parents out of this fixed mindset and encourage them to embrace teaching approaches that are truly responsive to research and best practices.

Teachers are constantly assessing and responding to data to provide the next step for students in their journey toward their goals. Therefore, they have to be better at sharing those data with parents and discussing the instructional content and approaches they suggest. Teachers have to communicate to parents that each student has to move forward—every learner doesn't start from the same position, but they all can achieve the necessary levels of learning and academic accomplishment to thrive in life. Differentiation is about offering their children choices and helping them find their own surest and best route to academic success.

Beyond general discussions of students' varying academic needs, teachers can provide parents access to surveys or learning inventories to discuss with their children. Grading offers another discussion point, which can be a hard sell. We are hoping schools move to competencies and continuous progress rather than grading every step of the way to really assess growth and then move forward. Teachers want parents to know that they will offer students choices, consider their learning preferences, and coach them to success. Teachers need to be certain that students understand this, as well.

Of course, teachers need their own framework of support in order to provide everything that students and their parents need to create a successful learning experience. Teaching is a complex task, and teachers need time and ongoing support to develop the mindset and dispositions necessary to sustain and persist in the sometimes arduous job of implementing best practices. Teachers must be realistic, optimistic, and persistent in their quest. They require a professional learning community, collaborative teams, and school support staff to offer help and support through trial and error, successes, and disappointments, as they work together. As we learned early in the book, all multitiered systems of instruction and intervention, including RTI, are based on the premise that schools can prevent roadblocks to academic progress with an early identification of needs followed by immediate, targeted intervention. The most important point to remember in putting those systems to work, however, is the belief that *all students can learn* when provided with appropriate, effective, evidence-based instruction. Effective practices at Tier 1 must offer *all* students high-quality curriculum and instruction. To accomplish that, teachers must have opportunities to be sufficiently trained in using research-based materials and strategies in a consistent manner.

If students learn the core curriculum from highly trained teachers, 75–80 percent (or more) of students should be able to master the standards-based content and skills for their grade-level benchmarks (Shapiro, n.d.). However, some schools wrongly assume that all students already receive effective research-based instruction in the general education classroom without addressing Tier 1, or the *forgotten tier* (Allain & Eberhardt, 2011). Many teachers may lack appropriate instructional resources or training in providing differentiated instruction within Tier 1. Differentiation, scaffolding, and the variety of skills and strategies we have described in this book must be in every teacher's repertoire in order to keep students from falling behind and to maximize learning opportunities for all students.

When teachers are not part of a professional learning community and do not share common goals with colleagues, they may feel isolated and reluctant to seek help from their peers. Within collaborative teams, teachers take collective responsibility for student learning, investigate the extensive body of research-based strategies, and receive the appropriate professional development as needed. In order to maximize student learning every year, teachers also need to continually improve their own skill sets. Attending high-quality professional development, seeking out high-impact differentiated strategies, and keeping current on new technology innovations are all part of a teaching professional's responsibility to continually get better at their craft. When a significant number of students do not demonstrate success with the core curriculum, collaborative teams analyze instructional strategies and the curriculum to determine where to strengthen the instructional program. Acknowledging that no single educational professional has all the answers and being willing to seek help from colleagues is often the first step toward making the journey of ongoing professional growth and development.

As stated early in this book, collaborative teams must come to terms with four critical questions of the PLC at Work process in order to create and teach the kind of powerful core curriculum necessary to bring academic achievement to all students at Tier 1. Those questions are (DuFour et al., 2010):

1. What do we want our students to learn?

2. How will we know if our students are learning?

3. How will we respond when student don't learn?

4. How will we respond when they do?

Ultimately, however, there's another question every teacher must answer as they prepare to implement the instructional approaches and strategies we've outlined in this book: "Do I believe that all students can learn at high levels?" We believe that in a culture of collaboration with support from the educational leadership and with sufficient training to build teacher confidence, the answer to this question should always be, "Yes!"

The Journey Ahead

As educators travel along their professional journey, how will they know that they have done the best they can for as many students as possible? Taking time to really reflect on past processes, purpose, and progress will provide valuable data that teachers can use to increase the chances for future success. Routinely examining their efforts will help them thoughtfully assess their successes and guide them in planning next steps. Here are some questions we encourage all educators to ask themselves when determining how they currently approach the task of differentiating instruction to maximize student success and how they can plan for a more effective path forward.

▽ **"Who have I taught well?"** Teachers should identify those students who have benefited greatly from the use of a particular process or strategy and note whether this success was true for many or just a few. They also should take time to celebrate all students' learning—even if the growth is incremental.

▽ **"What aspects have I taught well?"** Are there parts of a lesson or unit that went particularly smoothly? If so, teachers should note the strategy and the classroom management systems they put in place around that experience. If they can identify the reasons why students learned those parts of the lesson effectively, educators can look for future opportunities to apply a similar technique.

▽ **"What needs revision?"** Even master teachers consider how a lesson might be better the next time they teach it. Elementary teachers may not have an opportunity to teach the same lesson again until the following year, so they must carefully consider the strategies that were successful and see how they can be adapted for upcoming lessons.

▽ **"What would *I* do differently?"** The key here is remembering the *I* in this question, to go beyond the situational blame game, as in "The students were so excited about Spirit Week that they couldn't pay attention" or "The lesson was in the afternoon on a really hot day." It also doesn't allow for "Yeah, but" statements, such as "Yeah, but these students are real behavior problems" or "Yeah, but my students are ELs." Instead, teachers must look for specific techniques, strategies, and organization they might do differently the next time to maximize student success.

▽ **"Should I adapt my next purpose and target?"** This reflection question asks teachers to consider the next step in the learning game plan. Perhaps the teacher already determined the lesson purpose or target, but as the lesson progresses, he or she considers whether to modify the next steps: "Should I reteach this lesson, add more student practice, or skip the next step altogether to avoid redundancy?"

These are just some of the questions teachers can ask themselves as they think of the yearly journey they take as educators. Teaching isn't a lockstep process that can be remotely paced or prescribed. It is a continuous process of decision making and a commitment to using best strategies first based on clear expectations and data from ongoing formative assessment. No teacher needs to make this journey alone; in almost every learning environment, there are other committed colleagues who share the collective focus on helping all learners be successful. If teachers become complacent, we run the risk of lowering the quality of our commitment, our work, and our end product. That complacency can put student achievement at risk. We have offered this in-depth look at best practices for delivering daily differentiated instruction to give teachers the ideas, techniques, and tools they need to continue to learn and grow their educational repertoire even as they help their students learn and progress toward their own academic achievement. We hope these offerings will help every educator strive to be the best teacher he or she can be.

References and Resources

Achieve the Core. (2015). *Professional development: Understanding text-dependent questions.* Accessed at http://achievethecore.org/page/396/professional-development-understanding -text-dependent-questions-detail-pg on April 7, 2015.

ACT. (2006). *Reading between the lines: What the ACT reveals about college readiness in reading.* Iowa City, IA: Author. Accessed at www.act.org/research/policymakers/pdf/reading_report.pdf on March 30, 2015.

Adams, M. J. (2009). The challenge of advanced texts: The interdependence of reading and learning. In E. H. Hiebert (Ed.), *Reading more, reading better: Are American students reading enough of the right stuff?* (pp. 163–189). New York: Guilford Press.

Aikens, N. L., & Barbarin, O. (2008). Socioeconomic differences in reading trajectories: The contribution of family, neighborhood, and school contexts. *Journal of Educational Psychology, 100*(2), 235–251.

Ainsworth, L. (2003a). *Power standards: Identifying the standards that matter the most.* Denver, CO: Advanced Learning Press.

Ainsworth, L. (2003b). *"Unwrapping" the standards: A simple process to make standards manageable.* Englewood, CO: Lead + Learn Press.

Ainsworth, L. (2007). Common formative assessments: The centerpiece of an integrated standards-based assessment system. In D. Reeves (Ed.), *Ahead of the curve: The power of assessment to transform teaching and learning.* Bloomington, IN: Solution Tree Press.

Ainsworth, L. (2011, April 19). *Rigorous curriculum design for the future* [Keynote address]. Englewood, CO: Leadership and Learning Center. Presented at the 2011 Common Core State Standards Conference—Moving to Action.

Allain, J. K., & Eberhardt, N. C. (2011). *RtI: The forgotten tier: A practical guide for building a data-driven Tier 1 instructional process.* Stockton, KS: Rowe.

Almarode, J., & Miller, A. M. (2013). *Captivate, activate, and invigorate the student brain in science and math, grades 6–12.* Thousand Oaks, CA: Corwin Press.

Anderson, L. W., & Krathwohl, D. R. (Eds.). (2001). *A taxonomy for learning, teaching, and assessing: A revision of Bloom's taxonomy of educational objectives.* New York: Longman.

Anderson, T. H., & Armbruster, B. B. (1984). Studying. In P. D. Pearson, R. Barr, M. L. Kamil, & P. Mosenthal (Eds.), *Handbook of reading research* (Vol. 1, pp. 657–679). New York: Longman.

Armstrong, J. S. (2012). Natural learning in higher education. In N. M. Seel (Ed.), *Encyclopedia of the sciences of learning* (Vol. 1, pp. 2426–2433). New York: Springer.

Aronson, E., Blaney, N., Stephan, C., Sikes, J., & Snapp, M. (1978). *The jigsaw classroom*. Beverly Hills, CA: SAGE.

Assouline, S. G., Nicpon, M. F., & Huber, D. H. (2006). The impact of vulnerabilities and strengths on the academic experiences of twice-exceptional students: A message to school counselors. *Professional School Counseling, 10*(1), 14–24.

Ausubel, D. P. (1968). *Educational psychology: A cognitive view*. New York: Holt, Rinehart, and Winston.

Bailey, K., Jakicic, C., & Spiller, J. (2014). *Collaborating for success with the Common Core: A toolkit for Professional Learning Communities at Work*. Bloomington, IN: Solution Tree Press.

Barron, B., & Darling-Hammond, L. (2008). *Teaching for meaningful learning: A review of research on inquiry-based and cooperative learning*. San Rafael, CA: Edutopia. Accessed at www.edutopia .org/pdfs/edutopia-teaching-for-meaningful-learning.pdf on April 7, 2015.

Battistich, V., Schaps, E., & Wilson, N. (2004). Effects of an elementary school intervention on students' "connectedness" to school and social adjustment during middle school. *Journal of Primary Prevention, 24*(3), 243–262.

Baumann, J. F., & Kame'enui, E. J. (Eds.). (2004). *Vocabulary instruction: Research to practice*. New York: Guilford Press.

Beck, I. L., McKeown, M. G., & Kucan, L. (2008). *Creating robust vocabulary: Frequently asked questions and extended examples*. New York: Guilford Press.

Beck, I. L., McKeown, M. G., & Kucan, L. (2013). *Bringing words to life: Robust vocabulary instruction* (2nd ed.). New York: Guilford Press.

Beck, R. H. (1956). *The three R's plus: What today's schools are trying to do and why*. Minneapolis: University of Minnesota Press.

Beers, K. (2003). *When kids can't read, what teachers can do: A guide for teachers 6–12*. Portsmouth, NH: Heinemann.

Bennett, B., & Rolheiser, C. (2001). *Beyond Monet: The artful science of instructional integration*. Toronto, Canada: Bookation.

Bennett, B., Rolheiser, C., & Stevahn, L. (1991). *Cooperative learning: Where heart meets mind*. Toronto, Canada: Educational Connections.

Berry, D., & O'Connor, E. (2010). Behavioral risk, teacher–child relationships, and social skill development across middle childhood: A child-by-environment analysis of change. *Journal of Applied Developmental Psychology, 31*(1), 1–14.

Birch, S. H., & Ladd, G. W. (1997). The teacher–child relationship and children's early school adjustment. *Journal of School Psychology, 35*(1), 61–79.

Birch, S. H., & Ladd, G. W. (1998). Children's interpersonal behaviors and the teacher–child relationship. *Developmental Psychology, 34*(5), 934–946.

Black, S. (2006). Respecting differences: Diverse learners can blossom in culturally responsive classrooms. *American School Board Journal, 193*(1).

Black, P., Harrison, C., Lee, C., Marshall, B., & Wiliam, D. (2004). Working inside the black box: Assessment for learning in the classroom. *Phi Delta Kappan, 86*(1), 8–21.

Blackburn, B. R. (2008). *Rigor is not a four-letter word*. Larchmont, NY: Eye on Education.

Blakemore, S.-J. (2010). The developing social brain: Implications for education. *Neuron, 65*(6), 744–747.

Blakemore, S.-J., Burnett, S., & Dahl, R. E. (2010). The role of puberty in the developing adolescent brain. *Human Brain Mapping, 31*(6), 926–933.

Bloom, B. S. (1968). Learning for mastery. *Evaluation Comment, 1*(2), 1–12.

Boss, S. (2014, September 16). The Hattie effect: What's essential for effective PBL? *Edutopia*. Accessed at www.edutopia.org/blog/hattie-effect-whats-essential-effective-pbl-suzie-boss July 10, 2015.

Bower, H. A., & Powers, J. D. (2009). What is rigor? A qualitative analysis of one school's definition. *Academic Leadership Live: The Online Journal, 7*(4). Accessed at https://literacymethods .wikispaces.com/file/view/rigor+academic+leadership.pdf on November 24, 2014.

Brooks, R., & Goldstein, S. (2008). The mindset of teachers capable of fostering resilience in students. *Canadian Journal of School Psychology, 23*(1), 114–126.

Brown, D. F. (2003). Urban teachers' use of culturally responsive management strategies. *Theory Into Practice, 42*(4), 277–282.

Brown, S. (2009). *Play: How it shapes the brain, opens the imagination, and invigorates the soul.* New York: Avery.

Buffum, A., Mattos, M., & Weber, C. (2010). The why behind RTI. *Educational Leadership, 68*(2), 10–16.

Buffum, A., Mattos, M., & Weber, C. (2012). *Simplifying response to intervention: Four essential guiding principles.* Bloomington, IN: Solution Tree Press.

Burgess, D. (2012). *Teach like a pirate: Increase student engagement, boost your creativity, and transform your life as an educator.* San Diego, CA: Dave Burgess Consulting.

Caine, R. N., & Caine, G. (1994). *Making connections: Teaching and the human brain.* Menlo Park, CA: Addison-Wesley.

Cammarota, J. (2007). A social justice approach to achievement: Guiding Latina/o students toward educational attainment with a challenging, socially relevant curriculum. *Equity and Excellence in Education, 40*(1), 87–96.

Center for Public Education. (2006). *High-stakes testing and effects on instruction: Research review.* Accessed at www.centerforpubliceducation.org/Main-Menu/Instruction/High-stakes -testing-and-effects-on-instruction-At-a-glance/High-stakes-testing-and-effects-on -instruction-Research-review.html#sthash.wOMz5z8L.dpuf on July 22, 2015.

Chall, J. S. (1996). American reading achievement: Should we worry? *Research in the Teaching of English, 30*(3), 303–310.

Chall, J. S., & Dale, E. (1995). *Readability revisited: The new Dale-Chall readability formula.* Cambridge, MA: Brookline Books.

Chaltain, S. (2014, October 7). We're failing to prepare our kids for the impending robot takeover. Here's what we should teach them. *Washington Post*. Accessed at www.washingtonpost .com/posteverything/wp/2014/10/07/were-failing-to-prepare-our-kids-for-the-impending -robot-takeover-heres-what-we-should-teach-them on March 30, 2015.

Chapman, C., & Vagle, N. (2011). *Motivating students: 25 strategies to light the fire of engagement.* Bloomington, IN: Solution Tree Press.

Charney, R. S. (2002). *Teaching children to care: Classroom management for ethical and academic growth, K–8* (Revised ed.). Turners Fall, MA: Northeast Foundation for Children.

Chen, J. (2006). *Flow in games: Introduction.* Accessed at www.jenovachen.com/flowingames /introduction.htm on May 16, 2008.

Cole, R. W. (Ed.). (2008). *Educating everybody's children: Diverse teaching strategies for diverse learners* (Revised and expanded 2nd ed.). Alexandria, VA: Association for Supervision and Curriculum Development.

Coleman, M. R. (2005). Academic strategies that work for gifted students with learning disabilities. *Teaching Exceptional Children, 38*(1), 28–32.

Coley, R. J. (2002, March). *An uneven start: Indicators of inequality in school readiness* (Policy Information Report). Princeton, NJ: Educational Testing Service. Accessed at www.ets.org /Media/Research/pdf/PICUNEVENSTART.pdf on March 30, 2015.

Collins, J. (2005). *Good to great and the social sectors: A monograph to accompany Good to Great.* New York: HarperCollins.

Collins, J. (2009). *How the mighty fall: And why some companies never give in.* New York: HarperCollins.

Costa, A. L., & Kallick, B. (2008). *Learning and leading with habits of mind: 16 essential characteristics for success.* Alexandria, VA: Association for Supervision and Curriculum Development.

Covey, S. R. (1989). *The seven habits of highly effective people: Restoring the character ethic.* New York: Simon & Schuster.

Croninger, R. G., & Lee, V. E. (2001). Social capital and dropping out of high school: Benefits to at-risk students of teachers' support and guidance. *Teachers College Record, 103*(4), 548–581.

Csikszentmihalyi, M. (1990). *Flow: The psychology of optimal experience.* New York: Harper & Row.

Cunningham, A. E., & Stanovich, K. E. (1997). Early reading acquisition and its relation to reading experience and ability 10 years later. *Developmental Psychology, 33*(6), 934–945.

Cunningham, H. (2005). *Children and childhood in western society since 1500* (2nd ed.). New York: Routledge.

Daggett, W. R. (2008). *Achieving academic excellence through rigor and relevance.* Rexford, NY: International Center for Leadership in Education. Accessed at www.leadered.com/pdf/Achieving _Academic_Excellence_2014.pdf on March 30, 2015.

Damasio, A. R. (1994). *Descartes' error: Emotion, reason, and the human brain.* New York: Putnam.

Damasio, A. (2003). *Looking for Spinoza: Joy, sorrow, and the feeling brain.* New York: Harcourt.

Daniels, D. H., & Perry, K. E. (2003). "Learner-centered" according to children. *Theory Into Practice, 42*(2), 102–108.

Daniels, H., & Bizar, M. (2005). *Teaching the best practice way: Methods that matter, K–12.* Portland, ME: Stenhouse.

Darling-Hammond, L. (2006). Securing the right to learn: Policy and practice for powerful teaching and learning. *Educational Researcher, 35*(7), 13–24.

Dean, C. B., Hubbell, E. R., Pitler, H., & Stone, B. J. (2012). *Classroom instruction that works: Research-based strategies for increasing student achievement* (2nd ed.). Alexandria, VA: Association for Supervision and Curriculum Development.

Deci, E. L., & Ryan, R. M. (1985). *Intrinsic motivation and self-determination in human behavior.* New York: Plenum Press.

Deci, E. L., & Ryan, R. M. (Eds.). (2002). *Handbook of self-determination research.* Rochester, NY: University of Rochester Press.

Denton, C. A., Cirino, P. T., Barth, A. E., Romain, M., Vaughn, S., Wexler, J., et al. (2011). An experimental study of scheduling and duration of "Tier 2" first-grade reading intervention. *Journal of Research on Educational Effectiveness, 4*(3), 208–230.

Dewey, J. (1902). *The child and the curriculum.* Chicago: University of Chicago Press.

Dewey, J. (1933). *How we think: A restatement of the relation of reflective thinking to the educative process.* Boston: D. C. Heath.

Dewey, J. (1938). *Experience and education.* New York: Kappa Delta Pi.

Diamond, M. C., & Hopson, J. (1998). *Magic trees of the mind: How to nurture your child's intelligence, creativity, and healthy emotions from birth through adolescence.* New York: Plume.

Diamond, M. C., Lindner, B., & Raymond, A. (1967). Extensive cortical depth measurements and neuron size increases in the cortex of environmentally enriched rats. *Journal of Comparative Neurology, 131*(3), 357–364.

Donohue, K. M., Perry, K. E., & Weinstein, R. S. (2003). Teachers' classroom practices and children's rejection by their peers. *Journal of Applied Developmental Psychology, 24*(1), 91–118.

Donovan, M. S., & Bransford, J. D. (Eds.). (2005). *How students learn: History, mathematics, and science in the classroom.* Washington, DC: National Academies Press.

Doyle, M., & Straus, D. (1976). *How to make meetings work.* New York: Playboy Press.

Drapeau, P. (2014). *Sparking student creativity: Practical ways to promote innovative thinking and problem solving.* Alexandria, VA: Association for Supervision and Curriculum Development.

Draper, A. G., & Moeller, G. H. (1971). We think with words (therefore, to improve thinking, teach vocabulary). *Phi Delta Kappan, 52*(8), 482–484.

Duch, B., Groh, S. E., & Allen, D. E. (Eds.). (2001). *The power of problem-based learning.* Sterling, VA: Stylus.

Duffett, A., Farkas, S., Rotherham, A. J., & Silva, E. (2008, May). *Waiting to be won over: Teachers speak on the profession, unions, and reform* (Education Sector Reports). Washington, DC: Education Sector. Accessed at www.educationsector.org/usr_doc/WaitingToBeWonOver.pdf on March 30, 2015.

DuFour, R., DuFour, R., Eaker, R., & Many, T. (2010). *Learning by doing: A handbook for Professional Learning Communities at Work* (2nd ed.). Bloomington, IN: Solution Tree Press.

DuFour, R., & Marzano, R. J. (2011). *Leaders of learning: How district, school, and classroom leaders improve student achievement.* Bloomington, IN: Solution Tree Press.

DuFour, R., & Mattos, M. (2013). How do principals really improve schools? *Educational Leadership, 70*(7), 34–40.

Dunn, R., & Dunn, K. (1993). *Teaching secondary students through their individual learning styles: Practical approaches for grades 7–12.* Boston: Allyn & Bacon.

Dunn, R., & Dunn, K. (Eds.). (1998). *Practical approaches to individualizing staff development for adults.* Westport, CT: Praeger.

Dunn, R., & Dunn, K. (1999). *The complete guide to the learning styles inservice system.* Boston: Allyn & Bacon.

Dunn, R., Thies, A. P., & Honigsfeld, A. (2001). *Synthesis of the Dunn and Dunn learning-style model research: Analysis from a neuropsychological perspective.* New York: Center for the Study of Learning and Teaching Styles, St. John's University.

Dweck, C. S. (2006). *Mindset: The new psychology of success.* New York: Ballantine Books.

Eber, P. A., & Parker, T. S. (2007). Assessing student learning: Applying Bloom's taxonomy. *Human Service Education, 27*(1), 45–53.

Echevarria, J., Vogt, M., & Short, D. J. (2012). *Making content comprehensible for English learners: The SIOP model* (4th ed.). Boston: Pearson.

Edmonds, R. (1979, October). Effective schools for the urban poor. *Educational Leadership, 37*, 15–27.

Elkind, D. (2007). *The hurried child: Growing up too fast too soon* (25th anniversary ed.). Cambridge, MA: Da Capo Press.

Elley, W. B. (1992). *How in the world do students read?: IEA study of reading literacy.* The Hague, the Netherlands: International Association for the Evaluation of Educational Achievement.

Erkens, C., & Twadell, E. (2012). *Leading by design: An action framework for PLC at Work leaders.* Bloomington, IN: Solution Tree Press.

Fensterwald, J. (2014, October 21). *Report urges revamping student testing.* Accessed at http://edsource.org/2014/report-urges-revamping-student-testing/68811#.VRrFi_nF8xM on March 30, 2015.

Fisher, D., & Frey, N. (2008). *Better learning through structured teaching: A framework for the gradual release of responsibility.* Alexandria, VA: Association for Supervision and Curriculum Development.

Fisher, D., & Frey, N. (2012). Text-dependent questions. *Principal Leadership, 13*(1), 70–73.

Fisher, D., & Frey, N. (2013). *Common Core English language arts in a PLC at Work, grades 3–5.* Bloomington, IN: Solution Tree Press.

Fisher, D., & Frey, N. (2015). *Unstoppable learning.* Bloomington, IN: Solution Tree Press.

Flynn, H. (n.d.). *Tiered lesson plan: "Polygon scavenger hunt."* Accessed at www.diffcentral.com /examples/2ndMath.pdf on April 7, 2015.

Ford, D. Y. (2005). Welcome all students to room 202: Creating culturally responsive classrooms. *Gifted Child Today, 28*(4), 28–30.

Four corners. (n.d.). *Four corners.* Accessed at www.angelfire.com/ok/freshenglish/fourcorners.html on June 9, 2015.

Frayer, D., Fredrick, W. C., & Klausmeier, H. J. (1969). *A schema for testing the level of concept mastery: Report from the project on situational variables and efficiency of concept learning.* Madison, WI: Wisconsin Center for Education Research.

Freedman, J. (2007). *At the heart of leadership: How to get results with emotional intelligence.* Freedom, CA: Six Seconds.

Fullan, M. (2007). *The new meaning of educational change* (4th ed.). New York: Teachers College Press.

Fullan, M. (2013). The new pedagogy: Students and teachers as learning partners. *LEARNing Landscapes, 6*(2), 23–29.

Gallagher, S. A. (1997). Problem-based learning: Where did it come from, what does it do, and where is it going? *Journal for the Education of the Gifted, 20*(4), 332–362.

Gallimore, R., Ermeling, B. A., Saunders, W. M., & Goldenberg, C. (2009). Moving the learning of teaching closer to practice: Teacher education implications of school-based inquiry teams. *Elementary School Journal, 109*(5), 537–553.

Gardner, H. (2004). *Frames of mind: The theory of multiple intelligences* (10th anniversary ed.). New York: Basic Books.

Gauthier, A., Laurence, M., Thirkill, L., & Dorman, S. (2012). Examining school-based pedometer step counts among children in grades 3 to 6 using different timetables. *Journal of School Health, 82*(7), 311–317.

Gay, G. (2000). *Culturally responsive teaching: Theory, research, and practice.* New York: Teachers College Press.

Gay, G. (2002). Preparing for culturally responsive teaching. *Journal of Teacher Education, 53*(2), 106–116.

Geake, J. G. (2009). *The brain at school: Educational neuroscience in the classroom.* New York: Open University Press.

Gee, J. P. (2005). Learning by design: Good video games as learning machines. *E-Learning and Digital Media, 2*(1), 5–16.

Gee, J. P. (2012). Foreword. In C. Steinkuehler, K. Squire, & S. Barab (Eds.), *Games, learning, and society: Learning and meaning in the digital age* (pp. xvii–xx). New York: Cambridge University Press.

Gibbs, J. (1998). *Tribus: Una nueva forma de aprender y convivir juntos* [Spanish ed.]. Windsor, CA: CenterSource Systems.

Gibbs, J. (2001). *Discovering gifts in middle school: Learning in a caring culture called Tribes.* Windsor, CA: CenterSource Systems.

Gibbs, J. (2006). *Reaching all by creating Tribes learning communities.* Windsor, CA: CenterSource Systems.

Gibbs, J., & Ushijima, T. (2008). *Engaging all by creating high school learning communities.* Windsor, CA: CenterSource Systems.

Giedd, J. N., Blumenthal, J., Jeffries, N. O., Castellanos, F. X., Liu, H., Zijdenbos, A., et al. (1999). Brain development during childhood and adolescence: A longitudinal MRI study. *Nature Neuroscience, 2*(10), 861–863.

Given, B. K. (2002). *Teaching to the brain's natural learning systems.* Alexandria, VA: Association for Supervision and Curriculum Development.

Glasser, W. (1986). *Control theory in the classroom.* New York: Perennial Library.

Glasser, W. (1990). *The quality school: Managing students without coercion.* New York: Perennial Library.

Glasser, W. (1998). *Choice theory: A new psychology of personal freedom.* New York: HarperCollins.

Glasser, W. (2013). *Take charge of your life: How to get what you need with choice theory psychology.* Bloomington, IN: iUniverse.

Goleman, D. (2006a, December 27). Aiming for the brain's sweet spot [Blog post]. *New York Times.* Accessed at http://opinionator.blogs.nytimes.com/2006/12/27/aiming-for-the-brains-sweet-spot on May 12, 2011.

Goleman, D. (2006b). *Emotional intelligence: Why it can matter more than IQ* (10th anniversary ed.). New York: Bantam Books.

Goleman, D. (2006c). The socially intelligent leader. *Educational Leadership, 64*(1), 76–81.

Goleman, D. (2013). *Focus: The hidden driver of excellence.* New York: HarperCollins.

Gopnik, A., Meltzoff, A. N., & Kuhl, P. K. (1999). *The scientist in the crib: What early learning tells us about the mind.* New York: William Morrow.

Great Schools Partnership. (2013). Learning progression. *Glossary of Education Reform.* Accessed at http://edglossary.org/learning-progression on July 21, 2015.

Great Schools Partnership. (2015). Scaffolding. *Glossary of Education Reform.* Accessed at http://edglossary.org/scaffolding on April 7, 2015.

Gregorc, A. F. (1985). *Inside styles: Beyond the basics.* Maynard, MA: Gabriel Systems.

Gregory, A., & Ripski, M. B. (2008). Adolescent trust in teachers: Implications for behavior in the high school classroom. *School Psychology Review, 37*(3), 337–353.

Gregory, G. H. (2005). *Differentiating instruction with style: Aligning teacher and learner intelligences for maximum achievement.* Thousand Oaks, CA: Corwin Press.

Gregory, G. H. (2013). *Differentiated instructional strategies professional learning guide: One size doesn't fit all* (3rd ed.). Thousand Oaks, CA: Corwin Press.

Gregory, G. H., & Chapman, C. (2007). *Differentiated instructional strategies: One size doesn't fit all* (2nd ed.). Thousand Oaks, CA: Corwin Press.

Gregory, G. H., & Kaufeldt, M. (2012). *Think big, start small: How to differentiate instruction in a brain-friendly classroom.* Bloomington, IN: Solution Tree Press.

Gregory, G. H., & Parry, T. (2006). *Designing brain-compatible learning* (3rd ed.). Thousand Oaks, CA: Corwin Press.

Gurian, M. (2001). *Boys and girls learn differently!: A guide for teachers and parents.* San Francisco: Jossey-Bass.

Hallowell, E. M. (2011). *Shine: Using brain science to get the best from your people.* Boston: Harvard Business Review Press.

Hamre, B. K., & Pianta, R. C. (2001). Early teacher–child relationships and the trajectory of children's school outcomes through eighth grade. *Child Development, 72*(2), 625–638.

Harris, B. (2010). *Battling boredom: 99 strategies to spark student engagement.* Larchmont, NY: Eye on Education.

Hattie, J. (2009). *Visible learning: A synthesis of over 800 meta-analyses relating to achievement.* New York: Routledge.

Hattie, J. (2012). *Visible learning for teachers: Maximizing impact on learning.* New York: Routledge.

Hattie, J., & Timperley, H. (2007). The power of feedback. *Review of Educational Research, 77*(1), 81–112.

Hattie, J., & Yates, G. (2014). *Visible learning and the science of how we learn.* New York: Routledge.

Haystead, M. W., & Marzano, R. J. (2009). *Meta-analytic synthesis of studies conducted at Marzano Research on instructional strategies.* Englewood, CO: Marzano Resources. Accessed at www.marzano evaluation.com/files/Instructional_Strategies_Report_9_2_09.pdf on March 30, 2015.

Heick, T. (2013, September 27). *How to add rigor to anything.* Accessed at www.teachthought.com /learning/how-to-add-rigor-to-anything on March 30, 2015.

Herbst, S., & Davies, A. (2014). *A fresh look at grading and reporting in high schools.* Bloomington, IN: Solution Tree Press.

Hess, K. (2009). *Hess' cognitive rigor matrix & curricular examples: Applying Webb's depth-of-knowledge levels to Bloom's cognitive process dimensions—ELA.* Accessed at www.nciea.org /publications/CRM_ELA_KH11.pdf on July 22, 2015.

Hiebert, E., & Mesmer, H. A. (2013). Upping the ante of text complexity in the Common Core State Standards: Examining its potential impact on young readers. *Educational Researcher, 42*(1), 44–51. Accessed at www.researchgate.net/publication/258134755 on July 15, 2015.

Hill, J. D., & Flynn, K. M. (2006). *Classroom instruction that works with English language learners.* Alexandria, VA: Association for Supervision and Curriculum Development.

Hill, S., & Hancock, J. (1993). *Reading and writing communities.* Armadale, Australia: Curtin.

Himmele, P., & Himmele, W. (2011). *Total participation techniques: Making every student an active learner.* Alexandria, VA: Association for Supervision and Curriculum Development.

Hirst-Loucks, C., & Loucks, K. P. (2014). *Serious fun: Practical strategies to motivate and engage students.* New York: Routledge.

Honaker, J. (n.d.). *Using technology to differentiate instruction.* Accessed at www.wcs.k12.va.us/users /honaker/Differentiation.pdf on July 23, 2015.

Hord, S. M., Rutherford, W. L., Huling-Austin, L., & Hall, G. E. (1987). *Taking charge of change.* Alexandria, VA: Association for Supervision and Curriculum Development.

Hummel, T. (2014, June 19). Lesson planning with depth of knowledge and Bloom's taxonomy [Blog post]. *Thinkgate.* Accessed at www.thinkgate.com/lesson-planning-with-depth-of-knowledge on June 19, 2014.

Individuals With Disabilities Education Improvement Act of 2004, Pub. L. No. 108–446 § 300.115 (2004).

Jacobellis v. Ohio. (n.d.). In *Wikipedia.* Accessed at http://en.wikipedia.org/wiki/Jacobellis_v._Ohio on March 30, 2015.

Jensen, E., & Nickelsen, L. (2014). *Bringing the Common Core to life in K–8 classrooms: 30 strategies to build literacy skills.* Bloomington, IN: Solution Tree Press.

John Dewey. (n.d.). In *Wikipedia.* Accessed at http://en.wikipedia.org/wiki/John_Dewey on March 30, 2015.

Johnson, D. W., Johnson, R. T., & Holubec, E. J. (1998). *Cooperation in the classroom* (Rev. ed.). Edina, MN: Interaction Book.

Johnson, D. W., & Johnson, F. P. (2009). *Joining together: Group theory and group skills* (10th ed.). Upper Saddle River, NJ: Pearson.

K–3 North Carolina Assessment Think Tank. (2013). *Assessment for learning and development in K–3*. Raleigh, NC: North Carolina Department of Public Instruction. Accessed at www.dpi.state.nc.us/docs/earlylearning/k3-assessment.pdf on April 7, 2015.

Kaplan, S. N., Gould, B., & Siegel, V. (1995). *The flip book: A quick and easy method for developing differentiated learning experiences*. Calabasas, CA: Educator to Educator.

Kariuki, P., & Nash, J. (1999, November). *The relationship between multiple school transfers during elementary years and student achievement*. Paper presented at the annual conference of the Mid-South Educational Research Association, Point Clear, AL.

Kaufeldt, M. (2005). *Teachers, change your bait!: Brain-compatible differentiated instruction*. Norwalk, CT: Crown House.

Kaufeldt, M. (2010). *Begin with the brain: Orchestrating the learner-centered classroom* (2nd ed.). Thousand Oaks, CA: Corwin Press.

King, E. W. (2005). Addressing the social and emotional needs of twice-exceptional students. *Teaching Exceptional Children, 38*(1), 16–20.

King, M. B., Newmann, F. M., & Carmichael, D. L. (2009). Authentic intellectual work: Common standards for teaching social studies. *Social Education, 73*(1), 43–49.

Klem, A. M., & Connell, J. P. (2004). Relationships matter: Linking teacher support to student engagement and achievement. *Journal of School Health, 74*(7), 262–273.

Kolb, D. (1984). *Experiential learning: Experience as the source of learning and development*. Englewood Cliffs, NJ: Prentice Hall.

Lamb, A. (2007). Intellectual freedom for youth: Social technology and social networks. *Knowledge Quest, 36*(2), 38–45.

Lamb, A., & Johnson, L. (2007). An information skills workout: Wikis and collaborative writing. *Teacher Librarian, 34*(5), 57.

Langhout, R. D., Drake, P., & Rosselli, F. (2009). Classism in the university setting: Examining student antecedents and outcomes. *Journal of Diversity in Higher Education, 2*(3), 166–181.

Levine, M. (1993). *All kinds of minds: A young student's book about learning abilities and learning disorders*. Cambridge, MA: Educators Publishing Service.

Lezotte, L. (1991). *Correlates of effective schools: The first and second generation*. Okemos, MI: Effective Schools Products.

Lou, Y., Alorami, P. C., Spence, J. C., Paulsen, C., Chambers, B., & d'Apollonio, S. (1996). Within-class grouping: A meta-analysis. *Review of Educational Research, 66*(4), 423–458.

Mann, R. L. (2006). Effective teaching strategies for gifted/learning-disabled students with spatial strengths. *Journal of Secondary Gifted Education, 17*(2), 112–121.

Marlowe, C. A. (2012). *The effect of the flipped classroom on student achievement and stress*. Master's paper, Montana State University, Bozeman, Montana. Accessed at http://scholarworks.montana.edu/xmlui/bitstream/handle/1/1790/MarloweC0812.pdf?sequence=1 on July 23, 2015.

Marzano, R. J. (2003). *What works in schools: Translating research into action*. Alexandria, VA: Association for Supervision and Curriculum Development.

Marzano, R. J. (2007). *The art and science of teaching: A comprehensive framework for effective instruction*. Alexandria, VA: Association for Supervision and Curriculum Development.

Marzano, R. J. (2010). The art and science of teaching/using games to enhance student achievement. *Educational Leadership, 67*(5), 71–72.

Marzano, R. J. (2013, May 23). *Proficiency scales for the Common Core* [Webinar]. Accessed at http://pages.solution-tree.com/rs/solutiontree/images/LOWRES_35MEU_MRL_ProficiencyScalesForCC_webinar.pdf on March 30, 2015.

Marzano, R. J., & Brown, J. L. (2009). *A handbook for the art and science of teaching.* Alexandria, VA: Association for Supervision and Curriculum Development.

Marzano, R. J., & Pickering, D. J. (2005). *Building academic vocabulary: Teacher's manual.* Alexandria, VA: Association for Supervision and Curriculum Development.

Marzano, R. J., Pickering, D. J., & Pollock, J. E. (2001). *Classroom instruction that works: Research-based strategies for increasing student achievement.* Alexandria, VA: Association for Supervision and Curriculum Development.

Marzano, R. J., Yanoski, D. C., Hoegh, J. K., & Simms, J. A. (2013). *Using Common Core standards to enhance classroom instruction and assessment.* Bloomington, IN: Marzano Resources.

Maslow, A. H. (1968). *Toward a psychology of being* (2nd ed.). Princeton, NJ: Van Nostrand.

Mayer, R. E. (2010). Applying the science of learning to instruction in school subjects. In R. J. Marzano (Ed.), *On excellence in teaching* (pp. 93–111). Bloomington, IN: Solution Tree Press.

McCarthy, B. (2000). *About teaching: 4MAT in the classroom.* Wauconda, IL: About Learning.

McCarthy, B., & McCarthy, D. (2006). *Teaching around the 4MAT cycle: Designing instruction for diverse learners with diverse learning styles.* Thousand Oaks, CA: Corwin Press.

McTighe, J., & Lyman, F. T. (1988). Cueing thinking in the classroom: The promise of theory-embedded tools. *Educational Leadership, 45*(7), 18–24.

McTighe, J., & Wiggins, G. (2013). *Essential questions: Opening doors to student understanding.* Alexandria, VA: Association for Supervision and Curriculum Development.

Medina, J. (2008). *Brain rules: 12 principles for surviving and thriving at work, home, and school.* Seattle, WA: Pear Press.

Mindset Works. (2002). *Mindset Works EducatorKit: Tools for teachers.* Accessed at http://oagct.org/wp-content/uploads/growth-mindset-feedback-tool.pdf on April 7, 2015

Mistry, R. S., Benner, A. D., Tan, C. S., & Kim, S. Y. (2009). Family economic stress and academic well-being among Chinese-American youth: The influence of adolescents' perceptions of economic strain. *Journal of Family Psychology, 23*(3), 279–290.

Mitra, S. (2013a, February). *Sugata Mitra: Build a school in the cloud* [Video file]. Accessed at www.ted.com/talks/sugata_mitra_build_a_school_in_the_cloud on April 7, 2015.

Mitra, S. (2013b, February 27). We need schools . . . not factories. *Huffington, 39.* Accessed at www.huffingtonpost.com/sugata-mitra/2013-ted-prize_b_2767598.html on March 30, 2015.

Montgomery, W. (2000). Literature discussion in the elementary school classroom: Developing cultural understanding. *Multicultural Education, 8*(1), 33–36.

Morgan, P. L., Farkas, G., Hillemeier, M. M., & Maczuga, S. (2009). Risk factors for learning-related behavior problems at 24 months of age: Population-based estimates. *Journal of Abnormal Child Psychology, 37*(3), 401–413.

Morrison, W. F., & Rizza, M. G. (2007). Creating a toolkit for identifying twice-exceptional students. *Journal for the Education of the Gifted, 31*(1), 57–76.

Muijs, D., Harris, A., Chapman, C., Stoll, L., & Russ, J. (2004). Improving schools in socioeconomically disadvantaged areas: A review of research evidence. *School Effectiveness and School Improvement, 15*(2), 149–175.

Murphy, C. (2011). *Why games work and the science of learning.* Accessed at www.gametools.dk/files/papers/WhyGamesWork_TheScienceOfLearning_CMurphy_2011.pdf on March 30, 2015.

Nakamura, J. (1988). Optimal experience and the uses of talent. In M. Csikszentmihalyi & I. Csikszentmihalyi (Eds.), *Optimal experience* (pp. 319–326). Cambridge, England: Cambridge University Press.

Nakamura, J., & Csikszentmihalyi, M. (2009). Flow theory and research. In S. J. Lopez & C. R. Snyder (Eds.), *The Oxford handbook of positive psychology* (2nd ed., pp. 195–206). New York: Oxford University Press.

National Center for Education Statistics. (2008). Percentage of high school dropouts among persons 16 through 24 years old (status dropout rate), by income level, and percentage distribution of status dropouts, by labor force status and educational attainment: 1970 through 2007. In *Digest of Education Statistics*. Accessed at http://nces.ed.gov/programs/digest/d08/tables/dt08_110.asp on March 30, 2015.

The National Center for Fair and Open Testing. (2009, March). *Position paper on assessment for learning from the Third International Conference on Assessment for Learning.* Paper presented at the Third International Conference on Assessment for Learning, Dunedin, New Zealand. Accessed at www .fairtest.org/position-paper-assessment-learning on October 20, 2014.

National Council of Teachers of English. (2013, October 21). *Formative assessment that* truly *informs instruction* (NCTE position statement). Accessed at www.ncte.org/positions/statements/formative -assessment on April 7, 2015.

National Governors Association Center for Best Practices & Council of Chief State School Officers. (n.d.a). *Common Core State Standards for English language arts and literacy in history/social studies, science, and technical subjects: Appendix A—Research supporting key elements of the standards.* Washington, DC: Author. Accessed at www.corestandards.org/assets/Appendix_A.pdf on March 30, 2015.

National Governors Association Center for Best Practices & Council of Chief State School Officers. (n.d.b). *Common Core State Standards for English language arts and literacy in history/social studies, science, and technical subjects: Appendix B—Text exemplars and sample performance tasks.* Washington, DC: Author. Accessed at www.corestandards.org/assets/Appendix_B.pdf on March 30, 2015.

National Governors Association Center for Best Practices & Council of Chief State School Officers. (2010a). *Common Core State Standards for English language arts and literacy in history/social studies, science, and technical subjects.* Washington, DC: Authors. Accessed at www.corestandards.org/ELA -Literacy on May 21, 2015.

National Governors Association Center for Best Practices & Council of Chief State School Officers. (2010b). *Common Core State Standards for mathematics.* Washington, DC: Author. Accessed at www.corestandards.org/Math on May 21, 2015.

National Institute of Mental Health. (2011). *The teen brain: Still under construction* (NIH Publication No. 11–4929). Bethesda, MD: Author. Accessed at www.nimh.nih.gov/health/publications/the -teen-brain-still-under-construction/teen-brain_141903.pdf on March 30, 2015

NGSS Lead States. (2013). *Next Generation Science Standards: For states, by states.* Washington, DC: The National Academies Press.

Nebraska Department of Education. (2009). *Student-friendly language arts standards for grade five.* Lincoln, NE: Author. Accessed at www.education.ne.gov/read/StudentFriendly Standards/5thNumberingTable.pdf on April 7, 2015.

Nebraska Department of Education. (2014). *Nebraska English language arts standards.* Lincoln, NE: Author. Accessed at www.education.ne.gov/AcademicStandards/index.html on July 8, 2015.

Newmann, F. M. (1990). Higher order thinking in teaching social studies: A rationale for the assessment of classroom thoughtfulness. *Journal of Curriculum Studies, 22*(1), 41–56.

Nieto, S. (1996). *Affirming diversity: The sociopolitical context of multicultural education* (2nd ed.). White Plains, NY: Longman.

Northwestern University Feinberg School of Medicine. (n.d.). *Problem based learning (PBL).* Accessed at www.feinberg.northwestern.edu/sites/pa/education/problem-based-learning.html on April 7, 2015.

Oakes, J. (1985). *Keeping track: How schools structure inequality.* New Haven, CT: Yale University Press.

Oczkus, L. D. (2003). *Reciprocal teaching at work: Strategies for improving reading comprehension.* Newark, DE: International Reading Association.

Odden, A. R., & Archibald, S. J. (2009). *Doubling student performance . . . and finding the resources to do it.* Thousand Oaks, CA: Corwin Press.

Orr, A. J. (2003). Black-white differences in achievement: The importance of wealth. *Sociology of Education, 76*(4), 281–304.

Palardy, G. J. (2008). Differential school effects among low, middle, and high social class composition schools: A multiple group, multilevel latent growth curve analysis. *School Effectiveness and School Improvement, 19*(1), 21–49.

Paley, V. G. (1992). *You can't say you can't play.* Cambridge, MA: Harvard University Press.

Palincsar, A. S., & Brown, A. L. (1984). Reciprocal teaching of comprehension-fostering and comprehension-monitoring activities. *Cognition and Instruction, 1*(2), 117–175.

Panksepp, J. (1998). *Affective neuroscience: The foundations of human and animal emotions.* New York: Oxford University Press.

Peebles, L., & Kirkwood, K. J. (2011). The views of teachers toward the balanced day schedule in five elementary pilot schools in southern Ontario. *Teaching & Learning, 6*(1), 83–94.

Perry, K. E., & Weinstein, R. S. (1998). The social context of early schooling and children's school adjustment. *Educational Psychologist, 33*(4), 177–194.

Pfeffer, J., & Sutton, R. I. (2006). *Hard facts, dangerous half-truths, and total nonsense: Profiting from evidence-based management.* Boston: Harvard Business School Press.

Piaget, J. (1997). *The child's conception of the world* (J. Tomlinson & A. Tomlinson, Trans.). New York: Routledge.

Piaget, J., & Inhelder, B. (1969). *The psychology of the child* (H. Weaver, Trans.). New York: Basic Books.

Pianta, R. C. (1999). *Enhancing relationships between children and teachers.* Washington, DC: American Psychological Association.

Pianta, R. C., & Hamre, B. (2001). *Students, teachers, and relationship support: User's guide.* Lutz, FL: Psychological Assessment Resources.

Piolat, A., Olive, T., & Kellogg, R. T. (2005). Cognitive effort during note taking. *Applied Cognitive Psychology, 19*(3), 291–312.

Pluralize. (n.d.). In *Oxford Dictionaries.* Accessed at www.oxforddictionaries.com/us/definition/american_english/pluralize on April 7, 2015.

Posner, M. I., & Rothbart, M. K. (2007). Research on attention networks as a model for the integration of psychological science. *Annual Review of Psychology, 58*, 1–23.

Prasse, D. P. (n.d.). *Why adopt an RTI model?* Accessed at www.rtinetwork.org/learn/what/whyrti on March 31, 2015.

Prensky, M. (2001). *Digital game-based learning.* New York: McGraw-Hill.

Ratey, J. J. (2008). *Spark: The revolutionary new science of exercise and the brain.* New York: Little, Brown.

Reeves, D. B. (2002). *Making standards work: How to implement standards-based assessments in the classroom, school, and district* (3rd ed.). Denver, CO: Advanced Learning Press.

Reis, S. M., & Renzulli, J. S. (n.d.). *Curriculum compacting: A systematic procedure for modifying the curriculum for above average ability students.* University of Connecticut: The Neag Center for Gifted

Education and Talent Development. Accessed at www.gifted.uconn.edu/sem/semart08.html on July 15, 2015.

Resnick, L. B., & Klopfer, L. E. (Eds.). (1989). *Toward the thinking curriculum: Current cognitive research* (ASCD Yearbook). Alexandria, VA: Association for Supervision and Curriculum Development.

Reynolds, G. (2010, September 15). Phys ed: Can exercise make kids smarter? [Blog post]. *New York Times.* Accessed at http://well.blogs.nytimes.com/2010/09/15/phys-ed-can-exercise-make-kids -smarter/?emc=eta1 on May 4, 2011.

Rhodes, V. L. (2005). Kids on the move: The effects of student mobility on NCLB school accountability ratings. *PennGSE Perspectives on Urban Education, 3*(3). Accessed at www.urban edjournal.org/printpdf/206 on April 7, 2015.

Riby, L. M., Law, A. S., McLaughlin, J., & Murray, J. (2011). Preliminary evidence that glucose ingestion facilitates prospective memory performance. *Nutrition Research, 31*(5), 370–377.

Rice, J. K. (2010). *The impact of teacher experience: Examining the evidence and policy implications* (Brief No. 11). Washington, DC: Urban Institute.

Ridgewood Public Schools. (2003). *Analogies: Sampler for grades K–12.* Cambridge, MA: Educators Publishing Service. Accessed at http://eps.schoolspecialty.com/EPS/media/Site-Resources /downloads/program-overviews/s-analogies.pdf on July 23, 2015.

Riggs, E. G., & Gholar, C. R. (2009). *Strategies that promote student engagement: Unleashing the desire to learn* (2nd ed.). Thousand Oaks, CA: Corwin Press.

Rimm-Kaufman, S. E., & Chiu, Y.-J. I. (2007). Promoting social and academic competence in the classroom: An intervention study examining the contribution of the *Responsive Classroom* approach. *Psychology in the Schools, 44*(4), 397–413.

Rimm-Kaufman, S. E., Curby, T. W., Grimm, K. J., Nathanson, L., & Brock, L. L. (2009). The contribution of children's self-regulation and classroom quality to children's adaptive behaviors in the kindergarten classroom. *Developmental Psychology, 45*(4), 958–972.

Rimm-Kaufman, S. E., Early, D. M., Cox, M. J., Saluja, G., Pianta, R. C., Bradley, R. H., et al. (2002). Early behavioral attributes and teachers' sensitivity as predictors of competent behavior in the kindergarten classroom. *Journal of Applied Developmental Psychology, 23*(4), 451–470.

Ritchhart, R., Church, M., & Morrison, K. (2011). *Making thinking visible: How to promote engagement, understanding, and independence for all learners.* San Francisco: Jossey-Bass.

Rodgers, R. (2011, March 2). Technology, creativity, and rigor [Blog post]. *Moss-Free Stone.* Accessed at http://mossfreestone.com/2011/03/02/technology-creativity-and-rigor on March 30, 2015.

Rohde, M. (2013). *The sketchnote handbook: The illustrated guide to visual note taking.* San Francisco: Peachpit Press.

Rogers Public Schools. (2015). *Fourth grade year at a glance.* Accessed at http://cloud.rpsar.net/edocs /YearAtGlance/4th_year_at_a_glance.pdf on July 28, 2015.

Rollins, S. P. (2014). *Learning in the fast lane: 8 ways to put all students on the road to academic success.* Alexandria, VA: Association for Supervision and Curriculum Development.

Ronis, D. L. (2007). *Problem-based learning for math and science: Integrating inquiry and the Internet.* Thousand Oaks, CA: Corwin Press.

Rowe, M. B. (1986). Wait time: Slowing down may be a way of speeding up! *Journal of Teacher Education, 37*, 43–50.

Rudasill, K. M., Prokasky, A., Tu, X., Frohn, S., Sirota, K., & Molfese, V. J. (2014). Parent vs. teacher ratings of children's shyness as predictors of language and attention skills. *Learning and Individual Differences, 34*, 57–62.

Rutledge, P. (n.d.). The positive side of video games: Part III [Blog post]. *Paperblog.* Accessed at http://en.paperblog.com/the-positive-side-of-video-games-part-iii-294723 on November 28, 2012.

Sanderson, D. R. (2003). Engaging highly transient students. *Education, 123*(3), 600–605.

Santrock, J. W. (2004). *Child development* (10th ed.). Boston: McGraw-Hill.

Schafft, K. A. (2003, April). *Low income student transiency and its effects on schools and school districts in upstate New York*. Paper presented at the Promoting the Economic and Social Vitality of Rural America: The Role of Education conference, New Orleans, LA.

Schlechty, P. C. (2011). *Engaging students: The next level of working on the work*. San Francisco: Jossey-Bass.

Schmoker, M. (2004). Tipping point: From feckless reform to substantive instructional improvement. *Phi Delta Kappan, 85*(6), 424–432.

Schoenherr, A. B. (n.d.). *Four corners teaching strategy*. Accessed at www.ehow.com/way_5809507 _four-corners-teaching-strategy.html on June 9, 2015.

Schreck, M. K. (2011). *You've got to reach them to teach them: Hard facts about the soft skills of student engagement*. Bloomington, IN: Solution Tree Press.

Shapiro, E. S. (n.d.). *Tiered instruction and intervention in a Response-to-Intervention model*. Accessed at www.rtinetwork.org/essential/tieredinstruction/tiered-instruction-and-intervention-rti-model on March 30, 2015.

Shaw, P., Greenstein, D., Lerch, J., Clasen, L., Lenroot, R., Gogtay, N., et al. (2006). Intellectual ability and cortical development in children and adolescents. *Nature, 440*(7084), 676–679.

Sheppard, R. L., & Stratton, B. D. (1993). *Reflections on becoming: Fifteen literature-based units for the young adolescent*. Columbus, OH: National Middle School Association.

Smilkstein, R. (2003). *We're born to learn: Using the brain's natural learning process to create today's curriculum*. Thousand Oaks, CA: Corwin Press.

Smith, G. E., & Throne, S. (2007). *Differentiating instruction with technology in K–5 classrooms*. Washington, DC: International Society for Technology in Education.

Sousa, D. A., & Tomlinson, C. A. (2010). *Differentiation and the brain: How neuroscience supports the learner-friendly classroom*. Bloomington, IN: Solution Tree Press.

Sowell, E. R., Thompson, P. M., Holmes, C. J., Jernigan, T. L., & Toga, A. W. (1999). In vivo evidence for post-adolescent brain maturation in frontal and striatal regions. *Nature Neuroscience, 2*(10), 859–861.

Spillane, J. P. (2000). A fifth-grade teacher's reconstruction of mathematics and literacy teaching: Exploring interactions among identity, learning, and subject matter. *Elementary School Journal, 100*(4), 307–330.

Springer, M. G., Ballou, D., Hamilton, L., Le, V.-N., Lockwood, J. R., McCaffrey, D. F., et al. (2010). *Teacher pay for performance: Experimental evidence from the Project on Incentives in Teaching*. Nashville, TN: National Center on Performance Incentives, Vanderbilt University.

Stager, G. (n.d.). *Less us, more them*. Accessed at www.the creativeeducator.com/v10/articles/Less_ Us_More_Them on July 9, 2015.

Stahl, S. A. (1999). *Vocabulary development*. Cambridge, MA: Brookline Books.

Stahl, S. A., & Fairbanks, M. M. (1986). The effects of vocabulary instruction: A model-based meta-analysis. *Review of Educational Research, 56*(1), 72–110.

Stahl, S. A., & Kapinus, B. (2001). *Word power: What every educator needs to know about teaching vocabulary*. Washington, DC: National Education Association.

Stahl, S. A., & Nagy, W. E. (2006). *Teaching word meanings*. Mahwah, NJ: Erlbaum.

Sternberg, R. J. (1996). *Successful intelligence: How practical and creative intelligence determine success in life*. New York: Simon & Schuster.

Sternberg, R. J. (1998). Teaching and assessing for successful intelligence. *School Administrator, 55*(1), 26–27, 30–31.

Stiggins, R. (2007). Assessment *for* learning: An essential foundation of productive instruction. In D. Reeves (Ed.), *Ahead of the curve: The power of assessment to transform teaching and learning* (pp. 59–76). Bloomington, IN: Solution Tree Press.

St. Louis Post-Dispatch. (2014, September 14). *Groups say monarch butterfly needs protecting.* Accessed at https://newsela.com/articles/butterfly-gmos/id/5103 on April 7, 2015.

Stormont, M., Stebbins, M. S., & Holliday, G. (2001). Characteristics and educational support needs of underrepresented gifted adolescents. *Psychology in the Schools, 38*(5), 413–423.

Teacher. (n.d.). In *Dictionary.com.* Accessed at http://dictionary.reference.com/browse/teacher on November 4, 2014.

Tenkely, K. (2015). *Using technology to differentiate instruction.* Accessed at http://teaching.monster .com/benefits/articles/8484-using-technology-to-differentiate-instruction? on July 23, 2015.

Thorndike, E. (1932). *The fundamentals of learning.* New York: AMS Press.

Tomlinson, C. A. (2003). Deciding to teach them all. *Educational Leadership, 61*(2), 6–11.

Torp, L., & Sage, S. (2002). *Problems as possibilities: Problem-based learning for K–16 education* (2nd ed.). Alexandria, VA: Association for Supervision and Curriculum Development.

Utting, D. (Ed.). (2007). *Parenting and the different ways it can affect children's lives: Research evidence.* York, England: Joseph Rowntree Foundation. Accessed at www.jrf.org.uk/system/files/2132 -parenting-literature-reviews.pdf on March 30, 2015.

Vygotsky, L. S. (1978). *Mind in society: The development of higher psychological processes.* Cambridge, MA: Harvard University Press.

Vygotsky, L. S. (1987). Thinking and speech. In R. W. Rieber & A. S. Carton (Eds.), *The collected works of L. S. Vygotsky: Problems of general psychology* (N. Minick, Trans.; Vol. 1, pp. 39–285). New York: Plenum Press.

Wagner, T. (2008a). Rigor redefined. *Educational Leadership, 66*(2), 20–25.

Wagner, T. (2008b). *The global achievement gap: Why even our best schools don't teach the new survival skills our children need—and what we can do about it.* New York: Basic Books.

Walls, C. A. (2003). *Providing highly mobile students with an effective education.* New York: ERIC Clearinghouse on Urban Education. (ERIC Document Reproduction Service No. ED482918)

Walsh, J. A., & Sattes, B. D. (2005). *Quality questioning: Research-based practice to engage every learner.* Thousand Oaks, CA: Corwin Press.

Webb, N. L. (1997). *Criteria for alignment of expectations and assessments in mathematics and science education (Research monograph No. 6).* Washington, DC: Council of Chief State School Officers.

Weisberg, D., Sexton, S., Mulhern, J., & Keeling, D. (2009). *The widget effect: Our national failure to acknowledge and act on differences in teacher effectiveness* (2nd ed.). New York: New Teacher Project. Accessed at http://tntp.org/assets/documents/TheWidgetEffect_2nd_ed.pdf on March 30, 2015.

Wentling, R. M., & Waight, C. L. (2001). Initiatives that assist and barriers that hinder the successful transition of minority youth into the workplace in the USA. *Journal of Education and Work, 14*(1), 71–89.

Westera, J., & Moore, D. W. (1995). Reciprocal teaching of reading comprehension in a New Zealand high school. *Psychology in the Schools, 32*(3), 225–232.

White, H. (1995). "Creating problems" for PBL. *About Teaching, 1995*(47). Accessed at www.udel .edu/pbl/cte/jan95-chem.html on April 7, 2015.

Wiggins, G. (2012). Seven keys to effective feedback. *Educational Leadership, 70*(1), 10–16.

Wiggins, G., & McTighe, J. (2005). *Understanding by design* (Expanded 2nd ed.). Alexandria, VA: Association for Supervision and Curriculum Development.

Williamson, R., & Blackburn, B. R. (2010). *Rigorous schools and classrooms: Leading the way.* Larchmont, NY: Eye on Education.

Williamson, R., & Blackburn, B. R. (2011). Recognizing rigor in classrooms: Four tools for school leaders. *Principal Leadership, 11*(6). Accessed at www.principals.org/tabid/3788/default.aspx?topic=Recognizing_Rigor_in_Classrooms_Four_Tools_for_School_Leaders_ on March 30, 2015.

Willingham, D. T. (2009). *Why don't students like school?: A cognitive scientist answers questions about how the mind works and what it means for the classroom.* San Francisco: Jossey-Bass.

Willis, J. (2006). *Research-based strategies to ignite student learning: Insights from a neurologist and classroom teacher.* Alexandria, VA: Association for Supervision and Curriculum Development.

Winebrenner, S. (2001). *Teaching gifted kids in the regular classroom* (Rev ed.). Minneapolis, MN: Free Spirit.

Woolfolk, A. (2006). *Educational psychology* (10th ed.). Boston: Allyn & Bacon.

Wylie, E. C. (2008). *Formative assessment: Examples of practice.* Washington, DC: Council of Chief State School Officers. Accessed at http://ccsso.org/documents/2008/formative_assessment_examples_2008.pdf on March 30, 2015.

Yeh, S. S. (2005). Limiting the unintended consequences of high-stakes testing. *Education Policy Analysis Archives, 13*(43). Accessed at http://epaa.asu.edu/epaa/v13n43 on September 29, 2015.

Zull, J. E. (2002). *The art of changing the brain: Enriching the practice of teaching by exploring the biology of learning.* Sterling, VA: Stylus.

Index

A

ability grouping, 13
About Teaching (McCarthy), 140–141
acceleration, 149
ACT, 193
active processing, 178
added-value lessons
    creating, 199–200
    teaching, 201–202
add-ons, 198
advance organizers, 31, 131, 134
Ainsworth, L., 18, 79–80, 180–181
analogies, 138, 141
analysts, 58
Armstrong, J. S., 33
Art and Science of Teaching, The (Marzano), 6
assessments
    common, 18, 157–159
    commonsense approach to, 173–174
    convergent, 18–19, 145
    for learning, 19, 151–152
    formative, 18–19, 146, 151–161
    of learning, 19
    pre-, 146, 149–151
    self-, 153
    summative, 146, 161
    See also data collection
assignments, adjusting, 166–173
attention, 56, 57
Ausubel, D., 31, 134
authentic learning, 95–96

B

Bailey, K., 82
Barron, B., 103
basal ganglia, 28
Beck, I., 119
behaviors, expectations for classroom, 26
best practices
    defined, 5
    See also evidence-based best practices
Black, P., 45
Bloom's Revised Taxonomy, 84, 184–185, 186–190
Bloom's Taxonomy of the Cognitive Domain, 184
body-kinesthetic intelligence, 60–61
body language, 37
Bower, H., 177
brain-derived neurotrophic factor (BDNF), 28
brain development
    stress and, 25–26
    See also learning environment
Buffum, A., 17, 79
Building Academic Vocabulary (Marzano and Pickering), 122–123

C

Caine, G., 177–178
Caine, R., 177–178
Carmichael, D., 95
CCSS (Common Core State Standards)
    4Cs, 93
    learning progressions, 80–81, 86–87, 88

proficiency scales, 87, 89–92

rewriting (unwrapping, unpacking, deconstructing), 81–84

using complex texts and text-dependent questions to increase instructional rigor, 193–197

Center for Applied Research in Educational Technology (CARET), 116

chaining, 31

classroom environment. *See* learning environment

class-size reduction programs, 14

climate, creating, 128, 129–131

close observation, 194

close reading, 193–195

cognitive dissonance, 183

Coleman, M. R., 68

Collaborating for Success With the Common Core (Bailey, Jakicic, and Spiller), 82

collaboration, 153

classroom, 26–27

teams, role of, 16–19

Collins, J., 15

common assessments, 18, 157–159

Common Core State Standards. *See* CCSS

compacting, 69, 165

complex texts, to increase instructional rigor, 193–197

concentrated instruction, 17

concept maps, 135, 137

constructivism, 113–114

contact urge, 35

convergent assessments, 18–19, 145

cooperative group learning (CGL), 40, 41–50

cooperative learning tasks, 131

core curriculum. *See* curriculum

Costa, A., 98

"Creating Problems for PBL" (White), 102

cross-classification, 140

Csikszentmihalyi, M., 72, 73–74

cues, 131–132

cultural responsivity, 38–39

curriculum

components of, 78

concentrating, 103–108

content relevancy, 32, 94–96

engaging instruction, providing, 31–32

evidence-based best practices, 97–103

learning progressions, 80–81, 86–87, 88, 153

maps, 106

mastery, criteria for, 84, 86–92

past efforts to improve, 12–15

proficiency scales, 87, 89–92

relevancy of, 32, 94–96

standards, incorporating, 79–84

streamlining, 106–108

21st century skills, integrating, 92–94

D

Damasio, A., 25

Darling-Hammond, L., 103

data collection

diagnostic preassessments, 146, 149–151

formative assessments, 18–19, 146, 151–161

making adjustments based on, 161–173

prerequisite screenings, 146, 148–149

student profiles, 63–66, 146, 147

summative assessments, 146, 161

Dean, C. B., 128, 141

deconstructing standards, 81–84

dendrites, 32, 113

depth and complexity, 191–193

Depth of Knowledge (DOK) model, 84, 185–190,

Dewey, J., 32, 112, 182

diagnostic preassessments, 146, 149–151

diamante poems, 156

Diehl, E., 34

differentiation

ability grouping, 13

flexible grouping, 13–14, 43

learning centers and, 43, 123–127

role of, 6, 203–206

Doyle, M., 43

draw-pair-share, 46

Dweck, C., 33–34, 38, 130

E

Edmonds, R., 11

Education Place, 134–135

Education Support Systems, 116

effective teaching

elements of good, 5–6

how will we know if students are learning, 18–19

how will we respond to learning outcomes, 19

what constitutes, 15–19

what do we want students to learn, 17–18

effect size, 12, 36, 41, 42, 70, 159

Elkind, D., 29

emotional intelligence, 30, 36

Emotional Intelligence (Goleman), 30

emotions, 57

engagement, role of student, 20, 56, 57

engaging instruction, providing, 31–32

English learners (ELs), 65, 66–67

enrichment centers, 124

environmental stressors, 26–27

essential questions, 105

essential standards. *See* standards

evidence-based best practices

problem-based learning, 97–102

project-based learning, 102–103

existential intelligence, 62

exit tickets, 37, 70–71, 154

F

feedback, 37–38, 130, 153, 159–161

feelings, positive, 57

Fisher, D., 163, 197

fixed mindset, 33, 38

flexible grouping, 13–14, 43

Flip Book, The (Kaplan, Gould, and Siegel), 191

flipped classrooms, 117–118

flow, theory of, 72–74

Flubaroo, 156

formative assessments, 18–19

defined, 151

developing effective, 152–153

feedback, 159–161

flowchart, 152

implementing, 153–157

role of, 146, 151–152, 157–159

4Cs, 93, 197–202

Frayer method, 122

Frey, N., 163, 197

front-loading, 164

G

Gallimore, R., 17

Gardner, H., 59–62, 98

Geake, J., 23, 58

Glasser, W., 27

Goleman, D., 30

good teaching. *See* effective teaching

Google Forms, 156

Gould, B., 191

gradual release of responsibility model, 162–163

graphic organizers, 134–135

Great Minds, 106

groups

ability, 13

adjusting, 165–166

cooperative group flow, 73–74

cooperative group learning, 40, 41–50

flexible, 13–14, 43

problems with, 46–49

student pairs, 43–46

growth mindset, 33–35, 38

H

habits of mind, 92

Hallowell, E., 27

Harrison, C., 45

Hattie, J., 1, 4, 11, 12, 13, 14, 16, 19, 20, 21, 36, 41, 42, 70, 83, 103, 138, 159

Hawn Foundation, 30

Heick, T., 178

Hiebert, E., 196

higher-level thinking skills, developing, 182–191

hippocampus, 28

homework, 137–138, 181

Honaker, J., 116

horizontal threading, 31

How the Mighty Fall (Collins), 15

Hummel, T., 186

Hurried Child, The (Elkind), 29

hypotheses, generating and testing, 41

I

individualized education programs (IEPs), 65

Individuals With Disabilities Education Improvement Act (IDEIA), 3

instructional methods, moving from traditional to progressive, 112–114
intelligences
  defined, 98
  multiple, 59–63
interest, 56–57
interest or exploratory centers, 124
International Society for Technology, 116
interpersonal intelligence, 62
interpersonal learners, 58
intrapersonal intelligence, 62

J

Jakicic, C., 82
jigsaw tasks, 49–50, 154
Johnson, D., 42
Johnson, R., 42
journals, 70–71
J Taylor Education, 191
jumpstarting, 164

K

Kallick, B., 98
Kaplan, S. N., 191
Keeping Track (Oakes), 3
Kennedy, J. F., 179
Khan Academy, 118
kinesthetic representations, 136
King, M. B., 95–96
knowledge, helping students extend and apply, 128, 138–141
Kucan, L., 119

L

learning
  active, 113
  student ownership of, 32–33
learning centers, 43, 123–127, 168
learning environment
  classroom behaviors, expectations for, 26
  classroom collaboration, 26–27
  classroom routines and procedures, 27
  cooperative group learning, 40, 41–50
  creating rigorous, 179–182
  cultural responsivity, 38–39
  engaging instruction, providing, 31–32
  environmental stressors, 26–27
  growth mindset, 33–35, 38
  guidelines, 51–53
  maintaining a safe, 24–30
  mindfulness, 29–30
  physical movement and nutrition, role of, 27–29
  recording issues, 52, 53
  social interaction, supporting, 35–41
  social skills, 39–41
  stress and brain development, 25–26
  student ownership of learning, 32–33
Learning in the Fast Lane: 8 Ways to Put All Students on the Road to Academic Success (Rollins), 149
learning preferences
  English learners, 65, 66–67
  flow, theory of, 72–74
  helping students identify their own, 70–72
  multiple intelligences, 59–63
  recognizing, 58–59
  student profiles, creating, 63–66
  surveys, 63
  teaching to each student's sweet spots, 56–58
  twice-exceptional students, 67–69
learning progressions, 80–81, 86–87, 88, 148, 153, 186
learning styles, 58
learning sweet spot. *See* learning preferences
learning targets, 82
learning tasks, cooperative, 131
Lee, C., 45
Levine, M., 31
Lezotte, L., 11
listening chart, 40, 41
logical-mathematical intelligence, 61
Lou, Y., 43

M

Making Connections: Teaching and the Human Brain (Caine and Caine), 177–178
Making Standards Work (Reeves), 18
Marshall, B., 45
Marzano, R., 6, 11, 17, 42, 89, 122–123, 128, 130–131, 136, 137
Maslow, A., 27
MasteryConnect, 157
mastery, criteria for, 84, 86–92
maximal cognitive efficiency, 25

Mayer, R., 31

McCarthy, B., 140–141

McKeown, M., 119

McTighe, J., 18, 105

Medina, J., 31–32

Mesmer, H. A., 196

metaphors, 140–141, 156

mindfulness, 29–30

mindset, growth, 33–35, 38

Mindset: The New Psychology of Success (Dweck), 33

Mindset Works, 34

mirror neurons, 35

Mitra, S., 118–119

models, constructed, 135

Morrison, W., 68

multiple intelligences, 59–63

multitiered system of support (MTSS), 2

musical-rhythmic intelligence, 60

myelination, 32

N

National Council of Teachers of English, 151

naturalist intelligence, 61

needs theories, 27

neuroeducation, 23

neuroscience, 23–24

Newmann, F., 95, 182

No Child Left Behind (NCLB), 12

nonlinguistic representations, 134–136

note taking, 136–137

nutrition, role of, 29

O

Oakes, J., 3

one-on-one time with students, 37

organizers, 58, 131–134

advance organizers, 31, 131, 134

graphic, 134–135

P

Panksepp, J., 35

Partnership for 21st Century Skills (P21), 93

physical movement, role of, 27–29

Piaget, J., 32

Pickering, D. J., 122–123

pictographs, 135

placemat charts, 156–157

pluralized instructional strategies, 69, 111

flipped classrooms, 117–118

implementation stages, 142

learning centers, 43, 123–127

mixed modality, 128–142

technology, use of, 115–119

vocabulary development, 119–123

Polacco, P., 194

Poll Everywhere, 156

Powers, J., 177

power standards, 79–80

Power Standards (Ainsworth), 18, 79–80

praise, 130–131

Prasse, D., 4

preassessments, diagnostic, 146, 149–151

prerequisite screenings, 146, 148–149

probes and prompts, 132

problem-based learning (PBL)

benefits of, 99

defined, 97–98

facilitating, 101–102

process steps, 99–101

professional learning communities, four

questions of, 17–20, 207

proficiency scales, 87, 89–92, 191

project-based learning, 102–103

Q

questions, 132–133

R

random learners, 58

Ratey, J., 28, 31

Reading Between the Lines (ACT), 193

recognition, 130–131

Reeves, D., 18, 80

Reis, S., 165

relevancy, content, 32, 94–96

Renzulli, J., 165

response cards, 154

response to intervention (RTI)

critical questions, 15–19

goals of, 2–3

multitiered system of support, 2

problems with implementing, 3–5

pyramid, 2
role of, 1
rewriting (unwrapping, unpacking,
    deconstructing) standards, 81–84
rigor
    defined, 177
    importance of, 178
    learning environments and, 179–182
    myths about, 181
    using complex texts and text-dependent
        questions to increase instructional,
        193–197, 198
    using 21st century skills to increase, 197–202
Rizza, M., 68
Rogers Public Schools, 106–107
Rohde, M., 136–137
Rollins, S., 149

S

Sacramento County Office of Education, 116
scaffolding, 66–67, 162–164
Schmoker, M., 5–6
School in the Cloud, 118
screenings, prerequisite, 146, 148–149
seeking system, 32
self-assessment, 153
self-determination theory, 33
self-grading, 20
Siegel, V., 191
similarities and differences, identifying, 138–141,
    155
Sketchnote Handbook, The (Rohde), 136–137
skill centers, 124
Smilkstein, R., 32
social interaction, supporting, 35–41
social skills, 39–41
Socrative, 157
Spark: The Revolutionary New Science of Exercise
    and the Brain (Ratey), 28
SPATE (specific, personal, actionable, task, and
    effort), 160–161
Spiller, J., 82
SQ3R (survey, question, read, recite, review), 133
Stager, G., 96
standards
    charting, 84, 85

identifying, 79–81
incorporating, 79–84
power, 79–80
rewriting (unwrapping, unpacking,
    deconstructing), 81–84
step-and-column pay scales, 13
Sternberg, R., 98
Stiggins, R., 19
stimulus-driven attention, 25
Straus, D., 43
stress, brain development and, 25–26
stressors, environmental, 26–27
student-centered instruction, 96
student-centered responsibility, 32–33, 77
student ownership of learning, 32–33
student pairs, 43–46
student profiles, creating, 63–66, 146, 147
successes, prior, 57
summarizing and note taking, 136–137
summative assessments, 146, 161
surveys, student preferences, 71
sweet spot. See learning preferences

T

task and workflow, adjusting, 162–165
teacher-compensation pay scales, 13
teacher evaluation and merit pay, 14
teacher-preparation programs, 12–13
teacher-student relationships, developing, 36–38
teacher talk, 31
teaching
    art of, 6, 203–207
    elements of good, 5–6
    science of, 5–6
    what constitutes effective, 15–19
Teaching for Meaningful Learning (Darling-
    Hammond and Barron), 103
technology
    creative use of, 116–117
    flipped classrooms, 117–118
    role of, 115
    student self-guided, 118–119
TED, 118
Tenkely, K., 116
text-dependent questions, to increase
    instructional rigor, 193–197, 198

think-pair-share, 45

Third International Conference on Assessment for Learning, 151–152

Thorndike, E., 72

thumbs-up or thumbs-down, 154

Tier 1, purpose of, 2

Tier 3, purpose of, 2

Tier 2, purpose of, 2

TIPS (total class, independent students, partners, and small groups) chart, 43, 44

Tomlinson, C. A., 146

21st century skills
    increasing rigor using, 197–202
    integrating, 92–94

twice-exceptional students, 67–69

U

Understanding by Design (Wiggins and McTighe), 18

understanding, helping students develop, 128, 131–138

unpacking standards, 81–84

unwrapping standards, 81–84

"Unwrapping" the Standards (Ainsworth), 18

Using Technology to Differentiate Instruction (Honaker), 116

Using Technology to Differentiate Instruction (Tenkely), 116

V

Venn diagrams, 139–140

verbal-linguistic intelligence, 59

viable curriculum, 17

Visible Learning (Hattie), 83

visual-spatial intelligence, 60

vocabulary development, 119–123

Vygotsky, L., 32, 73, 162, 164

W

Webb, N., 185

Webb's Depth of Knowledge model, 84, 185–190

What Works in Schools (Marzano), 11

White, H., 102

Wiggins, G., 18, 105, 159

Wiliam, D., 45

write-pair-share, 45

Wylie, C., 151

Z

zone of proximal development, 73, 162, 181

It's About Time, Elementary
Austin Buffum and Mike Mattos
Carve out effective intervention and extension time at all three tiers of the RTI pyramid. Explore more than a dozen examples of creative and flexible scheduling, and gain access to tools you can use immediately to overcome implementation challenges.
BKF609

Think Big, Start Small
Gayle Gregory and Martha Kaufeldt
You don't have to be a neuroscientist to understand how your students absorb knowledge. This easy-to-understand guide pares down the vast field of neuroscience and provides simple brain-compatible strategies that will make a measurable difference in your differentiated classrooms.
BKF471

Simplifying Response to Intervention
Austin Buffum, Mike Mattos, and Chris Weber
The sequel to *Pyramid Response to Intervention* advocates that effective RTI begins by asking the right questions to create a fundamentally effective learning environment for every student. Understand why paperwork-heavy, compliance-oriented, test-score-driven approaches fail. Then learn how to create an RTI model that works.
BKF506

The RTI Toolkit
Learn how to control the intensity of your interventions while addressing learning gaps and meeting the needs of individual students. Loaded with dynamic strategies, this toolkit will keep your school culture healthy for years to come.
KTF133

Solution Tree | Press a division of
Solution Tree

Visit solution-tree.com or call 800.733.6786 to order.

" WOW!

I liked how I was given
an effective, organized plan
to help EVERY child. "

—Linda Rossiter, teacher,
Spring Creek Elementary School, Utah

 PD Services

Our experts draw from decades of research and their own experiences to bring you
practical strategies for providing timely, targeted interventions. You can choose from a
range of customizable services, from a one-day overview to a multiyear process.

Book your RTI PD today!
888.763.9045

Solution Tree